Scottish-American Heirs,
1683 - 1883

Scottish-American H E I R S

1683-1883

David Dobson

CLEARFIELD

Printed by Genealogical Publishing Company,
Baltimore, Maryland
1990, 1992

Library of Congress Catalogue Card Number 90-80875

Reprinted for Clearfield Company
by Genealogical Publishing Company
Baltimore, Maryland
2010

ISBN 978-0-8063-1278-1

Made in the United States of America

Introduction

he records of the Services of Heirs in Scotland are of immense value to the genealogist as they provide authentic and reliable confirmation of the relationship between deceased individuals and their heirs. These records survive, albeit in a fragmentary form, from the late Medieval period; however, those dating after 1600 are virtually complete. Abstracts of most of those prior to 1699 have been published in a three-volume work entitled *Inquisitionum ad Capellum Regis Retornatarum Abbreviato,* while those dating from 1700 onwards have published indexes, decennial up to 1860 and annual thereafter. On the death of a landowner the local sheriff held an inquest to establish the credentials of a person claiming to be the true and rightful heir to lands in the possession of the deceased at the time of his or her death. The sheriff's decision was then recorded in the Record of Retours, which is now in the Scottish Record Office. The documentary evidence associated with the inquest—the records of the Services of Heirs—generally contains information pertaining to the deceased and to the heir which is of paramount importance to the family historian.

The Services of Heirs is a particularly useful source for those who wish to make a trans-Atlantic connection, as many of the entries link families in North America with Scotland (the earliest of these is dated 19 November 1683 when Alexander Ross or Garge, a dyker in Kirkwall, Orkney Islands, was serviced as heir to his father, William Ross or Garge, in New Scotland Parish, Barbados). This volume contains over 2,600 such links between Scots and their descendants in North America.

David Dobson

Abbreviations

USA

Ala	Alabama
Cal	California
Col	Colorado
Ct	Connecticut
Del	Delaware
Fla	Florida
Ga	Georgia
Ia	Iowa
Ida	Idaho
Ill	Illinois
Ind	Indiana
Kan	Kansas
Ky	Kentucky
La	Louisiana
Mass	Massachusetts
Md	Maryland
Me	Maine
Mich	Michigan
Miss	Mississippi
Mo	Missouri
NC	North Carolina
Nev	Nevada
NH	New Hampshire
NJ	New Jersey
NY	New York
Oh	Ohio
Ore	Oregon
Pa	Pennsylvania
RI	Rhode Island
SC	South Carolina
Tenn	Tennessee
Tex	Texas
Ut	Utah
Va	Virginia
Vt	Vermont
Wisc	Wisconsin

CANADA

Can	Canada
BC	British Columbia
BNA	British North America
Man	Manitoba
NB	New Brunswick
NS	Nova Scotia
Ont	Ontario
PEI	Prince Edward Island
Up Can	Upper Canada

OTHERS

NA	North America
NSW	New South Wales
NZ	New Zealand
WI	West Indies

MISCELLANEOUS

HEICS	Honorable East India Company Service
RN	Royal Navy
SSC	Solicitor to the Supreme Court
USN	United States Navy
WS	Writer to the Signet

TERMS

Feuar	lease holder
Portioner	co-inheritor
Writer	lawyer
Baillie	burgh official
Provost	mayor

Scottish-American Heirs,
1683-1883

1. Adair, Thomas, sailor, in Creetown Kirkcudbrightshire, heir to bro John Adair, sailor in Creetown then Quebec, reg. 27 June 1837.
2. Adam, David, in Falkirk Stirlingshire, heir to bro John Adam, in NY then Falkirk, d. 6 Jan.1865, reg. 2 Feb.1865.
3. Adam, James, in Ill then Glasgow, heir to bro John Adam, in Garnavel Glasgow, reg. 28 Feb.1833.
4. Adam, James, in Ill then Glasgow, heir to grandfa James Adam, portioner of Hurlford, reg. 5 Feb.1851.
5. Adam, James, in Ill then Glasgow, heir to bro Robert Adam, in Randolph Co Ill, reg. 28 Feb.1853.
6. Adam or McKellar, Mary Ann, w of Archibald McKellar, in Whiteinch Glasgow, heir to uncle James Wright, seaman in Paisley Renfrewshire then America, reg. 28 Nov.1860.
7. Adams, Alexander Hanson, in Wilmington Del, heir to mo Isabella Bogie or Adams, in Wilmington Del, reg. 28 Oct.1859.
8. Adamson, Peter, farmer, in Bayfield Can W, heir to fa William Adamson, in Whaligoe Caithness, d. 4 Nov.1856, reg. 27 Mar.1863.
9. Addison, James, in North York Ont, heir to fa James Addison, spirit dealer in Edinburgh, d. 5 Feb.1863, reg. 26 Oct.1875.
10. Agnew, William, shoemaker, in Toronto, heir to bro James Agnew, shoemaker in Stranraer Wigtownshire, d. 31 Oct.1878, reg. 16 Oct.1879.
11. Aikman, Jane, in Burlington NJ, heir to cousin Alexander Aikman, in Hollandbush Hamilton Lanarkshire, d. 13 May 1879, reg. 5 Dec.1879.
12. Ainslie, George, in Ky, heir to mo Janet Ainslie, w of Hew Ainslie in Ky, d. 28 Mar.1863, reg. 1 June 1875.
13. Aird or Jamieson, Elizabeth, w of Rev John Aird, in Jamaica, heir to cousin John Jamieson, grocer in Greenock Renfrewshire, reg. 4 May 1849.
14. Aird, John Mackenzie, in Grenada, heir to fa Alexander Aird, merchant in Invergordon Ross & Cromarty, reg. 13 Mar.1850.
15. Aird, John Mackenzie, in Grenada, heir to uncle George Mackenzie, in Culcragie, reg. 19 Feb.1856.

16. Aird, John Mackenzie, in Grenada, heir to cousin Margaret Mackenzie, in Invergordon Ross & Cromarty, reg. 19 Feb.1856.
17. Aird, John Mackenzie, in Grenada, heir to grand-uncle George Mackenzie, in Invergordon Ross & Cromarty, reg. 20 Feb.1860.
18. Airston, William, yeoman, in Leith Sydenham NA, heir to cousin Elizabeth Hunter, w of William Baird-Airston in St Andrews Fife, d. 12 Feb.1870, reg. 7 July 1870.
19. Aitchison, Andrew, in Up Can, heir to fa Andrew Aitchison, innkeeper in Lauder, reg. 4 Dec.1854.
20. Aitchison, Anne, in Lauder, heir to bro Andrew Aitchison, in Jackson USA, reg. 18 Dec.1854.
21. Aitchison, William, in Hamilton Can, heir to bro Adam Aitchison, joiner in Annan Dumfries-shire, d. 19 Oct.1875, reg. 17 Jan.1877.
22. Aitken, Robert, in America, heir to bro William Aitken, s of R Aitken in Camlachie Lanarkshire, d. 1835, reg. 25 Sep.1849.
23. Aitken, Robert, in America, heir to sis Jean Aitken, da of R Aitken in Camlachie Lanarkshire, d. 1822, reg. 25 Sep.1849.
24. Aitken, Robert, in America, heir to sis Mary Aitken, da of R Aitken in Camlachie Lanarkshire, d. 1831, reg. 25 Sep.1849.
25. Aitken, Robert, in America, heir to bro James Aitken, s of R Aitken in Camlachie Lanarkshire, d. 1831, reg. 25 Sep.1849.
26. Alexander or Lloyd, Christina, in St Lucia, heir to Marie Jean Alexander, in St Lucia, reg. 22 Feb.1839.
27. Alexander or Lloyd, Christina, wid of Ebenezer Lloyd merchant London, in St Lucia, heir to sis Robertina Alexander, in St Lucia, d. 14 Jan.1866, reg. 14 Feb.1867.
28. Alexander, David, in Petersburg Va, heir to bro James Alexander, wright in Montrose Angus, reg. 27 July 1809.
29. Alexander, George Andrew, in Toronto, heir to fa George Alexander, farmer in Can, reg. 9 Feb.1858.
30. Alexander, James, merchant, in St Johns Can, heir to mo Margaret Morison or Alexander, in Alloa Clackmannanshire, reg. 20 Oct.1830.
31. Alexander, James, in Camden Mills America, heir to mo Mary Gardiner or Alexander, in Ferguston of Arbroath Angus, reg. 25 Jan.1860.
32. Alexander, Janet, heir to Marie Jean Alexander, in St Lucia, reg. 22 Feb.1839.
33. Alexander or Lyon, Jean, in Greenock Renfrewshire, heir to fa William Alexander, cooper in Greenock then Tobago, reg. 21 Apr.1837.
34. Alexander, Jeanette Mary, in St Lucia, heir to sis Robertina Alexander, in St Lucia, d. 14 Jan.1866, reg. 14 Feb.1867.
35. Alexander, John, in Sterling Col, heir to grand-uncle William Alexander, merchant in Stanley Perthshire, d. 4 Sep.1865, reg. 20 Sep.1882.

2

36. Alexander, Joseph, in Delhi Delaware Co NY, heir to fa William Alexander, cooper in Castle Douglas Kirkcudbrightshire, d. 6 Apl.1861, reg. 16 Dec.1870.
37. Alexander, Maxwell, in Jackson NA, heir to bro Robert Alexander, in Battenville NA, d. 25 May 1861, reg. 2 Feb.1863.
38. Alexander, Robert, in Jamaica, heir to mo Janet Black or Alexander, w of Thomas Alexander merchant in Maybole Ayrshire, reg. 17 Apr.1804.
39. Alexander, Robert, in Jamaica, heir to grandfa Quintin Black, in Brockloch & Lochstoun Ayrshire, reg. 17 Apr.1804.
40. Alexander, Robertina, heir to Marie Jean Alexander, in St Lucia, reg. 22 Feb.1839.
41. Allan or Duncan, Ann, wid of John Duncan, in NB, heir to William Stewart, farmer in Woodhead, reg. 29 Jan.1852.
42. Allan or McLeish, Ann, wid of James McLeish, in Aberfoil Can W, heir to bro Archibald Allan, in Logie Almond Perthshire, d. 28 May 1870, reg. 13 Mar.1871.
43. Allan or Buddo, Annie, wife of George Buddo gardener, in Montreal, heir to James Allan, forester in Cumbernauld, reg. 1 Mar.1877.
44. Allan, George, in St Croix, heir to cousin George Allan, s of Rev Alexander Allan in Edinburgh, reg. 28 Feb.1820.
45. Allan, James, teacher, in Philadelphia, heir to fa James Allan, weaver in Paisley Renfrewshire, reg. 5 Jan.1824.
46. Allan or Knox, Jean Gibbon, in NB, heir to grandfa Arthur Gibbon, shipowner in Aberdeen, reg. 3 June 1837.
47. Allan or Knox, Jean Gibbon, in NB, heir to aunt Isabella Gibbon, in Aberdeen, reg. 2 Nov.1839.
48. Allan or Knox, Jean Gibbon, in NB, heir to aunt Christien Gibbon, reg. 2 Nov.1839.
49. Allan, John, in Richfield Ut, heir to fa Robert Allan, manufacturer in Kirkintilloch Dunbartonshire, d. 6 Sep.1874, reg. 23 Mar.1878.
50. Allan, John Henry, merchant, in Pictou Ont, heir to uncle Robert Allan, in Greenock Renfrewshire, reg. 20 Sep.1878.
51. Allan or Moore, Margaret, heir to aunt Elizabeth Dennistoun or Bell, w of Archibald Bell in Can, d. 1847, reg. 5 Dec.1883.
52. Allan, Robert Gillespie, in Can, heir to mo Catherine Dennistoun or Allan, w of James Allan in Glasgow, d. 1843, reg. 5 Dec.1883.
53. Allan, Robert Gillespie, in Can, heir to aunt Elizabeth Dennistoun or Bell, w of Archibald Bell in Can, d. 1847, reg. 5 Dec.1883.
54. Allan, William, merchant, in Paisley Renfrewshire, heir to cousin George Allan, in Grenada, reg. 26 Dec.1834.
55. Allardice or Ritchie, Margaret B, wid of Samuel Ritchie, in NY, heir to fa Robert Barclay of Ury, in Kincardineshire, reg. 12 Jan.1859.

3

56. Allason, William, heir to fa William Allason, surgeon in Port Royal Va, reg. 12 Oct.1770.
57. Allen, Robert, merchant, in Barbados, heir to sis Christien Allen or Stewart, wid of Rev Peter Stewart in Auchtergaven, reg. 15 Feb.1755.
58. Allison, James, blacksmith, in NY, heir to fa James Allison, blacksmith in Greenock Renfrewshire, d. 13 Jan.1843, reg. 17 Apr.1851.
59. Allison, James, in Wisc, heir to fa John Allison, ginger beer brewer in Paisley Renfrewshire, d. 28 Nov.1850, reg. 31 Aug.1852.
60. Allston, Joseph Blythe, in SC, heir to Margaret Allan or Hutchison, w of Provost John Hutchison in Renfrew, reg. 27 June 1846.
61. Alves, Thomas, in Jamaica, heir to gt grandfa Thomas Alves of Shipland, merchant in Inverness, reg. 8 Feb.1792.
62. Anderson, Alexander, in Can, heir to uncle John Anderson, in Candacraig, reg. 9 Nov.1855.
63. Anderson, Alexander, in Thornville NA, heir to grandfa John Kerr, mason in Camelon Stirlingshire, d. 1817, reg. 2 Dec.1865.
64. Anderson, Alexander, farmer, in Gloucester Ottawa Can, heir to fa John Anderson, mason in Selkirk, d. 10 Oct.1849, reg. 30 June 1874.
65. Anderson, Alexander, in Clarence Can, heir to mo Elizabeth Philip or Anderson, wife of G Anderson in Clarence Can, d. 28 July 1834, reg. 6 Jan.1875.
66. Anderson, Alexander, engineer, in Clinton Ia, heir to fa Alexander Anderson, mason in Will Co Ill, d. Feb.1860, reg. 18 July 1877.
67. Anderson, Alexander, in Portage la Prairie Man, heir to fa Robert Anderson, mason in Forres Morayshire, d. 24 Apr.1845, reg. 24 July 1878.
68. Anderson, Andrew, naval architect, in Antigua, heir to niece Alexandrina Anderson, da of Alexander Anderson of Newton, reg. 28 July 1769.
69. Anderson, Andrew, teacher, in NY, heir to bro Thomas Anderson, in Dundee Angus then New Orleans, reg. 11 Feb.1835.
70. Anderson, Arthur, MD, in America, heir to uncle Andrew Anderson, hairdresser in St Andrews Fife, reg. 16 Feb.1833.
71. Anderson or Christie, Catherine, w of Ebenezer Christie, in USA, heir to bro William Anderson, teacher in Cowdenbeath Fife, reg. 27 Apr.1858.
72. Anderson, Charles Alexander, in Silchar Cachar, heir to bro James Anderson, engineer in NY, d. 1 Nov.1868, reg. 20 Sep.1869.
73. Anderson, David Sim, in Brooklyn NY, heir to grandfa George Anderson, mason in Kinglassie Fife, d. 3 Oct.1855, reg. 20 Oct.1863.
74. Anderson or Clayton, Eliza, in Montreal, heir to grandfa David Anderson, laborer in Tyrie Bleachfield Fife, d. 3 Oct.1830, reg. 26 Oct.1872.

75. Anderson or Watson, Elizabeth, wid of H Watson of Torsonce WS, heir to uncle John Watson, merchant in Jamaica, d. 20 Aug.1850, reg. 11 Nov.1851.
76. Anderson, George, in Greenhaugh, heir to uncle George Smith, in Ga, reg. 6 Nov.1850.
77. Anderson, Henry John, in Falmouth Jamaica, heir to uncle John Anderson, in Belleville, d. 10 May 1847, reg. 21 May 1866.
78. Anderson, James, clerk, in Rhonds, heir to brother William Anderson, teacher in Airdrie Lanarkshire then America, reg. 9 Nov.1847.
79. Anderson, James, farmer, in Can W, heir to mo Elspet Gow or Anderson, wid of James Anderson in Scroggiemill Elgin Morayshire, reg. 12 June 1856.
80. Anderson, James, in Hudson Bay, heir to fa James Anderson, in Bridgend of Brechin Angus, d. 4 Apl.1864, reg. 13 Mar.1867.
81. Anderson, James, in Alleghany USA, heir to grandfa James Anderson, farmer in Boghouse Kilsyth Stirlingshire, d. 1833, reg. 10 June 1876.
82. Anderson, John, merchant, in Leith Midlothian, heir to bro James Anderson, merchant in Va, reg. 27 May 1790.
83. Anderson or Kirton, John, heir to mo Barbara Anderson or Castor of Tushielaws, wid of Alexander Kirton in Barbados, d. Nov.1790, reg. 20 Dec.1793.
84. Anderson, John Paterson, in Quebec, heir to fa John Anderson, in Dalgarroch House Colmonell, reg. 21 June 1851.
85. Anderson, John, in NY , heir to fa John Anderson, carpenter in Garmouth Morayshire, reg. 1 Feb.1856.
86. Anderson, Margaret, heir to fa David Anderson, wright in Antigua, reg. 20 Nov.1777.
87. Anderson, Polly, heir to fa David Anderson, wright in Antigua, reg. 20 Nov.1777.
88. Anderson, Robert, in NY, heir to fa Robert Anderson, fruit merchant in Corstorphine Mid Lothian, d. 13 Sep.1872, reg. 2 June 1874.
89. Anderson, Thomas, doctor of medicine, in Trinidad, heir to fa James Anderson, surgeon in Antigua, reg. 20 Oct.1829.
90. Anderson, Thomas, insurance clerk, in New Orleans, heir to fa George Anderson, feuar & wright in Stanley Perthshire, d. Oct.1832, reg. 29 Nov.1868.
91. Anderson, William, in Dominica, heir to fa William Anderson, merchant in London, reg. 28 Jan.1822.
92. Anderson, William, in Dominica, heir to aunt Rachel Anderson, da of Henry Anderson farmer in Broughton Edinburgh, reg. 22 Mar.1824.

93. Anderson, William, in Dominica, heir to aunt Jean Anderson or Sommers, w of William Sommers innkeeper in Edinburgh, reg. 22 Mar.1824.
94. Anderson, William, in Dominica, heir to aunt Margaret Anderson or Bogue, w of John Bogue WS in Edinburgh, reg. 22 Mar.1824.
95. Anderson, William, in Dominica, heir to aunt Mary Anderson, da of Henry Anderson farmer in Broughton Edinburgh, reg. 22 Mar.1824.
96. Anderson, William, in Dominica, heir to uncle Henry Anderson, s of Henry Anderson farmer in Broughton Edinburgh, reg. 22 Mar.1824.
97. Anderson, William, in NY, heir to grandfa William Anderson, minister in Auchterarder Perthshire, d. 8 May 1855, reg. 7 July 1856.
98. Anderson, William George, in USA, heir to mo Jean Jamieson or Anderson, w of James Anderson shoemaker in Denburn Aberdeen, reg. 18 Sep.1860.
99. Angus, Andrew, in St Kitts, heir to Alexander Mein, surgeon in Dalkeith Midlothian, reg. 18 Dec.1754.
100. Annan, Robert, minister, in Mount Pleasant Pa, heir to bro John Annan, in Lebanon Cupar Fife, reg. 16 Jan.1818.
101. Arbuckle, William, in Falkirk Stirlingshire, heir to uncle John Steven, millwright in Trinidad, reg. 21 Mar.1845.
102. Archer, James, stocking-weaver, in Nottingham, heir to bro Andrew Archer, in Jamaica, reg. 6 Nov.1826.
103. Archibald, James, in La Porte America, heir to fa John Archibald, platelayer in Clackmannan, d. 31 Jan.1871, reg. 22 Jan.1876.
104. Archibald, John, farmer, in Ind, heir to fa John Archibald, laborer in Dundee Angus, d. 22 Jan.1801, reg. 23 July 1863.
105. Armour, Robert, surgeon, in Trinidad, heir to bro Hugh Armour, shipmaster in Irvine Ayrshire, reg. 1 May 1823.
106. Armour, William, in Providence RI, heir to fa William Armour, in Glasgow, d. 8 Jan.1849, reg. 11 Feb.1864.
107. Armstrong, John, in Madoc Ont, heir to cousin Elizabeth Armstrong or Campbell, wid of James Campbell in Girvan Ayrshire, d. 26 Dec.1879, reg. 10 Nov.1881.
108. Arnot, Lamont, farmer, in MacNab Bathurst Can, heir to grandfa John Arnot, in Prestonpans then Musselburgh E Lothian, reg. 9 Mar.1853.
109. Arnott, David Shiress, in NY, heir to fa George Arnott, weaver in Brechin Angus, d. 15 May 1842, reg. 4 Aug.1862.
110. Arnott, David Shiress, marble worker, in S Brooklyn NY, heir to uncle John Arnott, cowfeeder in Brechin Angus, d. 8 July 1869, reg. 29 Sep.1869.

111. Arrol jr, William, in Rond Eau Can W, heir to bro Thomas Arrol, in Enniskillen Can W, d. 16 Nov.1863, reg. 12 May 1864.

112. Arrol jr, William, in Rond Eau Can W, heir to sis Margaret Arrol, in London, d. 3 May 1850, reg. 12 May 1864.

113. Arrott, William, merchant, in Philadelphia, heir to mo Anne Stewart or Arrott, da of Thomas Stewart of Boghall, reg. 21 Oct.1831.

114. Arthur, William, in Brooklyn NY, heir to bro Archibald Arthur, s of Archibald Arthur calico printer in Glasgow, reg. 7 May 1870.

115. Arthur, William, in Brooklyn NY, heir to sis Cecilia Young Arthur, da of Archibald Arthur calico printer in Glasgow, reg. 7 May 1870.

116. Arthur, William, in Brooklyn NY, heir to bro Henry Monteath Arthur, s of Archibald Arthur calico printer in Glasgow, reg. 7 May 1870.

117. Arthur, William, in Brooklyn NY, heir to bro James Young Arthur, s of Archibald Arthur calico printer in Glasgow, reg. 7 May 1870.

118. Arthur, William, in Brooklyn NY, heir to mo Cecilia Young or Arthur, wid of Archibald Arthur calico printer in Glasgow, reg. 7 May 1870.

119. Ashton, Edward, in Cal, heir to mo Jane Thompson or Ashton, in South Shields Northumberland, reg. 2 Feb.1857.

120. Ashton, Edward, in Cal, heir to George Weatherhead, physician in London, reg. 2 Feb.1857.

121. Ashton, Edward, in Cal, heir to William Weatherhead, physician in Coldstream Berwickshire, reg. 2 Feb.1857.

122. Athol, Francis, in Halifax NS, heir to uncle John Athol, in Stranraer Wigtownshire, reg. 30 Oct.1838.

123. Auchenvole, David, merchant, in NY, heir to fa Alexander Auchenvole, in Kilsyth Stirlingshire, reg. 5 Sep.1800.

124. Auchterlonie, John, dyer, in Kingston Jamaica, heir to bro Thomas Auchterlonie, dyer in Edinburgh, reg. 15 Nov.1826.

125. Auld, John, WS, in Edinburgh, heir to uncle James Auld, in Jamaica then Edinburgh, reg. 4 May 1857.

126. Austin, Adam, merchant, in Charleston SC, heir to fa Joseph Austin of Kilspindie, in Perthshire, reg. 3 July 1782.

127. Austin or Dow, Henrietta Munro, w of James Dow carpenter, in NY, heir to sis Margaret Isabella Austin, in Dublin, d. 3 Jan.1851, reg. 29 Mar.1881.

128. Badenoch, Alexander, merchant, in Quebec, heir to grandfa Alexander Forsyth, tailor in Calton, reg. 15 Nov.1825.

129. Baillie, Andrew, merchant, in Va, heir to sis Margaret Baillie, in Port Glasgow Renfrewshire , reg. 15 June 1790.

130. Bain, Alexander, in Raensselaer Iron Works Troy NY, heir to w Margaret Adamson or Bain, d. 11 May 1840, reg. 20 Feb.1867.

131. Bain, Jane Ann, in Oquanka Ill, heir to bro John Bain, in Forres Morayshire, d. 26 May 1850, reg. 1 Sep.1870.

132. Bain, John, cabinet-maker, in Can, heir to grandfa Thomas Bain, wright in Keith Banffshire, reg. 28 Sep.1854.

133. Bain, John, cabinet-maker, in Can, heir to gt grandfa Archibald Bain, wright in Keith Banffshire, reg. 9 Nov.1854.

134. Bain, William E, in Cherokee Flat Cal, heir to fa Edward Bone or Bain, laborer in Greenlaw, d. 25 Jan.1868, reg. 22 Dec.1882.

135. Baine, David, in Hamilton Can W, heir to bro Colin Baine, in Orillia Can W, d. 13 Apr.1857, reg. 11 Apr.1864.

136. Baine, David, in Hamilton Can W, heir to sis Susan Baine, in Orillia Can W, d. 6 Apr.1857, reg. 11 Apr.1864.

137. Baine, David, in Hamilton Can W, heir to bro Anderson Baine, in Orillia Can W, d. 12 Apr.1857, reg. 11 Apr.1864.

138. Baird, Alexander, in New Annan Colchester Co NS, heir to fa George Bain, mason in Kilmarnock Ayrshire, d. 30 Jan.1850, reg. 11 Mar.1869.

139. Baird, Andrew Wood, doctor, in Ipswich England, heir to uncle Andrew Baird, bookseller in Edinburgh then Jamaica, reg. 7 Sep.1827.

140. Baird, Samuel, merchant, in St Kitts then Barbados, heir to uncle John Paterson, in Kildrochat then Stranraer Wigtownshire, d. 16 June 1844, reg. 27 June 1862.

141. Baird, Samuel, merchant, in Barbados, heir to aunt Catherine Robertson, in Stranraer Wigtownshire, d. 10 Nov.1848, reg. 30 Apl.1869.

142. Baird or Munro, Sarah Bell, in Washington USA, heir to aunt Mary Bell, in Glasgow then Helensburgh Dunbartonshire, reg. 29 Sep.1851.

143. Baird, William, in Va, heir to bro John Baird, son of John Baird merchant in Va, reg. 18 Apr.1807.

144. Baird, William, marblecutter, in NJ, heir to fa Archibald Baird, mason in Kilmarnock Ayrshire, reg. 15 Sep.1858.

145. Bald, William Telfer, in Can, heir to fa Adam Bald, merchant in Glasgow, reg. 20 Nov.1846.

146. Ballantyne, James Burn, in Fort Clark Tex, heir to Thomas Vair, merchant in Kelso Roxburghshire, d. 15 Oct.1830, reg. 7 Nov.1871.

147. Ballantyne, Robert, merchant, in Albany NA, heir to bro James Ballantyne, wright in Perth, reg. 16 June 1829.

148. Ballingall, James, in San Francisco, heir to uncle James Ballingall, cabinetmaker in Perth, reg. 25 July 1854.

149. Ballingall, Laurence, baker, in Mo, heir to uncle William Ballingall, accountant in Edinburgh, reg. 1 Apr.1857.

150. Ballingall, Laurence, baker, in Mo, heir to uncle Laurence Ballingall, in Cupar Fife, reg. 3 Apr.1857.

151. Balmanno, Robert, in Brooklyn NY, heir to sis Helen Balmanno, in Aberdeen, reg. 23 Oct.1857.

152. Balmer, Robert, merchant, in Montreal, heir to fa Richard Balmer, mason in Cessford Roxburghshire, d. 11 Apr.1849, reg. 27 Dec.1859.
153. Banks, Charles Benjamin, in Wilmington NC, heir to grandmo Marion Shaw or Banks, wid of Charles Banks in Stevenston, d. 20 Dec.1854, reg. 3 Dec.1868.
154. Barbour or Lyle, Margaret, in Houston Renfrewshire, heir to bro Robert Lyle, in Lottery Jamaica, reg. 26 Aug.1839.
155. Barclay, Ann, in USA, heir to mo Ann Auld or Barclay, wife of Charles Barclay in Old Meldrum Aberdeenshire, reg. 17 June 1853.
156. Barclay, Ann, in USA, heir to fa Charles Barclay, saddler in Old Meldrum Aberdeenshire, reg. 17 June 1853.
157. Barclay or Houton, Beatrix Bessy, w of Andrew Houton, in Kelty Fife, heir to bro James Barclay, merchant in Jamaica, reg. 14 July 1750.
158. Barclay, Charles George, merchant, in Jamaica, heir to fa Charles Barclay, farmer in Inchbroom Elgin Morayshire, d. 27 Oct.1854, reg. 9 July 1855.
159. Barclay or Chalmers, Christian, w of James Chalmers, in America, heir to bro John Barclay, in Cupar Fife, reg. 13 July 1849.
160. Barclay or Cockerton, Clementina, w of R Cockerton, in Trinidad, heir to fa Thomas Barclay, auctioneer in Glasgow, d. 22 May 1853, reg. 28 Oct.1854.
161. Barclay, James, in Jamaica, heir to bro George Barclay of Cairnes, in Aberdeenshire, d. June 1756, reg. 23 Aug.1757.
162. Barclay or Henderson, Janet, w of George Henderson gardener, in Kirkland, heir to bro James Barclay, merchant in Jamaica, reg. 15 Nov.1750.
163. Barclay, John, mason, in America, heir to fa James Barclay, shoemaker in Dornoch Ross & Cromarty, reg. 15 Nov.1830.
164. Barclay, Patrick, merchant, in Va, heir to fa Andrew Barclay, writer in Edinburgh, reg. 24 Aug.1745.
165. Barclay, Patrick, merchant, in Va, heir to bro William Barclay, s of Andrew Barclay writer in Edinburgh, reg. 24 Aug.1745.
166. Barclay, Patrick, merchant, in Va, heir to bro Henry Barclay, s of Andrew Barclay writer in Edinburgh, reg. 14 Mar.1749.
167. Barland, Thomas, in Wisc, heir to fa John Barland, tacksman in Stormontfield Perthshire, d. 7 Dec.1827, reg. 10 Jan.1862.
168. Barnet, John, builder, in London, heir to uncle John Mackay, mason in Jamaica, reg. 4 Oct.1854.
169. Barr, Agnes, in Mass, heir to grandfa Archibald Barr, farmer in Linn of Cathcart Lanarkshire, reg. 4 Jan.1812.
170. Barr, Sarah, in Mass, heir to grandfa Archibald Barr, farmer in Linn of Cathcart Lanarkshire, reg. 4 Jan.1812.

171. Barrie, Robert, son of Robert Barrie surgeon, in Pensacola Fla, heir to grandmo Isabella Forsyth, in Sanquhar Dumfries-shire, reg. 3 Jan.1791.

172. Barrie, Robert, in Blair Mich, heir to mo Mary Findlay or Barrie, w of John Barrie in Lanfine Tileworks Newmilns Ayrshire, d. 23 Sep.1863, reg. 14 Oct.1870.

173. Bartlett or Mackay, Agnes, w of James Mackay, in NY, heir to fa James Bartlett, farmer in Nether Mains of Muchalls Kincardineshire, d. 1 Sep.1858, reg. 15 Oct.1869.

174. Barton, William, in Edinburgh, heir to mother Margaret Mossman or Barton, w of P Barton in Toronto, reg. 22 Feb.1860.

175. Baxter or Greenfield, Ann, wid of William Greenfield, in NY, heir to fa David Baxter, millwright in Glasgow, reg. 4 June 1824.

176. Bayne, Thomas, in Ida, heir to mo Agnes Blair or Bayne, w of William Bayne grocer in Doune Stirlingshire, reg. 27 Apr.1859.

177. Bayne, Thomas, in Halifax NS, heir to Margaret Neilson or Bayne, w of Rev Andrew Bayne in E Barns East Lothian, reg. 2 June 1881.

178. Beattie, Ann Hardie, in Miramachi NS, heir to fa James Beattie, wright in Annan Dumfries-shire, reg. 3 Mar.1826.

179. Beattie, Elizabeth Margaret, in Penrith Cumberland, heir to granduncle Francis Beattie, hat manufacturer in Dumfries then Montreal, d. 29 Sep.1828, reg. 2 Oct.1862.

180. Beatton or Bethune, William, farmer, in Walpole Haldimand Can, heir to fa Alexander Beaton, schoolmaster in Kinghorn Fife, d. 3 June 1850, reg. 13 Aug.1853.

181. Begbie or Yarrel, Elizabeth, w of Capt G Yarrel, in Carolina, heir to granduncle William Begbie of Giffordvale, reg. 6 Nov.1827.

182. Begbie, Thomas, in Williamstown NC, heir to granduncle William Begbie of Giffordvale, reg. 6 Nov.1827.

183. Begrie, Edward William, in Nassau New Providence, heir to Alexander Begrie, in Edinburgh, reg. 11 Nov.1881.

184. Begrie, Edward William, in Nassau New Providence, heir to William Begrie, in Edinburgh, reg. 11 Nov.1881.

185. Begrie, Edward William, in Nassau New Providence, heir to David Begrie, in Edinburgh, reg. 11 Nov.1881.

186. Beith, John, in Toronto, heir to fa John Beith, in Rothesay Bute, d. 6 Dec.1872, reg. 30 Apl.1874.

187. Beith, John, in San Francisco, heir to fa John Beith, merchant in Rothesay Bute, d. 6 Dec.1872, reg. 9 Mar.1877.

188. Bell or Combe, Ann, in NY, heir to sis Catherine Bell or Roy, w of William Brown Roy in Dundee Angus, d. 27 May 1858, reg. 15 Dec.1864.

189. Bell or Haig, Jane, w of Stephenson Haig, in NY, heir to uncle William Bell, roadman in Duns Berwickshire, d. 29 Sep.1871, reg. 8 Aug.1873.
190. Bell or Wilson, Janet, in Brooklyn NY, heir to uncle William Bell, roadman in Duns Berwickshire, d. 29 Sep.1871, reg. 8 Aug.1873.
191. Bell, John, weaver, in Schagticoke NA, heir to fa David Bell, weaver in Paisley Renfrewshire, reg. 28 Dec.1832.
192. Bell, John, s of Alexander Bell tobacconist, in Edinburgh, heir to sis Jean Bell or Minor, w of Dr Minor in Va, reg. 6 May 1835.
193. Bell of Carruthers, William, heir to uncle William Bell, in Falmouth Jamaica, reg. 29 Mar.1828.
194. Bell, William, in Falmouth Jamaica, heir to bro Thomas Bell, in Carruthers Dumfries-shire, reg. 28 Nov.1818.
195. Bell, William, in Jamaica then Lockerbie Dumfries-shire, heir to uncle William Bell, in Falmouth Jamaica, reg. 29 Sep.1827.
196. Bell, William, in Niagara, heir to grandfa Robert Renwick, deacon of wrights in Jedburgh Roxburghshire, reg. 12 Oct.1842.
197. Bell, William Pierce, in Washington DC, heir to grandfa William Bell, architect in Fayetteville NC, d. 17 Sep.1865, reg. 6 Oct.1868.
198. Bell, William, in San Francisco, heir to mo Janet Jardine or Bell, innkeeper in Kirkcudbright, d. 29 Sep.1861, reg. 20 Sep.1876.
199. Bennet, William, merchant, in Can W, heir to William Schoolbred, in Kinnesswood Kinross-shire, reg. 27 Oct.1858.
200. Bennet, William, merchant, in Can W, heir to uncle William Schoolbred or Schoolbraid, portioner of Kinnesswood in Kinross-shire, reg. 22 Oct.1861.
201. Bennett, George William, merchant, in Antigua, heir to bro James Henry Bennett, engineer in Leith Mid Lothian, d. 11 Apl.1874, reg. 9 May 1876.
202. Berford, William R F, in Elmsley Can, heir to sis Ann Mary Berford or Brown, w of David Brown of Rawflat, reg. 26 Nov.1830.
203. Berrie, George, farmer, in USA, heir to grandfa James Berrie of Thomaston, reg. 1 Sep.1856.
204. Bertram, James, in Salem NJ, heir to bro William Bertram, in ship THAMES, reg. 28 Mar.1806.
205. Berwick, Andrew, teacher, in Oh, heir to fa David Berwick, mason in Kettlebridge Fife then Islay Argyll , reg. 6 Sep.1860.
206. Berwick or Brown, Elizabeth, wid of William Brown, in Cumberland St Glasgow, heir to fa Newall Berwick, in Jamaica, reg. 12 Mar.1860.
207. Berwick, Mary, in Cumberland St Glasgow, heir to fa Newall Berwick, in Jamaica, reg. 12 Mar.1860.
208. Best, Isabella, in Wolfville NS, heir to aunt Barbara Playfair, da of R Playfair writer in Edinburgh, reg. 26 Feb.1844.

11

209. Beveridge, James, brewer, in Albany America, heir to fa Francis
     Beveridge, shipmaster in Kirkcaldy Fife, reg. 6 May 1818.
210. Beveridge, Thomas, in Craighead of Aldie Kinross then Can, heir to
     uncle Benjamin Greig, silk-mercer in Edinburgh, d. 31 May 1858,
     reg. 6 Feb.1861.
211. Birnie, William, in Aberdeen, heir to uncle William Black, in Charleston
     SC, reg. 25 Aug.1835.
212. Birrell, Ebenezer, in Kinnesswood Greenwood Ont, heir to sis Mary
     Birrell, in Peckham, d. 25 Mar.1881, reg. 6 Sep.1882.
213. Birrell, George, manufacturer, in Dunfermline Fife, heir to bro William
     Birrell, MD in Barbados, d. 18 July 1849, reg. 7 June 1850.
214. Bisset, Robert, coachpainter, in Gonzales Tex, heir to sis Jane Bisset or
     Macdonald, w of William Macdonald in Glasgow, d. 1 Sep.1863,
     reg. 29 May 1863.
215. Bisset, Thomas, machinist, in Richmond NA, heir to mo Elizabeth Urie
     or Bisset, in Glasgow, d. 31 Oct.1847, reg. 9 Oct.1861.
216. Black, Andrew, in Westmoreland Jamaica, heir to fa Archibald Black,
     merchant tailor in Glasgow, reg. 26 July 1782.
217. Black, David, in Up Can, heir to sis Mary Black, reg. 22 Jan.1858.
218. Black, Hugh, oil merchant, in Can W, heir to sis Ann Black or Swaine,
     w of Thomas Swaine blockprinter in Paisley Renfrewshire, d. June
     1859, reg. 24 Nov.1863.
219. Black, John, in Toronto, heir to sis Marian Scotland Black or Stow, in
     Toronto, reg. 6 Nov.1850.
220. Black, Samuel, in Up Can, heir to sis Jessie Black, Up Can, reg. 27
     Jan.1858.
221. Black, William McMillan, in Montreal, heir to aunt Marion McMillan or
     Mundell, in Wallacehall, reg. 19 Mar.1852.
222. Black, William, joiner, in Patterson NJ, heir to fa David Black,
     messenger-at-arms in Falkirk Stirlingshire, d. 21 Jan.1866, reg. 21
     Oct.1874.
223. Black, William, in Toronto, heir to bro James Black, in Manchester, d.
     14 Dec.1871, reg. 11 May 1880.
224. Blackburn, John Baziel, heir to fa Hugh Blackburn, in Boston USA, reg.
     23 Jan.1837.
225. Blackburn, William, in Murraybay Can, heir to aunt Christiana Nairn, in
     Murraybay Can, reg. 7 Nov.1821.
226. Blackburn, William, in Murraybay Can, heir to mo Mary Nairne or
     Blackburn, w of Austin Blackburn in Murraybay Can, reg. 7
     Nov.1821.
227. Blacklock, Alexander, in Annan Dumfries-shire then Can, heir to sis
     Helen Blacklock or Jackson, w of Thomas Jackson in Annan, reg.
     27 Sep.1858.

228. Blacklock, John Carruthers, deputy postmaster, in Toronto, heir to bro James Blacklock, in Albie Chapel Middlebie Dumfries, d. 23 Sep.1882, reg. 9 Jan.1883.
229. Blackstock or McWilliam, Janet, wid of J Blackstock, in Dalton, heir to bro John McWilliam, planter in Grenada, reg. 16 May 1829.
230. Blackwood, John, weaver, in Johnstone Renfrewshire then NY, heir to grandfa Duncan McArthur, gardener in Glasgow, reg. 16 July 1841.
231. Blaikie, Andrew, engineer, in USA, heir to uncle Francis Blaikie, in St Helens Roxburghshire, d. 17 Aug.1857, reg. 28 May 1858.
232. Blaikie, Marion, wid of John Blaikie weaver, in Haddington East Lothian, heir to cousin John Williamson, planter in Va, reg. 17 Sep.1785.
233. Blain, Andrew, in Charlestown NA, heir to sis Margaret Blain or McNish, w of D McNish merchant in Newton Stewart, reg. 20 May 1828.
234. Blain, James, in St Thomas, heir to grandfa James Blain, smith in Bush of Girthon, reg. 6 Mar.1817.
235. Blain, James, merchant, in San Domingo, heir to bro Joseph Blain, shipmaster in Greenock Renfrewshire, reg. 22 Nov.1839.
236. Blair, Archibald, in Richmond Va, heir to fa James Blair, s of Archibald Blair writer in Edinburgh, reg. 21 Feb.1800.
237. Blair, Archibald, in Cayuga Up Can, heir to cousin Archibald Blair of Merchiston, reg. 19 Oct.1836.
238. Blair, James Scott, in Detroit, heir to grandfa Dugald Blair, in Lochgilphead Argyll, d. 1812, reg. 28 May 1878.
239. Blair, John, merchant, in Va, heir to bro James Blair, writer in Edinburgh, reg. 22 Aug.1719.
240. Blair, John, merchant, in Va, heir to aunt Elizabeth Blair, in Edinburgh, reg. 24 Dec.1737.
241. Blair, John, in Charlestown NA, heir to aunt Agnes Blair, dau of Rev George Blair in Edzell Angus, reg. 27 June 1806.
242. Blair-Ferguson of Balthayock, Adam J, barrister, in Guelph Can, heir to bro Neil Ferguson-Blair of Balthayock, d. 12 Jan.1862, reg. 13 May 1862.
243. Bland or Collard, Janet Millar, w of S D Collard, in Hudson City USA, heir to grandfa Alexander Bland, in Twynholm Kirk, d. 30 Dec.1853, reg. 1 Feb.1869.
244. Blount, James, in Dumfries, heir to Samuel Blount, in Jamaica, reg. 21 Mar.1829.
245. Blount or Robinson, Jessie, in Jamaica, heir to mo Barbara McKewn or Blount, w of Samuel Blount in Carsethorn, reg. 13 Sep.1855.
246. Blount, John, in Dumfries, heir to cousin Samuel Blount, in Hordly Est Jamaica, reg. 3 Feb.1829.

247. Bluntach, James, in Hastings Minn, heir to fa John Bluntach, Inspector of Poor in Forres Morayshire, d. 9 Feb.1867, reg. 17 July 1872.

248. Blyth, James, in Chance Inn, heir to fa Thomas Blyth, wright in Grenada, reg. 6 June 1783.

249. Blyth, Robert, farmer, in Racine Wisc, heir to sis Jane Blyth, in Crail Fife, d. 28 May 1882, reg. 9 Aug.1882.

250. Boag, Robert, mason, in Dundee Ill, heir to mo Jean Boag, w of Robert Boag in Easter Levan Inverkip Renfrewshire, d. 23 Mar.1825, reg. 27 July 1869.

251. Boddan, John, in Tuckersmith Can, heir to uncle James Clark, in Woodend, d. 3 Feb.1839, reg. 2 Nov.1866.

252. Bogart, David Brown, in Passiac NJ, heir to grand-aunt Margaret Lamond, in Aberdeen, d. Jan.1833, reg. 16 Feb.1878.

253. Bonnar, Thomas, sergeant 71st Regiment of Foot, in Can, heir to fa Thomas Bonnar, wright in Dunfermline Fife, reg. 15 Jan.1850.

254. Bontein, Thomas, in London, heir to fa William Bontein, Captain of Engineers in NA, reg. 6 May 1788.

255. Boreland, James, soldier 42nd(Black Watch)Regiment, in Can, heir to Alexander Campbell, chandler in Gorbals Glasgow, reg. 10 Dec.1828.

256. Boreland, Peter, soldier 42nd(Black Watch)Regiment, in Can, heir to Alexander Campbell, chandler in Gorbals Glasgow, reg. 10 Dec.1828.

257. Borthwick, Charles, in San Francisco, heir to bro David Borthwick, in Bute Valley Nev, d. 20 Feb.1873, reg. 27 Mar.1877.

258. Boswell or Reid, Elizabeth, w of David Reid merchant, in Jamaica, heir to fa David Boswell, merchant in Leven Fife, reg. 26 Dec.1797.

259. Boswell, Robert, in St James Jamaica, heir to fa David Boswell, merchant in Leven Fife, reg. 26 Dec.1797.

260. Bowie, Ann Andrew, da of Ralph Bowie, in America, heir to grandfa George Bartholemew, merchant in Linlithgow W Lothian, reg. 25 Sep.1805.

261. Bowie, John, heir to mo Ann Bartholemew or Bowie, w of Ralph Bowie attorney in Yorktown America, reg. 1805.

262. Bowman, Alexander Gordon, in Ayr, heir to fa John Bowman, in Jamaica, d. 9 July 1838, reg. 3 Apr.1851.

263. Bowman or Rollo, Andrew F C, in Can, heir to Margaret Bowman, in Ashgrove Kilwinning Ayrshire, reg. 8 Mar.1860.

264. Bowman, Emily Margaret, in Edinburgh, heir to fa John Bowman, in Jamaica, d. 9 July 1838, reg. 3 Apr.1851.

265. Bowman, James Oswald, in Georgetown Md, heir to fa David Bowman, s of David Bowman shipmaster in Kirkcaldy Fife, reg. 24 Feb.1796.

266. Bowman, James, architect, in Fosterdale NY, heir to cousin Ann Gordon or Martin, in Milton Villa Pittenweem Fife, d. 3 Apr.1862, reg. 12 Mar.1863.

267. Bowman, John, in St John NB, heir to grandfa William Thomson, in Halhill Old Monkland, d. 18 May 1831, reg. 10 Mar.1865.

268. Bowman, John, in Boston USA, heir to bro William Bowman, in Middleton Farm Kilbarchan Renfrewshire, d. 2 Nov.1858, reg. 13 July 1867.

269. Bowman, John, in Boston USA, heir to mo Mary Thomson or Bowman, w of Thomas Bowman in Halhill Old Monkland, d. 10 Jan.1837, reg. 18 Dec.1867.

270. Bowman, John, in St John NB, heir to mo Mary Thomson or Bowman, w of Thomas Bowman farmer in Halhill Lanarkshire, reg. 11 Jan.1867.

271. Boxil or Innes, Helen Eliza, w of William Boxil, in Barbados, heir to mo Isabella Lumsden or Innes, in Aberdeen, reg. 7 Dec.1816.

272. Boyce, Joseph, engineer, in NY, heir to gt-grandfa Joseph Boyce, mason in Hillhousefield, d. 1841, reg. 11 May 1870.

273. Boyd, John, in Vandale Minn, heir to fa Alexander Boyd, in Paisley Renfrewshire, d. 18 July 1845, reg. 6 Nov.1883.

274. Boyd, Maitland Wilson, heir to fa William Boyd, merchant in Charleston SC, reg. 24 Aug.1829.

275. Boyle, James Lawrence, s of John Boyle, in St Croix, heir to grand-uncle James Stewart, MD in Christwell, d. 1731, reg. 12 Feb.1777.

276. Boyle or Knott, Jessie Montgomerie, w of James Knott merchant, in Jersey NJ, heir to fa John Boyle, in NJ, d. 30 Apr.1866, reg. 15 Aug.1879.

277. Bradbury, Eleanora, w of Charles Bradbury, in Boston USA, heir to aunt Margaret Bell, in Ayr, reg. 8 Mar.1825.

278. Brander, Alexander, heir to mo Jean Brander or Muterer, in Cloves Morayshire then Pa, reg. 7 May 1838.

279. Brander, Ann, heir to mo Jean Muterer or Brander, in Cloves Morayshire then Pa, reg. 7 May 1838.

280. Brander or Mellis, Jean, in Pa, heir to mo Jean Muterer or Brander, in Cloves Morayshire then Pa, reg. 7 May 1838.

281. Brander or Muterer, Jean, in Pa, heir to mo Jean Muterer or Brander, in Cloves Morayshire then Pa, reg. 7 May 1838.

282. Brander or Muterer, Jean, in Pa, heir to uncle John Muterer, in Lingieston Morayshire, reg. 7 Sep.1839.

283. Brander, Margaret, heir to mo Jean Muterer or Brander, in Cloves Morayshire then Pa, reg. 7 May 1838.

284. Brander, Robert, heir to mo Jean Muterer or Brander, in Cloves Morayshire then Pa, reg. 7 May 1838.

285. Brander, Robina, heir to mo Jean Muterer or Brander, in Cloves
     Morayshire then Pa, reg. 7 May 1838.
286. Brander, William, heir to mo Jean Muterer or Brander, in Cloves
     Morayshire then Pa, reg. 7 May 1838.
287. Brands, Ann, heir to bro Robert Brands, physician in Jamaica, reg. 30
     May 1795.
288. Brands, Caroline, heir to bro Robert Brands, physician in Jamaica, reg.
     30 May 1795.
289. Brands, Isabella, heir to bro Robert Brands, physician in Jamaica, reg. 30
     May 1795.
290. Brands or Webster, Margaret, wid of Thomas Webster of Balkaithly, heir
     to bro Robert Brands, physician in Jamaica, reg. 30 May 1795.
291. Brasnell, William, in London, heir to fa William Brasnell, in Tobago,
     reg. 8 Aug.1833.
292. Breakinridge, John, in Campbelltown Argyll, heir to bro Thomas
     Breakinridge, merchant in Jamaica, reg. 11 May 1839.
293. Brebner, James, s of Alexander Brebner vintner, in Glasgow, heir to uncle
     James Cross, in Va, reg. 7 May 1788.
294. Brebner, James, Royal Canadian Rifle Regiment, heir to uncle Alexander
     Brebner, ironmonger in Stonehaven Kincardineshire, reg. 20
     Dec.1867.
295. Bremner, Thomas, shipcarpenter, in Philadelphia, heir to fa George
     Bremner, feuar in Greenlaw Berwickshire, reg. 31 Oct.1799.
296. Brims or Calder, Helen, w of William Calder, in Can, heir to fa Donald
     Brims, fisherman in Thurso Caithness, reg. 8 May 1857.
297. Brine, Robert, in San Francisco, heir to grandmo Katherine Grant or
     Stewart, reg. 29 Dec.1870.
298. Brock, William, heir to uncle Daniel Virtue, in Manchester Middlesex
     Jamaica, reg. 21 Apr.1824.
299. Brodie, Mathew, in Howick Can, heir to fa Andrew Brodie, surveyor in
     Edinburgh, reg. 3 May 1854.
300. Brotherston or Seton, Barbara, wid of Ludovic Brotherston, in St Kitts,
     heir to bro Archibald Seton of Touch, in Stirlingshire, d. 30
     Mar.1818, reg. 10 July 1818.
301. Brotherstone, Robert, in Paspebiac Gaspe Quebec, heir to gt-granduncle
     William Brotherstone, in Peebles, reg. 20 Oct.1841.
302. Brown, Archibald, tinsmith, in Petersburg Va, heir to Jean Cunningham,
     in Rothesay Bute, d. 8 Jan.1873, reg. 5 Dec.1876.
303. Brown, Charles, baker, in Petersburg Va, heir to Jean Cunningham, in
     Rothesay Bute, d. 8 Jan.1873, reg. 5 Dec.1876.
304. Brown, David, merchant, in NY, heir to grandfa George Dobie, cordiner
     in Selkirk, reg. 9 Aug.1826.
305. Brown, David, in Can, heir to grandmo Agnes Irving or Brown, in
     Castlebank Dumfrieshire, reg. 23 June 1871.

306. Brown, David, in Can, heir to granduncle Edward Irving, in Ecclefechan Dumfriesshire, reg. 23 June 1871.

307. Brown or Murison, Elizabeth, in Halifax NA, heir to Janet Morrison or Orr, wid of Thomas Orr shipmaster in Greenock Renfrewshire, reg. 2 Apr.1830.

308. Brown, George, in Selkirk, heir to bro David Brown, merchant in NY, reg. 1 Feb.1837.

309. Brown, Gustavus, MD, in Mainside Md, heir to grandfa Gustavus Brown, MD in Mainside Roxburghshire, d. Mar.1762, reg. 4 Dec.1792.

310. Brown, James, in Peebles then America, heir to uncle James Thomson, in Jamaica, reg. 1 Mar.1833.

311. Brown, James Emanuel, in RI then Lacrosse, heir to fa William James Brown, in Edinburgh then Ohio, reg. 13 Sep.1853.

312. Brown or Williamson, Jane C, in Halifax NS, heir to Janet Morrison or Orr, wid of Thomas Orr shipmaster in Greenock Renfrewshire, reg. 2 Apr.1830.

313. Brown, John, heir to fa Alexander Brown, merchant in St Kitts & London, reg. 10 Apr.1765.

314. Brown, John, merchant, in Montreal, heir to grandfa John Morton, mason in Ayr, reg. 15 Feb.1821.

315. Brown, John W C, in Halifax NS, heir to Janet Morrison or Orr, wid of Thomas Orr shipmaster in Greenock Renfrewshire, reg. 2 Apr.1830.

316. Brown, John Moore, in Can, heir to sis Helen Brown, da of Principal Brown in Marischal College Aberdeen, reg. 6 Feb.1849.

317. Brown, John James, captain of THE LISBON, in St John NB, heir to grandfa William Brown, sawyer in Pennyhole St Andrews Fife, reg. 4 Jan.1855.

318. Brown, John Caldwell, in Havanna, heir to mo Marion Robertson or Brown, in Irvine Ayrshire, d. 2 Aug.1849, reg. 28 Nov.1861.

319. Brown, John Caldwell, in Havanna, heir to aunt Elizabeth Robertson, in Irvine Ayrshire, d. 19 May 1854, reg. 28 Nov.1861.

320. Brown, Margaret, in USA, heir to fa Thomas Brown, in Pathhead Kirkcaldy Fife, reg. 7 Dec.1848.

321. Brown or Taylor, Mary, in Petersburg Va, heir to Jean Cunningham, in Rothesay Bute, d. 8 Jan.1873, reg. 5 Dec.1876.

322. Brown or Nicol, Mary, in NJ, heir to fa James Brown, weaver in Anstruther Fife, d. 29 July 1855, reg. 1 Sep.1876.

323. Brown or Arnold, Mary, in Lafayette RI, heir to fa Alexander Brown, in Aberdeen, d. 8 Jan.1862, reg. 29 May 1902.

324. Brown, Robert, heir to fa Dr John Brown, surgeon in Va then Coldstream Berwickshire, reg. 5 Oct.1731.

325. Brown, Robert Morrison, in Halifax NS, heir to Janet Morrison or Orr, wid of Thomas Orr shipmaster in Greenock Renfrewshire, reg. 2 Apr.1830.

326. Brown, Robert, tinsmith, in Petersburg Va, heir to Jean Cunningham, in Rothesay Bute, d. 8 Jan.1873, reg. 5 Dec.1876.

327. Brown, Robert, miner, in Pratt Mines Ala, heir to fa John Brown, coalhewer in Irvine Ayrshire, d. 22 July 1869, reg. 12 July 1882.

328. Brown, Samuel, in Boarland, heir to cousin Alexander Brown, in Jamaica, d. Oct.1770, reg. 16 Aug.1771.

329. Brown, William, in Up Can, heir to fa Henry Brown, mason in Thornton Fife, d. 1 June 1824, reg. 28 Jan.1850.

330. Brown, William, in Buffalo USA, heir to fa William Brown, farm-servant in Penicuik Mid Lothian, d. 27 Sep.1856, reg. 22 July 1873.

331. Brown, William, tinsmith, in Petersburg Va, heir to Jean Cunningham, in Rothesay Bute, d. 8 Jan.1873, reg. 5 Dec.1876.

332. Bruce, James, in Barbados, heir to sis Mary Bruce, da of Alexander Bruce of Garland, reg. 9 Jan.1728.

333. Bruce, Lawrence, in St Louis NA, heir to fa Alexander Bruce, mason in Burrelton Perthshire, d. 11 Feb.1847, reg. 5 July 1866.

334. Bruce, William, in Tobago, heir to bro Andrew Bruce, Lt Col 5th Regiment of Foot, d. Dec.1791, reg. 14 Sep.1792.

335. Bruce, William, in NY, heir to fa William Bruce, wright in St Andrews Fife, reg. 18 July 1843.

336. Bryan, Robert, sergeant-major 117th Regiment NY Volunteers, in Va, heir to fa William Bryan, druggist in Catrine Ayrshire, reg. 29 Dec.1864.

337. Bryce or Martin, Agnes, w of Hugh Martin enginedriver, in Ia, heir to grandmo Jean Grindlay or Finlay, wid of John Finlay in Airdrie Lanarkshire, d. 26 Oct.1847, reg. 3 Nov.1871.

338. Bryce, David, merchant, in Trinidad, heir to grandfa Andrew Gray, feuar in Greenock Renfrewshire, d. July 1807, reg. 1 Aug.1850.

339. Bryce or Smith, Janet, in America, heir to uncle John Lyon, in Society Hopetoun House W Lothian, reg. 18 Feb.1833.

340. Bryden, James, in America, heir to mo Mary McMurdo or Bryden, w of James Bryden in Canple Closeburn, d. 4 Feb.1856, reg. 13 Sep.1875.

341. Bryden, James, tailor, in Delhi Ont, heir to fa William Bryden, in Crosshill Kirkmichael, d. 3 Dec.1881, reg. 6 July 1882.

342. Bryden, John, in NB, heir to grandfa John Bryden, farmer in Tardoars Ayrshire, reg. 25 Oct.1844.

343. Brydon or Todd, Margaret, in Glasgow then Trinidad, heir to mo Margaret Smith or Brydon, w of Andrew Brydon bookseller in Glasgow, reg. 8 Nov.1861.

344. Brymer, George William, shipmaster, in NY, heir to mo Elizabeth Fairlie or Brymer, in Greenock Renfrewshire, reg. 25 Oct.1850.
345. Buchan, David, in Toronto, heir to Lawrence Buchan, manufacturer in Manchester, d. 21 July 1859, reg. 6 Jan.1877.
346. Buchan, James, in Owen Sound Can, heir to fa Walter Ewing Buchan, in Glasgow then Owen Sound, d. 27 Feb.1857, reg. 7 Aug.1861.
347. Buchan, William, in Jamaica, heir to sis Mary Buchan, in Stirling, reg. 5 Feb.1836.
348. Buchan, William, in Jamaica, heir to bro Richard Buchan, Royal Marines, reg. 5 Feb.1836.
349. Buchanan, George, in Shelbourne NS, heir to bro Robertson Buchanan, civil engineer in Glasgow, reg. 3 Mar.1820.
350. Buchanan, James, merchant, in Va, heir to bro Gilbert Buchanan, s of Archibald Buchanan of Drumhead in Dunbartonshire, reg. 16 Mar.1759.
351. Buchanan, James, in Jamaica, heir to bro William Buchanan of Buchanan & Auchmar, reg. 16 June 1800.
352. Buchanan, James, merchant, in Ottawa, heir to fa James Buchanan, in Tollcross Glasgow, d. 23 June 1880, reg. 13 Oct.1882.
353. Buchanan or Hair, Janet, w of John Hair, in Glasgow, heir to uncle Coll Turner, merchant in Tobago, reg. 26 Feb.1817.
354. Buchanan or McCulloch, Janet, wid of Dr M McCulloch, in Montreal, heir to sis Elizabeth Buchanan, in Glasgow, reg. 27 Apr.1860.
355. Buchanan or Lyon, Jessie, in East Newark NJ, heir to fa James Buchanan, in Tollcross Glasgow, d. 23 June 1880, reg. 13 Oct.1882.
356. Buchanan, John, in Rodgerville Can, heir to fa James Buchanan, farmer in Callendar Stirlingshire, d. 12 June 1873, reg. 17 Dec.1875.
357. Buchanan, Mary, in NY, heir to bro James Buchanan of Milncroft, reg. 19 Dec.1814.
358. Buchanan, Thomas, merchant, in NY, heir to fa George Buchanan, brewer in Glasgow, reg. 29 Sep.1794.
359. Buchanan-Kincaid, Charles, in Brantford Can W, heir to uncle John Buchanan-Kincaid, in Carbeth Stirlingshire, d. 14 Mar.1872, reg. 19 Dec.1872.
360. Buffum or Russell, Elizabeth, w of B Buffum, in NY, heir to grandfa William Russell of Whiteside, reg. 31 Mar.1813.
361. Buffum or Russell, Elizabeth, w of B Buffum, in NY, heir to William Russell jr of Whiteside, reg. 6 July 1814.
362. Buist or Smith, Catherine, in Bronzton Mich, heir to fa John Buist, weaver in Sinclairtown Kirkcaldy Fife, d. 7 Sep.1878, reg. 25 June 1879.
363. Burn, James, in Baltimore Md, heir to fa William Burn, merchant in Edinburgh, reg. 12 Aug.1802.

364. Burnet, Peter, provincial land surveyor, in Can W, heir to mo Elizabeth Tower or Burnet, wid of Francis Burnet in Aberdeen, reg. 15 June 1865.

365. Burnet, William, sailor, in Philadelphia, heir to bro Alexander Burnet, merchant in Aberdeen, reg. 23 Mar.1793.

366. Burnett or Strachan, Margaret, in America, heir to uncle Alexander Burnett, weaver in Old Aberdeen, reg. 12 June 1840.

367. Burnham or Hynd, Ann, in Va, heir to gt grandmo H Lowson or Morris, w of G Morris barber in Dundee Angus, reg. 30 June 1847.

368. Burns or Rae, Agnes, w of John Rae, in Savanna USA, heir to bro James Adam Burns, apothecary in Stirling, d. 5 Dec.1859, reg. 5 Feb.1861.

369. Burns, James, s of John Burns tailor, in Hamilton Lanarkshire, heir to uncle James Govan, wright in Jamaica, reg. 27 Nov.1789.

370. Burns or Thomson, Jean, in Whiteside Co Ill, heir to fa William Burns, laborer in Eglinton Ayrshire, d. 14 Oct.1845, reg. 21 May 1873.

371. Burns, John, s of John Burns tailor, in Hamilton Lanarkshire, heir to uncle James Govan, wright in Jamaica, reg. 27 Nov.1789.

372. Burns, Thomas, in Clinton Can W, heir to aunt Mary Oswald or Wilson, w of William Wilson in Larbert Stirlingshire then Belfast, d. Feb.1857, reg. 11 Feb.1862.

373. Burns, William, surgeon, in NJ, heir to bro James Burns, s of William Burns innkeeper in Hamilton Lanarkshire, reg. 29 Apr.1808.

374. Burtis or Phillips, Grace Ewing, in Buffalo USA, heir to uncle David Phillips, in Boston USA, d. 20 Oct.1806, reg. 22 Feb.1865.

375. Burton or Robertson, James, professor, in Dublin, heir to Cardelia Robertson, dau of Thomas Robertson in Grenada, reg. 13 May 1861.

376. Butler, William, in NY, heir to uncle George Chalmers, manufacturer in Stirling, reg. 26 June 1837.

377. Cairns, Emily Rebecca, in Birgham Roxburghshire, heir to uncle William Cairns of Torr, merchant in NY, d. 7 Oct.1860, reg. 12 May 1864.

378. Cairns, John, in Sabinhill NY, heir to fa James Cairns, weaver in Auchterarder Perthshire, reg. 5 Feb.1836.

379. Cairns, Louisa Sarah, in Crewcerne Somerset, heir to uncle William Cairns of Torr, merchant in NY, d. 7 Oct.1860, reg. 12 May 1864.

380. Cairns or Gilman, Mary Wilson, w of T Gilman druggist, in Birgham Roxburghshire, heir to uncle William Cairns of Torr, merchant in NY, d. 7 Oct.1860, reg. 12 May 1864.

381. Calder, William, in Hartfield Ct, heir to uncle Alexander Calder, in Asswanlie Aberdeenshire, reg. 6 July 1809.

382. Calderwood, John, in Ill, heir to cousin James Calderwood, s of James Calderwood in Rothesay Bute, d. 1819, reg. 24 May 1869.
383. Cameron or Porteous, Catherine, in Galt Ont, heir to sis Sarah Cameron or McMillan, w of Rev Dougald McMillan in Edinburgh, d. 8 Sep.1851, reg. 17 Apr.1879.
384. Cameron or Porteous, Catherine, in Galt Ont, heir to sis Agnes Cameron or Croall, w of Alexander Croall in NY, d. 1 June 1852, reg. 30 Apr.1879.
385. Cameron or Porteous, Catherine, in Galt Ont, heir to sis Martine Cameron, in Dundee Angus, d. 9 July 1872, reg. 31 May 1879.
386. Cameron, James, commission agent, in Detroit, heir to fa James Cameron, slater in Inverness, reg. 9 Jan.1857.
387. Cameron, James, in Can W, heir to fa James Cameron, contractor in Woodend, reg. 19 June 1857.
388. Cameron, John, in Cape Breton NS, heir to fa Duncan Cameron, workman in Johnstone Renfrewshire, reg. 29 Nov.1830.
389. Cameron, Robert, carrier, in NY, heir to fa Robert Cameron, teacher in Paisley Renfrewshire, d. 15 June 1854, reg. 17 Apr.1866.
390. Cameron, Robert, expressman, in S Brooklyn USA, heir to mo Elisabeth Willison Bennie or Cameron, w of Robert Cameron teacher in Paisley Renfrewshire, d. 27 Feb.1848, reg. 21 Mar.1871.
391. Campbell, Abram, in NY then Stranraer Wigtownshire, heir to bro John Campbell, mariner in Stranraer, reg. 23 June 1849.
392. Campbell, Agnes, in St John NB, heir to uncle James Hart, in St John NB, reg. 25 July 1825.
393. Campbell, Agnes, in St John NB, heir to grandfa James Hart, weaver in Paisley Renfrewshire, reg. 9 Feb.1829.
394. Campbell, Andrew Young, in Lake Superior America, heir to uncle William Campbell, portioner in Oakfield Fife, d. 1 June 1862, reg. 16 Aug.1864.
395. Campbell, Archibald, in Jamaica, heir to fa John Campbell, tacksman in Larksfield Inverkip Renfrewshire, reg. 25 Feb.1794.
396. Campbell, Calenus, in Newhope Jamaica, heir to nephew Price John Campbell, in St Vincent, reg. 21 May 1798.
397. Campbell, Catherine, da of Hugh Campbell of Lix, heir to uncle Colin Campbell, planter in SC, reg. 25 Jan.1791.
398. Campbell, Colin Coillain, master mariner, in NY, heir to uncle Farquhar MacIver, minister in Glenshiel Inverness-shire, d. 20 Sep.1863, reg. 3 Nov.1866.
399. Campbell, George, banker, in Piper City Ill, heir to bro John Campbell, MD in Glasgow, d. 25 Apr.1875, reg. 28 Dec.1882.
400. Campbell, Henry, in Charleston, heir to fa McMillan Campbell, merchant in Charleston SC, reg. 18 Feb.1818.

401. Campbell or Logan, Isobel, w of George Logan merchant, in Va, heir to Mary Campbell or White, wid J White merchant in Jamaica, reg. 20 Dec.1799.
402. Campbell, James, midshipman & master-mate, in Frigate *Dido*, heir to bro John Campbell, merchant in Va, reg. 16 Nov.1798.
403. Campbell, James, in Ct, heir to bro George Campbell, flesher in Newton Stewart Wigtownshire, reg. 29 Dec.1842.
404. Campbell, James, in Mobile Ala, heir to fa George Campbell, in Newton Stewart Wigtownshire, reg. 23 Jan.1851.
405. Campbell, James, in Mobile Ala, heir to bro Archibald Campbell, tanner in Newton Stewart Wigtownshire, reg. 12 June 1852.
406. Campbell, James, in Mobile Ala, heir to sis Helen Campbell or Mitchison, w of Joseph Mitchison in Carlisle Cumberland, reg. 6 Nov.1856.
407. Campbell or Easton, Jean, in Pittsburg, heir to fa John Campbell, sergeant, reg. 18 Jan.1839.
408. Campbell, John, merchant, in Va, heir to fa Peter Campbell, minister in Kilmichael Glassary Argyll, reg. 26 June 1792.
409. Campbell, John, tobacconist, in Philadelphia, heir to bro Robert Campbell, merchant in Arbroath Angus, reg. 5 June 1837.
410. Campbell, John, in Toronto then Stranraer Wigtownshire, heir to aunt Jean Campbell, in Stranraer, reg. 16 Aug.1841.
411. Campbell jr, James, in West Troy NY, heir to uncle George Drummond, ship carpenter, d. 11 Mar.1869, reg. 6 July 1875.
412. Campbell jr, John, in Chinquacousy Can, heir to grandfa John Campbell sr, in Glenmachry Islay Argyll, d. 1841, reg. 28 Feb.1872.
413. Campbell, Margaret, w of Dugald Campbell of Ederline, heir to uncle Colin Campbell, planter in SC, reg. 25 Jan.1791.
414. Campbell or Magan, Margaret Henrietta, w of Samuel Magan midshipman USN, heir to Ralph Foster , in Drummoyne Lanarkshire, d. Feb.1810, reg. 8 Nov.1853.
415. Campbell, Maxwell Trokes, in Charleston America, heir to cousin Janet Barr or Elder, wid of James Elder writer in Glasgow, reg. 19 Oct.1849.
416. Campbell or Scott, Rebecca, wid of Adam Scott, in Jamaica, heir to grandfa Alexander Campbell, merchant in Glasgow, reg. 24 Nov.1817.
417. Campbell, Robert, millwright, in Montreal, heir to mo Jean Torrie or Campbell, wid of James Campbell in Forres Morayshire, reg. 26 Mar.1855.
418. Campbell, William, upholsterer, in Toronto, heir to grandfa William Campbell, moulder in Glasgow, reg. 28 Jan.1853.

419. Candlish or Nawgel, Henrietta, w of Frederick C Nawgel farmer, in Bedford NA, heir to aunt Eliza Candlish, in Castle Douglas Kirkcudbrightshire, reg. 22 Sep.1866.

420. Cannon, James, in Annan Ont, heir to mo Elizabeth McCandlish or Cannon, w of James Cannon farmer in Annan Ont, d. 29 Apr.1874, reg. 29 June 1882.

421. Cant or Banks, Elizabeth, w of William Banks mason, in Edinburgh, heir to bro James Cant, in Angels Cal, d. 23 June 1859, reg. 19 Aug.1869.

422. Cantley, Alexander, mariner, in NS, heir to grand-uncle George Cantley, farmer in Berryden, reg. 31 Aug.1859.

423. Cargill, John Thomas, in NY, heir to fa Thomas Cargill, flaxspinner in Dundee Angus, d. 17 Sep.1869, reg. 19 May 1875.

424. Cargill, John, in Dundee Angus, heir to uncle David Cargill, in New Orleans, d. 10 Feb.1846, reg. 3 Nov.1880.

425. Carlyle, Archibald Campbell, in Can, heir to fa Thomas Carlyle, advocate in Edinburgh then Albury Surrey, d. 28 Jan.1855, reg. 6 Sep.1855.

426. Carmichael, Charles Daniel, steamboat purser, in Toronto, heir to aunt Mary Auld, in Carnoustie Angus, d. 11 Sep.1859, reg. 27 Feb.1862.

427. Carmichael, Stewart, in Jamaica, heir to bro Robert Stewart, in Balmblae, reg. 28 July 1800.

428. Carmichael, Stewart, in Jamaica, heir to niece Magdalene Carmichael, in Balmblae, reg. 9 Mar.1801.

429. Carmichael, William, in Kingston Jamaica, heir to cousin David Lindsay, writer in Edinburgh, reg. 19 Apr.1803.

430. Carmichael, William, in Worth Tuscola Co Mich, heir to sis Sophia Carmichael, in Edinburgh, reg. 28 Nov.1870.

431. Carmichael, William, in Worth Tuscola Co Mich, heir to sis Jane Carmichael, in Edinburgh, reg. 28 Nov.1870.

432. Carnochan, John Murray, physician, in NY, heir to aunt Jane Carnochan or McMaster, wid of William McMaster in Charleston SC, d. July 1850, reg. 6 Oct.1863.

433. Carnochan, Robert Halliday, in Maryfield Ont, heir to uncle John Halliday, in Mullock Kirkcudbright, d. 8 Apr.1872, reg. 31 Aug.1872.

434. Carrick, James, merchant, in Boston NE, heir to fa James Carrick, miller in Balveardmill Fife, reg. 5 Apr.1754.

435. Carrick, Robert, in USA, heir to mo Mary Johnstone or Carrick, wid of Charles Carrick farmer in Baad Blair Drummond Stirlingshire, d. Dec.1850, reg. 1 Sep.1873.

436. Carruth, James, in Ut, heir to fa William Carruth, farmer in Birkenhead Renfrewshire, d. Feb.1833, reg. 2 Feb.1864.

437. Carruthers or Bryden, Agnes, w of John Bryden, in NY, heir to grandfa William Jardine, in Priesthead Dumfries-shire, reg. 20 Sep.1864.
438. Carson, John, in Toruntum USA, heir to fa William Carson, farmer in Grange of Cree Kirkcudbrightshire, reg. 26 July 1842.
439. Carswell, John, in Barry Pike Co Ill, heir to aunt Esther Carswell, in High St Paisley Renfrewshire, d. 4 Sep.1869, reg. 29 Apr.1870.
440. Cassels, Archibald, in Brooklyn NY, heir to fa Archibald Cassels, weaver in Glasgow, d. June 1850, reg. 1 May 1875.
441. Cassels, Richard Scougal, in Ottawa, heir to sis Janet Cassels, da of Walter Gibson Cassels in Blackford House Edinburgh, d. 30 Sep.1850, reg. 21 June 1871.
442. Cassels, Walter Gibson, in Toronto, heir to bro Andrew Cassels, s of Walter Cassels in Blackford House Edinburgh, d. 10 Mar.1840, reg. 21 June 1871.
443. Cassels, Walter Gibson, in Toronto, heir to bro John Scougal Cassels, s of Walter Gibson Cassels in Blackford House Edinburgh, d. 17 July 1848, reg. 21 June 1871.
444. Caswell, Miles, farmer, in Union City Mich, heir to sis Esther Caswell, in Paisley Renfrewshire, reg. 6 July 1879.
445. Caughey, Charles, in Baltimore, heir to mo Jean Kenmore or Caughey, wid of Robert Caughey in Stranraer Wigtownshire, d. 20 May 1879, reg. 29 Nov.1883.
446. Caughey, Charles, in Baltimore, heir to fa Robert Caughey, in Stranraer Wigtownshire, d. 26 Feb.1879, reg. 18 May 1883.
447. Chalmers, James, in Savanna Ga, heir to sis Margaret Chalmers, in Edinburgh, d. 25 Aug.1877, reg. 8 Apr.1878.
448. Chalmers, John, farmer, in Clarence Up Can, heir to cousin John Rainnie, feuar in MacDuff Banffshire, d. 1 May 1857, reg. 1 Sep.1866.
449. Chalmers, John, in St Louis, heir to mo Elizabeth Christie or Chalmers, w of John Chalmers in Burntisland Fife, d. 5 Mar.1876, reg. 19 Apr.1883.
450. Chalmers, Watson, printer, in Chico Cal, heir to mo Janet Arnot or Chalmers, w of C Chalmers, d. 24 July 1835, reg. 1 Aug.1867.
451. Chaplain, George, in Huron Can, heir to fa George Chaplain, carpenter in Burntisland Fife, d. 20 Apr.1860, reg. 15 Mar.1876.
452. Chapman, John, in Washington Ill, heir to bro Charles Chapman, in Edinburgh, d. 17 Aug.1865, reg. 10 Mar.1880.
453. Chapman, Peter, weaving foreman, in Paterson NJ, heir to fa James Chapman, weaver in Kilbarchan Renfrewshire, d. 23 July 1877, reg. 16 Aug.1882.
454. Chiene or Berwick, Margaret, w of David Berwick brewer, in St Andrews Fife then Chicago, heir to bro William Chiene, mariner in Liverpool, d. 22 Dec.1870, reg. 17 May 1876.

455. Chisholm or Ruxton, Ann, in Schenectady NY, heir to grandfa John Chisholm, shanker in Arbroath Angus, d. Nov.1847, reg. 16 Sep.1882.

456. Chisholm, James Sutherland, in Montreal, heir to Duncan Macdonell Chisholm of Chisholm, d. 14 Sep.1858, reg. 14 Dec.1859.

457. Chisholm, James Taylor, in NY, heir to fa John Chisholm, in Plantation Fowlis Berbice, d. 3 May 1859, reg. 6 Apr.1870.

458. Christie or Anderson, Catherine, wife of Ebenezer Christie, in USA, heir to brother William Anderson, teacher in Cowdenbeath Fife, reg. 27 Apr.1858.

459. Christie, Duncan, in Montgomery Co NY, heir to uncle Donald Christie, in Edinburgh, reg. 14 Mar.1836.

460. Christie, John, in Chicago, heir to bro Andrew Christie, in Ferry-Port-on-Craig Fife, reg. 17 July 1850.

461. Christie, John, mason, in Trenton NJ, heir to fa John Christie, mason in Auchterarder Perthshire, d. 27 July 1882, reg. 5 Dec.1882.

462. Christie or Stafford, Mary J, w of Francis William Stafford painter, in NY, heir to grandmo Mary Diack or Christie, w of George Christie in Aberdeen, reg. 28 Jan.1859.

463. Christison, David, farmer, in Woodburn NS, heir to fa David Christison, in Blackburn Aberdeenshire, d. 24 Nov.1844, reg. 30 June 1862.

464. Chrystal, William, in USA, heir to fa Dr William Chrystal, Rector of Glasgow Grammar School in Glasgow, reg. 9 Feb.1850.

465. Claperton, Alexander, storekeeper, in Empire City Kan, heir to fa Thomas Claperton, cooper in Gorebridge Mid Lothian, d. 19 Aug.1875, reg. 6 Oct.1879.

466. Clark, Alexander Chivas, broker, in Montreal, heir to grandmo Margaret Lindsay or Airth, wid of John Airth merchant in Arbroath Angus, d. 5 Mar.1835, reg. 9 Sep.1880.

467. Clark, George, butcher, in Detroit, heir to uncle William Murray, smith in Fisherrow Edinburgh, d. 30 Oct.1851, reg. 19 Dec.1879.

468. Clark or Forbes, Helen, w of A Clark, in Norfolk Va, heir to bro David Forbes, carver in Edinburgh, reg. 25 Oct.1815.

469. Clark, Hugh, in Grand River Up Can, heir to uncle John Clark, plasterer in Edinburgh, d. 13 Apr.1836, reg. 12 June 1871.

470. Clark, Isaac, in Delaware Co NY, heir to grand-uncle Lawrence Clark, in Auchterarder Perthshire, d. Apr.1829, reg. 5 Jan.1878.

471. Clark or Duff, Isabella, w of William Clark engineer, in USA, heir to fa Robert Duff, in Loaningside, reg. 22 Dec.1851.

472. Clark, Janet, da of John Clark merchant, in Greenock Renfrewshire, heir to bro John Clark, in Jamaica, reg. 8 May 1783.

473. Clark, John, dyer, in Glasgow then America, heir to fa John Clark, dyer in America, reg. 19 Sep.1792.

474. Clark, John, ex gunner Royal Horse Artillery, in America, heir to mo
Mary Watt or Clark, wid of Peter Clark wright in Paisley
Renfrewshire, d. 20 May 1837, reg. 13 Dec.1848.
475. Clark, Margaret, da of John Clark merchant, in Greenock Renfrewshire,
heir to bro John Clark, in Jamaica, reg. 8 May 1783.
476. Clark, Mary, da of John Clark merchant, in Greenock Renfrewshire, heir
to bro John Clark, in Jamaica, reg. 8 May 1783.
477. Clark, Nelson, engineer, in Columbo America, heir to fa William Clark,
builder in Wallacetown Ayrshire, d. 28 July 1867, reg. 9
Sep.1876.
478. Clark, Robert, mercantile clerk, in Quebec, heir to fa John Clark,
physician in Quebec, d. 7 Oct.1847, reg. 13 Oct.1864.
479. Clark, Thomas White, in Fergus Can, heir to fa Quinten Clark, hillsman
in Ricarton, reg. 8 Jan.1860.
480. Clark, William, thread manufacturer, in Newark USA, heir to fa John
Clark, in Paisley Renfrewshire, d. 27 June 1864, reg. 22
Jan.1879.
481. Clayton, Thomas, plasterer, in Edinburgh, heir to bro Francis Clayton,
merchant in Wilmington NC, reg. 7 Sep.1791.
482. Cleghorn, William, in Montreal, heir to sis Isobel Cleghorn, in
Edinburgh, reg. 20 Jan.1841.
483. Cleghorn, William, in Ellaville Ga, heir to sis Jacky Cleghorn, da of
Richard Cleghorn in Edinburgh, d. 17 Sep.1843, reg. 5 Sep.1881.
484. Cleghorn, William, in Ellaville Ga, heir to sis Susan Cleghorn, da of
Richard Cleghorn in Edinburgh, d. 29 Jan.1874, reg. 5 Sep.1881.
485. Cleland, Daniel, Canadian Rifles, heir to mo Janet Douglas or Cleland,
wid of James Cleland in Whitburn W Lothian, reg. 28 Nov.1856.
486. Clunes, Colin, planter, in Jamaica, heir to fa John Clunes of Neilston,
reg. 17 July 1809.
487. Clyde, John, clerk, in NY, heir to fa Stephen Clyde, in Neilston
Renfrewshire, d. 24 Apr.1847, reg. 3 Oct.1854.
488. Clyde, Robert, in Camlachie Glasgow, heir to Andrew Ritchie, smith in
Jamaica, reg. 1 July 1829.
489. Clydesdale or Mitchell, C, in NY, heir to fa H Clydesdale, ex sailor RN
in Kirkhill of Penicuik Mid Lothian, reg. 5 Oct.1847.
490. Clyne, Helen Goldie, in Cleveland Oh, heir to grandfa William Clyne,
leather merchant in Aberdeen, d. 14 Oct.1843, reg. 1 Dec.1880.
491. Clyne or Marquitt, Isabella, in Richfield Oh, heir to grandfa William
Clyne, leather merchant in Aberdeen, d. 14 Oct.1843, reg. 1
Dec.1880.
492. Clyne or Waite, Rachel Elizabeth, in Charleston SC, heir to grandfa
William Clyne, leather merchant in Aberdeen, d. 14 Oct.1843, reg.
1 Dec.1880.

493. Coats, John, in Baltimore, heir to mo Ann MacLean or Coats, wid of James Coats shipmaster in Greenock Renfrewshire, reg. 6 Dec.1815.

494. Coats, John, in Baltimore, heir to bro James Coats, in Greenock Renfrewshire, reg. 6 Dec.1815.

495. Cobban, Matthew Whyte, in Milton Can, heir to grandfa James Cobban, merchant in Inverurie Aberdeenshire, d. 28 June 1827, reg. 21 Mar.1862.

496. Cochran or Hamilton, Helen, w of David Cochran merchant, in Glasgow, heir to bro William Hamilton, in Jamaica, reg. 29 Apr.1752.

497. Cochrane, John, in NY then London, heir to mo Isobella Hendry or Cochrane, in Craigmore Rothesay Bute, d. 19 Feb.1862, reg. 12 Dec.1862.

498. Cochrane, Matthew, patternmaker, in Paisley Renfrewshire then America, heir to sis Helen Cochrane, in Paisley, d. 8 Aug.1846, reg. 8 Dec.1861.

499. Cole or Stewart, Jennie Eliza, in Litchfield Mich, heir to gt grandfa Alexander Stewart, carter in Castle Douglas, d. 1808, reg. 23 Feb.1881.

500. Colquhoun, Catherine, w of John Colquhoun, in Camstradden Dunbartonshire, heir to uncle Coll Turner, merchant in Tobago, reg. 26 Feb.1817.

501. Colquhoun or Stewart, Margaret, w of Donald Colquhoun, in Mull Argyll, heir to bro Duncan Stewart, in Jamaica, reg. 8 Aug.1814.

502. Colville, Mary, in St Leonard's on Sea Sussex, heir to fa Thomas Low Colville, in Wilmington USA, d. 13 Nov.1870, reg. 20 Jan.1875.

503. Comrie, James, in Cincinnati, heir to fa Peter Comrie, innkeeper in Comrie Perthshire, d. 13 Apr.1855, reg. 7 Dec.1855.

504. Comrie, John, farmer, in Downville Del, heir to fa William Comrie, tenant farmer in Buchanty, d. 27 Sep.1844, reg. 26 Dec.1867.

505. Congreve or Henderson, Christina, in Jamaica, heir to bro Balfour Henderson, s of John Henderson merchant in Edinburgh, reg. 15 Dec.1830.

506. Conning or Thompson, Agnes, in NY, heir to sis Janet Conning or Milne, in Elgin Morayshire, d. 28 Feb.1860, reg. 16 Mar.1865.

507. Conning, Robert, mason, in Whithorn Wigtownshire, heir to William Conning, in Falmouth Jamaica, reg. 5 Jan.1830.

508. Conquergood, Daniel William, in New Orleans, heir to mo Catherine Heatherington or Conquergood, w of Peter Conquergood builder in New Orleans, d. 9 July 1867, reg. 5 June 1874.

509. Constable, John, in Can, heir to fa Alexander Constable, carrier in Cupar then Craigsanquhar, reg. 22 Aug.1855.

510. Cook, Alison, da of Hugh Cook tanner, in Edinburgh, heir to uncle John Baptist, surgeon in Va, reg. 24 July 1751.

511. Cook, Andrew, clerk, in NY, heir to fa John Cook, grocer in Forfar Angus, d. 6 July 1874, reg. 23 Apr.1875.
512. Cook, William Lawrence, in NY, heir to 2nd cousin Christina Johnston or Hastings, wid of George Hastings in Arbroath Angus, d. 9 Jan.1878, reg. 3 Oct.1883.
513. Cooper or Wilson, Janet, in Can, heir to mo Janet Alexander or Wilson, in Dunfermline Fife then Can, reg. 10 May 1871.
514. Cooper or Wilson, Janet, in Can, heir to fa Lawrence Wilson, in Dunfermline Fife then Can, reg. 10 May 1871.
515. Copland, James, house carpenter, in Orillia Simcoe Co Can, heir to fa James Copland, in Strichen Aberdeenshire, d. 25 July 1850, reg. 3 Aug.1869.
516. Corbet or Balfour, Janet, w of John Balfour, in Jamaica, heir to bro James Corbet of Kenmuir, d. Aug.1790, reg. 14 Apr.1807.
517. Cordiner, Christina, heir to fa John Cordiner, in Glasgow then Boston NE, reg. 17 Oct.1712.
518. Cormack, William, merchant, in Montreal, heir to sis Ann Cormack, in Thurso Caithness, reg. 10 June 1851.
519. Cormack, William, merchant, in Montreal, heir to bro James Cormack, merchant in Montreal then Tongue Sutherland, reg. 10 June 1851.
520. Corner, William Neilson, shipmaster, in NY, heir to uncle Samuel Neilson, builder & architect in Edinburgh, reg. 14 Nov.1781.
521. Corner, William Neilson, shipmaster, in NY, heir to cousin Isobel Neilson, da of Dr John Neilson in Edinburgh, reg. 14 Nov.1781.
522. Corrie, Joseph, merchant, in St Thomas, heir to uncle James Philp of Greenlaw, judge of the Admiralty Court, d. May 1782, reg. 12 Feb.1783.
523. Coupar, Bell, in St Andrews Fife, heir to bro John Coupar, teacher in America, reg. 3 Apr.1848.
524. Coupar, Jean, in St Andrews Fife, heir to bro John Coupar, teacher in America, reg. 3 Apr.1848.
525. Coupland, Samuel, engineer, in Can W, heir to fa Francis Coupland, tenant farmer in Boghead, reg. 13 Apr.1860.
526. Coupland, Samuel, farmer, in Can, heir to grandfa Samuel Morrin, farmer in Cairn of Craigs, d. 14 Nov.1834, reg. 18 Apr.1861.
527. Coutts, George, in Buxton Can W, heir to aunt Margaret Coutts or Clark, wid of George Clark in Possnet, d. 3 Dec.1866, reg. 2 June 1868.
528. Coutts, James, in Cincinnati, heir to gt grandfa James Coutts, flaxdresser in Perth, reg. 17 July 1879.
529. Coventry, James, heir to fa George Coventry of Fairhill, Captain NY Independent Company, reg. 7 Apr.1791.
530. Cowan, David, in Toronto, heir to mo Julia Sim or Cowan, in New Rattray, d. 11 Jan.1875, reg. 15 Oct.1881.

531. Cowan or Thomson, Janet Wood, in Can, heir to William Cowan, molecatcher in Glasgow, reg. 20 May 1846.

532. Cowie, John Reid, in Indianapolis, heir to fa Alexander Cowie, surgeon in Tanfield Aberdeen, d. 27 Jan.1851, reg. 20 Mar.1883.

533. Cowie, Robert, wright, in Aberdeen then NY, heir to grandfa William Watts, gardener in Aberdeen, reg. 26 Sep.1851.

534. Cowie, Robert, wright, in Aberdeen then NY, heir to mo Sarah Watts or Cowie, wid of William Cowie saddler in Aberdeen, d. 28 Mar.1851, reg. 26 Sep.1851.

535. Cowie, Thomas, cabinetmaker, in Hamilton Can W, heir to fa Walkinshaw Cowie, spirit dealer in Corstorphine Mid Lothian, d. 1843, reg. 15 Jan.1863.

536. Cowper, George Constable, in Owen Sound Can W, heir to bro James Alexander Robertson Cowper, MD in Dundee Angus, d. 19 Feb.1866, reg. 27 Sep.1866.

537. Cox, Eloise, in Fredericton NB, heir to grandfa Robert Lamb of Templehall, reg. 16 Oct.1829.

538. Crabb, Alexander, printer, in Cincinnati, heir to fa John Crabb, in Pleasance Edinburgh, reg. 12 Jan.1852.

539. Craig or Simpson, Agnes, in Burnbraes then America, heir to mo Esther Stewart or Craig, in Moffat Dumfriesshire, reg. 31 Mar.1837.

540. Craig, Alexander Turnbull, in Rangoon Burma, heir to bro James Arthur Craig, in Chicago, d. 16 May 1881, reg. 30 Sep.1881.

541. Craig, David, in New Providence, heir to grandfa David Craig, gardener in Pilrig, reg. 11 Jan.1802.

542. Craig, James, farmer, in Can, heir to fa James Craig, in Kirkford of Stewarton Ayrshire, d. 17 June 1863, reg. 11 Nov.1863.

543. Craig, James Arthur, in Chicago, heir to mo Anne Turnbull or Craig, w of James Craig jr in Glasgow, d. 17 Mar.1880, reg. 12 May 1880.

544. Craig, William, photographer, in St Catherine Ont, heir to fa James Craig, farmer in Cairnfield Wick Caithness, d. 23 July 1870, reg. 8 Mar.1875.

545. Cram or Jackson, Agnes, in USA, heir to fa George Jackson, in Todmorden then Stockton on Tees, reg. 13 Apr.1853.

546. Cram, William Frederick, in Oregon Ill, heir to mo Agnes Jackson or Cram, w of G C Cram in Boston, d. 4 Aug.1877, reg. 23 Oct.1878.

547. Cranston, Alexander, in Glasgow, heir to fa William Cranston, builder in Jamaica, reg. 7 Nov.1854.

548. Crawford, Hugh, s of William Crawford, in Chicago, heir to cousin William Shaw, only child of George Shaw sailor in Bo'ness W Lothian, reg. 15 Feb.1867.

549. Crawford, John, in Newton-on-Ayr Ayrshire, heir to bro Alexander Crawford, planter in Jamaica, reg. 6 Feb.1854.

550. Crawford, John, joiner, in Montreal, heir to grandmo Elizabeth Whyte or Crawford, w of William Crawford, d. 15 Apr.1837, reg. 1 July 1875.

551. Crawford, John, joiner, in Montreal, heir to grandfa William Crawford, weaver in Williamsburgh Paisley Renfrewshire, d. 10 Aug.1853, reg. 1 July 1875.

552. Crawford, Patrick, Governor, in Leeward Islands, heir to bro Hugh Crawford of Garrieve, reg. 6 Dec.1733.

553. Crawford, Robert, merchant, in St Kitts, heir to grandmo Magdalene Crawford, w of James Crawford in Greenock Renfrewshire, reg. 2 Apr.1784.

554. Cree, James, accountant, in Newfoundland, heir to mo Ann Hill or Cree, in Ayr, reg. 26 Sep.1850.

555. Crerar, John, baker, in NY, heir to fa John Crerar, boatman in Perth, reg. 9 Oct.1852.

556. Crichton, Alexander William, in Garey's Ferry then Jacksonville Fla, heir to cousin Margaret Crichton or Otto, in Newark Sanquhar Dumfriesshire, d. 18 June 1839, reg. 17 May 1854.

557. Crichton, Alexander William, in Garey's Ferry then Jacksonville Fla, heir to cousin John Crichton of Skeoch, in Sanquhar Dumfriesshire, d. 8 Feb.1834, reg. 15 June 1854.

558. Crichton, John, stock-keeper, in Iowanaa Ill, heir to grandfa John Crichton, in Crossgates Fife, d. 23 Mar.1860, reg. 13 Oct.1882.

559. Crighton, William, in Jamaica, heir to bro Thomas Crighton of Millhill, reg. 11 Apr.1786.

560. Crockart, William, in Tarborough USA, heir to grandmo Agnes Thomson or Crockart, in Dumfries, reg. 14 Nov.1850.

561. Crockatt, James, doctor, in SC, heir to fa George Crockatt, surgeon in Coupar Angus Perthshire, reg. 18 May 1763.

562. Crombie, William, saddler, in Boston NE, heir to sis Ann Crombie, da of William Crombie merchant in Elgin Morayshire, reg. 22 Feb.1764.

563. Crookston, William Law, in Ia, heir to fa Thomas Crookston, clerk in Brewsterford, reg. 24 Sep.1857.

564. Cross or Muir, Elizabeth, w of John Muir shoemaker, in Cambuslang Lanarkshire, heir to bro James Cross, in Va, reg. 7 May 1788.

565. Cross or Shiels, Janet, w of William Shiels farmer, in Shiels, heir to bro James Cross, in Va, reg. 7 May 1788.

566. Cross or McIndoe, Jean, w of James McIndoe, in Carmyle, heir to bro James Cross, merchant in Va, reg. 7 May 1788.

567. Cross, Margaret, heir to bro James Cross, in Va, reg. 7 May 1788.

568. Cross, Walter, merchant, in Vera Cruz, heir to fa Robert Cross, engineer in Glasgow, reg. 20 May 1836.

569. Crow or Mudie, Margaret, in Douglas NS, heir to mo Christian Robertson or Mudie, reg. 11 Nov.1825.
570. Crowley or Marshall, Hannah, in Carolina, heir to bro James Marshall, painter in Edinburgh, reg. 13 June 1831.
571. Cruickshank or Napier, Margaret, wid of Samuel Hawkins Napier , in Bathurst NB, heir to Helen Selbie, wid of John Selbie hosier in Aberdeen, reg. 15 June 1865.
572. Cruickshanks, Alexander, blacksmith, in Buckingham Can, heir to fa Alexander Cruickshanks, feuar in Fife-Keith, d. 25 Oct.1846, reg. 25 Jan.1864.
573. Cumming, Alexander, farmer, in Newton Hamilton Pa, heir to grandfa John Whytock, weaver in Perth, d. Mar.1825, reg. 20 Nov.1878.
574. Cumming, John, in NY, heir to fa John Cumming, weaver in Kilmarnock Ayrshire, reg. 4 Sep.1851.
575. Cumming, Joseph, in Carricou, heir to cousin Alexander Lumsden of Pitcaple, d. 16 Jan.1778, reg. 30 June 1786.
576. Cumming, William, in Jamaica, heir to fa William Cumming, writer in Edinburgh, reg. 9 June 1802.
577. Cumming, William, in Wappin Gas Falls Duchess Co NY, heir to uncle George Cumming, weaver in Hamilton Lanarkshire, d. 20 Nov.1850, reg. 3 Nov.1874.
578. Cummings, Edward, in Waverley NY, heir to fa Edward Cummings, stonecutter in Brooklyn, d. 21 July 1872, reg. 15 May 1878.
579. Cunningham, George, s of Henry Cunningham surgeon, in E Fla, heir to grandfa John Cunningham of Balbougie, reg. 15 June 1771.
580. Cunningham, James, in Cal, heir to bro Thomas Cunningham, in Edinburgh, reg. 2 Mar.1859.
581. Cunningham, John, surgeon, in St Kitts, heir to grandfa John Cunningham of Baidland, in Ayrshire, reg. 6 May 1740.
582. Cunningham, John, surgeon, in St Kitts, heir to bro Richard Cunningham of Baidland, in Ayrshire, d. Jan.1716, reg. 6 May 1740.
583. Cunningham, John, shipmaster, in Va, heir to fa Thomas Cunningham, shipmaster in NY, reg. 12 June 1793.
584. Cunningham, John, s of John Cunningham merchant, in NY, heir to grandfa John Cunningham of Stain, reg. 13 June 1817.
585. Cunningham, John, sailor, in Can, heir to grandfa James Millar, in Saltcoats Ayrshire, reg. 28 Feb.1843.
586. Currie, Alexander, in Birkenshaw then Oh, heir to fa Alexander Currie, in Birkenshaw, reg. 19 May 1853.
587. Cushnie, Georgina Vallance, in Charleston USA, heir to mo Jean Vallance or Cushnie, w of Alexander Cushnie glover in Edinburgh, d. 26 May 1841, reg. 18 Apr.1859.

588. Cushnie, Georgina Vallance, in Charleston USA, heir to sis Jane
    Cushnie or Fisher, w of George Fisher comedian in Edinburgh
    then NY, d. Nov.1856, reg. 11 May 1859.
589. Cushnie, John, in Quebec, heir to bro Peter Cushnie, wright in
    Clashmore Aberdeenshire, reg. 24 Nov.1838.
590. Cushnie, Thomas Stratton, in Jamaica, heir to aunt Ann Cushnie or
    Burnes, in Stonehaven Kincardineshire, reg. 25 Nov.1819.
591. Cuthbert, John, in Esarea Co Durham Can W, heir to mo Mary Jolly or
    Cuthbert, in Forfar Angus, d. 30 Dec.1859, reg. 10 June 1867.
592. Cuthbert, Joseph, in Ga, heir to grand-uncle Alexander Cuthbert, s of
    John Cuthbert of Castlehill in Inverness, reg. 6 July 1785.
593. Cuthbert or Thomson, Marion, w of William Thomson shoemaker, in
    Va, heir to fa William Cuthbert, in Newton-on-Ayr Ayrshire, reg.
    13 Feb.1798.
594. Dalhousie, Elizabeth, Countess of, heir to uncle James Glen of
    Longcroft, Governor in SC, d. July 1777, reg. 26 Aug.1777.
595. Dalmahoy, John Christie, s of John Dalmahoy, in Jamaica, heir to
    granduncle Alexander Dalmahoy, shoemaker in Edinburgh, reg. 28
    Dec.1824.
596. Dalmahoy, John Christie, s of John Dalmahoy, in Jamaica, heir to grand-
    aunt Elizabeth Dalmahoy or Wright, wid of Robert Wright master
    mariner RN, reg. 28 Dec.1824.
597. Dalrymple or Cunningham, Susan, w of H Dalrymple, in Nunraw, heir
    to mo Mary Gainer or Cunningham, wid of Robert Cunningham
    in Cayon St Kitts, reg. 25 Aug.1761.
598. Darling, Mary Jane, in Trinidad, heir to uncle George Drummond, ship
    carpenter in Southampton, d. 11 Mar.1869, reg. 22 Dec.1875.
599. David, Henry, in Delhi NY, heir to mo Margaret Duncan or Davie, in
    Wrae, reg. 18 Apr.1836.
600. Davidson, Agnes, in Glasgow then America, heir to bro James Davidson,
    s of Thomas Davidson farmer in Titwood then Kinninghouse, reg.
    11 Aug.1824.
601. Davidson, Agnes, in Glasgow then America, heir to sis Janet Davidson,
    da of Thomas Davidson in Kinninghouse, reg. 21 May 1828.
602. Davidson, Andrew, bookseller, in Louisville USA, heir to fa James
    Davidson, teacher in Tudhoe, reg. 3 Aug.1859.
603. Davidson, Bryce, postmaster, in Lake Opinicon Ont, heir to fa Bryce
    Davidson, painter in Leith Mid Lothian, d. 18 Feb.1831, reg. 1
    May 1877.
604. Davidson or Wallace, Elizabeth, w of John Davidson, in Jamaica, heir to
    bro William Wallace, in Jamaica, reg. 16 Feb.1788.
605. Davidson, James, in Baltimore, heir to fa John Davidson, in Ferryhill,
    reg. 30 June 1796.

606. Davidson, James, in Vancouver Washington Territory, heir to fa James Davidson, stonecutter in Montrose Angus, reg. 30 Dec.1864.
607. Davidson, James, master mariner, in Buffalo NY, heir to uncle John Smith, accountant & linguist in Liverpool, d. 19 Mar.1877, reg. 4 Nov.1878.
608. Davidson or McLaren, Janet, in Lincoln Center Me, heir to cousin Donald McLaren, merchant in Callendar Stirlingshire, d. 7 Feb.1880, reg. 20 Aug.1881.
609. Davidson, John, writer, in Aberdeen, heir to uncle John Blyth, planter in Jamaica, reg. 6 Aug.1849.
610. Davidson, Robert, in Meredith NY, heir to remote cousin John Fox, in Berwick-on-Tweed Northumberland, reg. 29 Dec.1840.
611. Davidson, William, MD, in Madison Ind, heir to uncle David Davidson, surgeon in Edinburgh then Elie Fife, d. 15 Feb.1858, reg. 7 Jan.1864.
612. Davidson, William, in Boston, heir to grandfa William Davidson, carrier in Lanton, reg. 8 May 1872.
613. Davidson, William, in Boston, heir to grandmo Agnes Turnbull or Davidson, reg. 8 May 1872.
614. Davie, Henry, in Delhi NY, heir to fa Andrew Davie, farmer in Porterside, reg. 19 Apr.1836.
615. Davie, James, in Deposit NY, heir to fa Andrew Davie, farmer in Porterside, reg. 19 Apr.1836.
616. Davie, James, in Deposit NY, heir to mo Margaret Duncan or Davie, in Wrae, reg. 19 Apr.1836.
617. Davies or Gordon, Harriet, w of James Gordon, in USA, heir to mo Margaret Davies, in Middlebie Dumfries-shire, reg. 20 Feb.1854.
618. Davies, John, surgeon, in Jamaica, heir to fa John Davies, surgeon in Glassrie, reg. 14 July 1772.
619. Dawson, John, engineer, in Can W, heir to granduncle George Bremner, feuar in Huntly Aberdeenshire, d. 8 May 1861, reg. 15 June 1863.
620. Dawson, William Thomas, in Philadelphia, heir to fa William Dawson, color-merchant in Leith Mid Lothian, d. 13 Sep.1854, reg. 18 June 1855.
621. Dawson, William, engineer, in Alloa Clackmannanshire, heir to aunt Janet Dawson, in USA then Edinburgh, d. 12 Jan.1873, reg. 6 Oct.1874.
622. Dean, John, in NJ, heir to granduncle Alexander Dunlop, sailor in Saltcoats Ayrshire, reg. 12 Aug.1816.
623. Deans, John, farmer, in Alexandria NY, heir to sis Margaret Deans or Henderson, w of D Henderson joiner in Roxburghshire, reg. 14 Dec.1864.
624. Deans, Walter, in NA, heir to fa Thomas Deans, in Hobkirk Glebe Roxburghshire, reg. 3 June 1831.

625. Dempster, George, merchant, in Montreal, heir to grandfa George Dempster, baker in Alloa Clackmannanshire, reg. 22 Apr.1848.

626. Dempster, George, merchant, in Montreal, heir to mo Helen Duncan or Dempster, in Alloa Clackmannanshire, reg. 13 Apr.1853.

627. Denholm or Gordon, Elizabeth, w of George Gordon surgeon, in Hanover Jamaica, heir to bro David Denholm, writer in Edinburgh, reg. 8 Feb.1753.

628. Dent, George, heir to fa William Dent, in Fauquier Co Va, reg. 11 Dec.1837.

629. Devine, Daniel, in America, heir to fa Dennis Devine, smith in Chapelhall Lanarkshire, d. 2 May 1858, reg. 23 Apr.1875.

630. Dewar, Andrew, customs officer, in Dominica, heir to sis Elizabeth Dewar or Moncrief, wid of G Moncrief wright in Campvere Netherlands, reg. 16 Jan.1767.

631. Dewar, James, patternmaker, in Chicago, heir to fa James Dewar, mason in Strathkinness Fife, d. 10 Mar.1858, reg. 4 Oct.1865.

632. Dewar, Mary, da of R Dewar merchant, in Antigua, heir to gt grandfa James Henderson of Laverockhall, reg. 15 Jan.1768.

633. Dewar, Mary, da of Robert Dewar merchant, in St Eustatia, heir to aunt Elizabeth Dewar, da of William Dewar merchant in Edinburgh, reg. 14 Jan.1772.

634. Dewar, Thomas, farmer, in East Whealand NA, heir to fa James Dewar, mason in Strathkinness Fife, d. 10 Mar.1858, reg. 4 Oct.1865.

635. Dick, David, seaman, in Leith Mid Lothian then America, heir to sis Jessey Dick, in Edinburgh, d. 14 Dec.1858, reg. 14 Oct.1861.

636. Dick, David, seaman, in Leith Mid Lothian then America, heir to uncle David Dick, in St George East London, reg. 14 Oct.1861.

637. Dick, James, farmer, in Walpole Can, heir to mo Jean Tulloch or Dick, w of Thomas Dick weaver in Kirkcaldy Fife, d. 11 Oct.1844, reg. 24 Nov.1870.

638. Dick, Mary, da of George Dick surgeon, in Carolina, heir to gt grandfa George Campbell of Croonan, reg. 29 July 1796.

639. Dick, Robert, in Trinidad, heir to bro Alexander Dick, merchant in Dundee Angus, reg. 4 Apr.1838.

640. Dick, Robert Lambly, in Can, heir to fa James Dick, in Quebec then Kilmarnock Ayrshire, reg. 23 May 1845.

641. Dick, Thomas, merchant, in Annapolis America, heir to fa Robert Dick, writer in Edinburgh, reg. 21 Mar.1758.

642. Dick, Thomas, farmer, in Ind, heir to fa James Dick, portioner in Pitquhanatrie, reg. 6 June 1836.

643. Dick, Thomas, farmer, in Ind, heir to bro James Dick, portioner of Pitquhanatrie, reg. 6 June 1836.

644. Dickison, George, joiner, in Mound City Ill, heir to fa Alexander Dickison, joiner in Dean Edinburgh, reg. 28 Apr.1864.

645. Dickson, Donald William, merchant, in Glasgow & London, heir to aunt Mary McDonald or Robinson, w of William Robinson in NY, d. Dec.1858, reg. 29 June 1882.
646. Dickson or Sinclair, Mary, w of James Sinclair, in St Mary's Can, heir to cousin Isabella Dickson, cooper in Airdrie Lanarkshire, d. 4 Sep.1862, reg. 7 June 1863.
647. Dickson, Peter, in Sanborn Dakota, heir to 2nd cousin James Dickson, in Roslyn Mid Lothian, d. 20 Dec.1882, reg. 1 Oct.1883.
648. Dickson, Robert, sailor, in NS, heir to fa James Dickson, smith in Stillenance, reg. 3 May 1842.
649. Dinnison, Andrew, in Jackson Pa, heir to fa James Dinnison, farmer in Copinshay then Little Corse Kirkwall Orkney, d. 30 July 1861, reg. 11 Dec.1862.
650. Dinwoodie, Agnes, in Mertoun Manse, heir to mo Ann Stevenson or Dinwoodie, in Buffalo USA, reg. 22 Sep.1852.
651. Dinwoodie, Ann, in Darnick, heir to mo Ann Stevenson or Dinwoodie, in Buffalo USA, reg. 22 Sep.1852.
652. Dinwoodie or Kerr, Mary, w of John Kerr, in Leith Mid Lothian, heir to mo Ann Stevenson or Dinwoodie, in Buffalo USA, reg. 22 Sep.1852.
653. Divins or Hopper, Isabella Jane, in Moncton NB, heir to grandfa Edward Divins, in Girvan Ayrshire, d. 30 Nov.1855, reg. 19 Sep.1882.
654. Divins, Jessie, in Moncton NB, heir to grandfa Edward Divins, in Girvan Ayrshire, d. 30 Nov.1855, reg. 19 Sep.1882.
655. Divins or Wall, Margaret, in Moncton NB, heir to grandfa Edward Divins, in Girvan Ayrshire, d. 30 Nov.1855, reg. 19 Sep.1882.
656. Dodds, William, in Gore Douglas NS, heir to fa George Dodds, carter in Whithorn Wigtownshire, reg. 17 May 1860.
657. Doig, James, in Antigua, heir to cousin Ann Doig or Kiddel, in Cookston Brechin Angus, reg. 8 Dec.1791.
658. Donald, Matilda, in Patterson NJ, heir to grandfa David Gourlay, in Ground of Woodside, reg. 30 Mar.1855.
659. Donald, William, merchant, in Ayr, heir to s Robert Donald, in Va, reg. 11 Apr.1788.
660. Donaldson or Alston, Ann, wid of Mr Alston, in Chicago, heir to cousin William Shaw, only child of George Shaw sailor in Bo'ness W Lothian, reg. 15 Feb.1867.
661. Donaldson or Henry, Anne, w of James Donaldson merchant, in Halifax NS, heir to uncle George Henry, merchant in Aberdeen, d. 3 Mar.1867, reg. 2 Oct.1867.
662. Donaldson, George Andrew, planter, in Jamaica, heir to mo Jane Bankhead or Donaldson, w of George Donaldson forester in Fochabers Morayshire, d. 27 Oct.1855, reg. 16 Dec.1863.

663. Donaldson or Williamson, Georgina, in Can, heir to bro Allan
Donaldson, s of Capt Alexander Donaldson 36th Regt, reg. 24
May 1841.

664. Donaldson, James, in Antigua, heir to gt grandfa Robert Donaldson, in
Manbeam Morayshire, reg. 24 June 1785.

665. Donaldson, John, machinist, in NJ, heir to grandmo Ann Gunn or
Young, wid of Alexander Young mechanic in Dundee Angus, reg.
7 Dec.1871.

666. Donaldson or Brown, Sarah, in Can, heir to bro Allan Donaldson, s of
Capt Alexander Donaldson 36th Regt, reg. 24 May 1841.

667. Donaldson or Brown, Sarah, in Can, heir to bro Allan Donaldson, s of
Capt Alexander Donaldson 36th Regt, reg. 24 May 1841.

668. Douglas, James, merchant, in Kingston Jamaica, heir to fa James
Douglas, MD in Carlisle Cumberland, reg. 3 July 1782.

669. Douglas, James, customs controller, in St Johns NA, heir to bro Samuel
Douglas, in Burnhouses Berwickshire, d. 17 Jan.1794, reg. 13
Nov.1794.

670. Douglas, John, Provost Marshal, in Grenada, heir to grandfa John
Douglas, laborer in Castle Douglas Kirkcudbrightshire, reg. 3
Feb.1837.

671. Douglas or Smith, Margaret, wid of Archibald Douglas of Burnbrae, heir
to bro John Smith, surgeon in St Vincent, reg. 22 Sep.1812.

672. Douglas, Robert, surgeon, in Tobago, heir to bro Henry Douglas,
minister in Kilsyth Stirlingshire, reg. 9 Jan.1850.

673. Dove or Kirkcaldy, Jean, wid of James Dove, in Kingston Jamaica, heir
to bro John Kirkcaldy, landwaiter in Kirkcaldy Fife, reg. 16
Aug.1805.

674. Dow, Alexander, in Halifax NS, heir to cousin John Dow, bookseller in
Montrose Angus, d. 13 Mar.1873, reg. 3 July 1873.

675. Dow or Watt, Isabella Glendinning, w of David Watt, in San Francisco,
heir to mo Jane Glendinning or Dow, in Edinburgh, reg. 22
Nov.1862.

676. Dow or Watt, Isabella Glendinning, w of David Watt, in Grass Valley
Nev, heir to bro Robert Dow, baker in Edmonston, d. 4 Apr.1865,
reg. 13 Dec.1877.

677. Dow or Watt, Isabella Glendinning, w of David Watt, in Grass Valley
Nev, heir to mo Jean Glendinning or Dow, w of James Dow
wright in Edinburgh, d. 18 Apr.1857, reg. 13 Dec.1877.

678. Dow, Robert, physician, in Greenock Renfrewshire then New Orleans,
heir to sis Grizzel Dow, in Saltcoats Ayrshire, reg. 12 July 1843.

679. Dower, Jane, in Millbank Can W, heir to sis Helen Dower or Mortimer,
wid of James Mortimer in Aberdeen, d. 17 Nov.1866, reg. 14
Mar.1868.

680. Dowie, Alexander, in Montreal, heir to fa William Dowie, sailor in St Monance Fife, reg. 11 Jan.1847.

681. Downie, John, farmer, in Standing Stones Old Machar Aberdeenshire, heir to bro Andrew Downie, in Oh, d. 13 May 1844, reg. 16 Jan.1854.

682. Downie, Robert Thomson, agent, in NY, heir to fa Robert Downie, in Gargunnock Stirlingshire, d. 1 July 1865, reg. 11 Aug.1866.

683. Downs, Alexander, in Montreal, heir to mo Ann Commins or Downs, w of John Downs in Edinburgh, d. 1 July 1867, reg. 8 Apr.1872.

684. Downs, Henry, in Montreal, heir to mo Ann Commins or Downs, w of John Downs in Edinburgh, d. 1 July 1867, reg. 8 Apr.1872.

685. Drummond, Andrew, coppersmith, in Glasgow, heir to uncle Andrew Drummond, in Clarendon Jamaica, reg. 24 Aug.1853.

686. Drummond, James, in St John NB, heir to grand-uncle Duncan Grahame, merchant in Glasgow, reg. 10 July 1816.

687. Drummond, Janet, in New Zealand, heir to fa John Drummond, millwright in Jamaica, reg. 17 Dec.1860.

688. Drummond, John, in Brunswick Va, heir to fa Robert Drummond, in Grangepans Linlithgow West Lothian, reg. 10 Aug.1807.

689. Drummond or McLean, Susan, in NB, heir to cousin Donald McGregor of Balhaldie, in Perthshire, d. 30 Dec.1854, reg. 10 Jan.1860.

690. Drysdale, Andrew, in Stratford Ont, heir to cousin James Taylor, in Denny Stirlingshire, d. 18 Mar.1865, reg. 28 Nov.1874.

691. Drysdale or Macintosh, Margaret, in Toronto, heir to fa William Drysdale, watchmaker in Edinburgh, reg. 28 Sep.1835.

692. Drysdale, Thomas, watchmaker, in Quebec, heir to fa William Drysdale, watchmaker in Edinburgh, reg. 28 Sep.1835.

693. Drysdale, William, watchmaker, in Philadelphia, heir to fa William Drysdale, watchmaker in Edinburgh, reg. 28 Sep.1835.

694. Drysdale, William, in Fremington USA, heir to mo Helen Dempster or Drysdale, in Alva Stirlingshire, reg. 6 Nov.1850.

695. Duff or Clark, Isabella, w of William Clark engineer, in USA, heir to fa Robert Duff, in Loaningside, reg. 22 Dec.1851.

696. Duff, Jane, mason, in Winnobogo City NA, heir to fa John Duff, quartermaster-sergeant 71st Foot, d. 10 Feb 1835, reg. 5 Sep.1868.

697. Duffus or Wylie, Jane, w of James Wylie, in Bemus Heights Saratoga USA, heir to uncle William Hutchison, writer in Forfar Angus, d. 9 Oct.1847, reg. 14 Feb.1851.

698. Duguid or Malcolm, Mary Ann, w of James Malcolm, in Hamilton Can W, heir to grandmo Janet Aiken or Duguid, wid of W Duguid manufacturer in Aberdeen, d. 3 Oct.1862, reg. 18 Jan.1864.

699. Dunbar, Alexander, in America, heir to uncle Donald McPherson, in Blairnaphat Nairnshire, reg. 3 July 1844.

700. Dunbar, Ann Gordon, in Jamaica, heir to grandfa Robert Dunbar, in Gordonstoun Morayshire then Peterhead Aberdeenshire, reg. 30 Sep.1833.

701. Dunbar, William, s of C Dunbar, in Antigua, heir to cousin Patrick Dunbar of Machemore, reg. 24 Nov.1762.

702. Duncan, Charles Erskine, s of Charles Duncan, in NY, heir to grand-uncle George Robertson of Fascally, in Perthshire, reg. 26 July 1780.

703. Duncan, Charles, in Montreal, heir to w Isabella Drummond, d. 14 Jan.1881, reg. 16 May 1881.

704. Duncan, James, currier, in NJ, heir to fa John Duncan, tanner in West Kilbride Ayrshire, d. 4 Apr.1836, reg. 23 July 1849.

705. Duncan, James, farmer, in Dalhousie Ont, heir to cousin Mary Dunn, in Kirkintilloch Dunbartonshire, d. 5 Dec.1873, reg. 22 May 1874.

706. Duncan, John, blacksmith, in Can, heir to fa James Duncan, laborer in Banchory Aberdeenshire then Can, d. 1 May 1838, reg. 4 Aug.1848.

707. Duncan, John, carpenter, in Coburg Can, heir to mo Martha Baillie or Duncan, in Haddington E Lothian, d. 10 Nov.1848, reg. 6 Jan.1863.

708. Duncan or Goodlet, Mary, in NY, heir to sis Jean Goodlet, in Linlithgow W Lothian then NY, reg. 6 Aug.1838.

709. Duncan, William, planter, in Jamaica, heir to mo Agnes Ronald or Duncan, w of Andrew Duncan baker in Glasgow, reg. 19 June 1789.

710. Duncan, William, in Woodhouse Talboat Can, heir to fa George Duncan, in Woodhouse Talboat, d. 16 Aug.1859, reg. 18 Aug.1864.

711. Duncanson, Catherine, da of Walter Duncanson town-clerk, in Dunbarton, heir to bro James Duncanson, in Jamaica, reg. 5 Mar.1798.

712. Duncanson, Robert, in NY, heir to fa William Duncanson, flesher in Stirling, reg. 14 June 1860.

713. Dundas, James, in Philadelphia, heir to cousin Ralph Peter Dundas of Manner, reg. 18 Feb.1829.

714. Dunlop, James, merchant, in Md, heir to cousin Christina Dunlop, in Glasgow, reg. 9 May 1799.

715. Dunlop, John, in NJ, heir to sis M Dunlop or Richmond, wid of J Richmond in Houletburn Loudoun Castle, reg. 9 Feb.1848.

716. Dunlop, Margaret, in Kingston St Vincent, heir to fa John William Dunlop, shipmaster in Irvine Aryshire, reg. 8 Dec.1851.

717. Dunlop, Robert, merchant, in Hamilton Can, heir to mo Jane Pennell or Dunlop, wid of Robert Dunlop shipmaster in Greenock Renfrewshire, d. 27 Jan.1865, reg. 17 Aug.1866.

718. Dunlop, William, papermaker, in NY, heir to fa William Dunlop, mason in Glasgow, reg. 28 Aug.1835.
719. Durie or Renton, Jemima, in SC, heir to fa James Durie, mariner in Rossie Island Montrose Angus, d. 18 Oct.1843, reg. 24 June 1875.
720. Dutch, George, ship carpenter, in NB, heir to uncle George Dutch, ship carpenter in Ferryport-on-Craig Fife, d. 14 Sep.1849, reg. 23 Feb.1866.
721. Duthie or Lawrence or Lee, Helen, w of R H Lee merchant, in Buffalo, heir to William Duthie, merchant in Aberdeen, reg. 27 Jan.1847.
722. Duthie or Lawrence or Lee, Helen, w of R H Lee merchant, in Buffalo, heir to Helen Milne or Duthie, w of William Duthie mason in Aberdeen, reg. 18 June 1847.
723. Duthie, William, smith, in Aberdeen then Buffalo, heir to William Duthie, merchant in Aberdeen, reg. 27 Jan.1847.
724. Duthie, William, smith, in Aberdeen then Buffalo, heir to Helen Milne or Duthie, w of William Duthie mason in Aberdeen, reg. 18 June 1847.
725. Earl of Stirling, Alexander, heir to gt gt grandfa Sir William Alexander of Menstrie, in Stirling & NS, d. 12 Feb.1640, reg. 2 July 1831.
726. Easson, James, bookbinder, in Brooklyn USA, heir to fa Robert Easson, carrier in Kirkcaldy Fife, reg. 18 May 1854.
727. Easson, William, in America, heir to mo Catherine Robertson or Easson, w of Robert Easson grocer in Dundee Angus, d. 11 May 1853, reg. 26 Dec.1866.
728. Easton or Rutherford, Janet, w of John Easton shoemaker, in Albany NA, heir to uncle William Turnbull of Longraw, reg. 22 Nov.1798.
729. Easton, John, in Southamptonville Pa, heir to cousin John Robson, in Dumfries, d. 9 Oct.1878, reg. 22 Sep.1882.
730. Eaton or Floyd, Margaret, w of Richard Floyd, in Christchurch Ga, heir to uncle James McIldoe, weaver in Glasgow, reg. 28 Nov.1774.
731. Edgar, Elizabeth Katherine, in Toronto, heir to grandmo Ann B Hamilton or Edgar, reg. 6 Aug.1866.
732. Edgar, Elizabeth Katherine, in Toronto, heir to gt grandfa John Hamilton of Broomfield, reg. 6 Aug.1866.
733. Edgar, Grace Matilda, in Toronto, heir to gt grandfa John Hamilton of Broomfield, reg. 6 Aug.1866.
734. Edgar, James, in Philadelphia, heir to uncle James Edgar, wheelwright in Milldamhead then Pleasance Dumfries, d. 9 Aug.1842, reg. 14 Nov.1851.
735. Edgar, James David, barrister, in Toronto, heir to gt grandfa John Hamilton of Broomfield, reg. 6 Aug.1866.

736. Edgar, James David, barrister, in Toronto, heir to grandmo Ann B Hamilton or Edgar, reg. 6 Aug.1866.

737. Edgar, Matilda Grace, in Toronto, heir to grandmo Ann B Hamilton or Edgar, reg. 6 Aug.1866.

738. Edmiston, Margaret, in Albion Ill, heir to grandmo Isobel Shields or Edmiston, w of Robert Edmiston in Govan Coalworks, reg. 2 May 1870.

739. Edmonstone, William, merchant, in Montreal, heir to bro Archibald Edmonstone, in Stirling, d. 28 Jan.1856, reg. 16 Apr.1856.

740. Edwards, William, judge, in Futtepore, heir to fa James Edwards, Receiver General in Jamaica, d. 18 Jan.1848, reg. 13 June 1861.

741. Edwards, William, in Agra East Indies, heir to fa John Edwards, Receiver General in Jamaica, reg. 2 Oct.1862.

742. Elder, Catherine, in NY, heir to grandfa John McNab, in New Scone Perthshire, reg. 6 Nov.1858.

743. Elder or Roy, Mary, w of Ebenezer Roy merchant, in Brantford Can, heir to sis Elizabeth Elder, in Dunfermline Fife, reg. 11 Mar.1851.

744. Elder, Peter, in Seven Rivers Jamaica, heir to fa John Elder, wright & feuar in Blairgowrie Perthshire, reg. 10 July 1789.

745. Elliot, Henry Anderson, in Oregon Washington Territory, heir to grandfa William Elliot, flesher in Edinburgh, d. July 1811, reg. 12 Oct.1868.

746. Elliot, John Jeffrey, in Oregon Washington Territory, heir to grandfa William Elliot, flesher in Edinburgh, d. July 1811, reg. 12 Oct.1868.

747. Elliot, Ralph Charles, in Oregon Washington Territory, heir to grandfa William Elliot, flesher in Edinburgh, d. July 1811, reg. 12 Oct.1868.

748. Elliot, Thomas Waugh, plumber & gas-fitter, in Montreal, heir to aunt Jean Elliot, in Jedburgh Roxburghshire, d. 10 Oct.1867, reg. 14 Feb.1868.

749. Ellis, Andrew, wright, in Banff, heir to bro Robert Ellis, wright in Strathmiglo Fife then America, reg. 6 Dec.1813.

750. Elmslie or Wallace, Jean, w of John Elmslie, in London, heir to bro William Wallace, in Jamaica, reg. 16 Feb.1788.

751. Erskine, John, in Toronto, heir to fa Alexander Erskine, in Toronto, d. 9 Nov.1865, reg. 7 June 1872.

752. Euing, William Duncan, in NY, heir to grandmo Susanna Morrison or Euing, in Inverkip Renfrewshire, reg. 1 Feb.1850.

753. Euing, William Duncan, in NY, heir to grand-aunt Margaret Morrison or Duguid, in Inverkip Renfrewshire, reg. 1 Feb.1850.

754. Ewart, George Graham, teacher, in Stratford Ont, heir to fa Robert Ewart, saddler in Edinburgh, reg. 4 Jan.1854.

755. Ewart, Robert Brunton, in Up Can, heir to bro Ritchie Ewart, in Knowtownhead Minto Roxburghshire, reg. 1 Sep.1848.

756. Ewing, Robert, housebuilder, in San Francisco, heir to fa Robert Ewing, wright in Dunbarton, d. 2 Oct.1863, reg. 12 Feb.1868.

757. Ewing, William, in Oh, heir to grandfa John Hervie, merchant in Aberdeen, reg. 4 Aug.1843.

758. Fairbairn, James, in Brooklyn NA, heir to fa Robert Fairbairn, writer in Duns Berwickshire, d. 22 Mar.1864, reg. 22 July 1864.

759. Fairbairn, Thomas, in St Vincent, heir to uncle Thomas Fairbairn, s of Rev Thomas Fairbairn in Gartly Aberdeenshire, reg. 22 Mar.1793.

760. Fairley or Malcolm, Janet, wid of Mr Fairley, in Jamaica, heir to aunt Janet Gordon Malcolm, reg. 26 June 1819.

761. Fairley, Robert Preston, planter, in Trinidad, heir to mo Euphemia Galloway or Fairley, w of Edward Fairley assistant bank cashier in Glasgow, d. 13 Apr.1846, reg. 4 Aug.1862.

762. Fairweather, George, in USA, heir to fa John Fairweather, flaxdresser in Arbroath Angus, reg. 10 Sep.1860.

763. Fairweather, George, in USA, heir to uncle David Fairweather, in Dundee Angus, reg. 10 Sep.1860.

764. Farish, James, in Hamilton Can, heir to fa Francis Farish, in Montreal, reg. 12 Apr.1850.

765. Farquhar, John, in Jamaica, heir to grand-uncle James Farquhar, land-surveyor in Aberdeen, reg. 16 Jan.1806.

766. Farquharson or Donald, Isabella, w of Alexander Donald, in NJ, heir to fa Peter Farquharson, in Padanarum Angus, d. 25 July 1854, reg. 20 Dec.1869.

767. Fechney, David, shipcarpenter, in NY, heir to fa Lawrence Fechney, warehouseman in Partick Glasgow, d. 6 Oct.1867, reg. 7 Feb.1868.

768. Fell, William Thomas, in Hamilton Can, heir to uncle Thomas Fell, coal merchant in Greenock Renfrewshire, d. 24 Oct.1873, reg. 25 July 1881.

769. Ferguson, David, manufacturer, in Kirkcaldy Fife then Waupan Wisc, heir to fa Drysdale Ferguson, in Kirkcaldy Fife, d. 8 June 1830, reg. 14 Apr.1853.

770. Ferguson, David, manufacturer, in Kirkcaldy Fife then Waupan Wisc, heir to mo Christian Forgan or Ferguson, wid of Drysdale Ferguson in Kirkcaldy Fife, reg. 5 Sep.1853.

771. Ferguson, Dougald, sailor, in Greenock Renfrewshire, heir to uncle Angus Ferguson, clerk in Newfoundland, reg. 25 Sep.1843.

772. Ferguson, Dougald, sailor, in Greenock Renfrewshire, heir to uncle Alexander Ferguson, merchant in Greenock then America, reg. 25 Sep.1843.

773. Ferguson or Gilchrist, Isabella, in Can, heir to uncle James Ferguson, excise officer in Thurso Caithness, reg. 5 Oct.1860.

774. Ferguson, James, in Baltimore, heir to bro William Ferguson of Dungalston, reg. 24 July 1821.

775. Ferguson or Young, Margaret, wid of John Duff Ferguson, in NY, heir to sis Isabella Young or Easson, wid of Robert Easson in Dundee Angus then Australia, reg. 10 Nov.1860.

776. Ferguson, Robert, in New Orleans, heir to fa Robert Ferguson, mason in Duns Berwickshire, reg. 1 June 1848.

777. Fergusson, Walter, in Edenton NC, heir to bro William Fergusson of Troston, reg. 31 May 1788.

778. Fergusson, William, merchant, in Philadelphia, heir to sis Jessie Fergusson, da of John Fergusson merchant in Ayr, reg. 3 Nov.1871.

779. Ferme, John, in NY, heir to fa George Ferme, in Crichton House Edinburgh, reg. 8 Aug.1842.

780. Ferrie or McLagan, Catherine, w of Peter McLagan, in NA, heir to fa John Ferrie, flesher in Paisley Renfrewshire, d. 21 Feb.1846, reg. 21 Jan.1862.

781. Ferrie or McLagan, Catherine, w of Peter McLagan, in NA, heir to mo Catherine Johnston or Ferrie, in Paisley Renfrewshire, d. 2 Aug.1859, reg. 21 Jan.1862.

782. Ferrier, Hugh, in Aquadilla Porto Rico, heir to cousin Peter Cochrane, in Clippen Renfrewshire, reg. 21 June 1836.

783. Ferrier, John Plain, in Big Oakflat Cal, heir to fa David Ferrier, bookbinder in Edinburgh, d. 13 June 1859, reg. 20 July 1865.

784. Ferrier, William, in Grenada, heir to bro Alexander Ferrier, in Grenada, reg. 29 Mar.1811.

785. Fife, Hannah, w of Samuel Fife sailor, in Bermuda, heir to grandfa William Fife, in Gilcomston, reg. 10 Feb.1755.

786. Findlay or Gourlay, Elizabeth, w of James Gourlay plasterer, in Can W, heir to grandmo Jean Findlay, wid of John Findlay in Airdrie Lanarkshire, d. 26 Oct.1847, reg. 3 Nov.1871.

787. Findlay, Helen, in St Michael's Barbados, heir to fa Thomas Findlay of Balkirsty, in Fife, d. June 1760, reg. 31 Oct.1765.

788. Findlay, John, in Akron Oh, heir to fa Robert Findlay, smith in Falkirk Stirlingshire, d. 4 Dec.1873, reg. 6 Apr.1876.

789. Findlay jr, John, joiner, in Chicago, heir to mo Margaret Fraser or Findlay, w of John Findlay sr in Isle of Whithorn Wigtownshire, d. 12 Sep.1862, reg. 6 June 1880.

790. Findlay or Forbes, Margaret, w of W Forbes barrister, in Barbados, heir to fa Thomas Finlay of Balkirsty, in Fife, d. June 1760, reg. 31 Oct.1765.

791. Findlay, Thomas, attorney & WS, in Barbados, heir to fa James Findlay, s of James Findlay of Balchristie in Fife, reg. 13 July 1741.

792. Findlay, William, gardener, in RI, heir to fa William Findlay, gardener in Edinburgh, d. 21 Feb.1859, reg. 20 Oct.1859.

793. Findlay, William, in Montreal, heir to mo Ellen Todd or Findlay, w of John Findlay farmer in Breckenbrae, d. 19 June 1850, reg. 26 Oct.1866.

794. Finlay, Gavin, in Ut, heir to grandmo Jean Grindlay or Finlay, wid of John Finlay in Airdrie Lanarkshire, d. 26 Oct.1847, reg. 3 Nov.1871.

795. Finlay, Thomas, in Barbados, heir to fa Thomas Finlay of Balkirsty, attorney & WS in Barbados, d. June 1760, reg. 4 Feb.1762.

796. Finlay, William Loutit, railway clerk, in Galt NA, heir to fa Hugh Finlay, shipmaster in Cottascarth Orkney, d. Jan.1838, reg. 12 Mar.1863.

797. Finlayson, Alexander, storekeeper, in Charleston USA, heir to bro John Finlayson, woolspinner in Inverurie Aberdeenshire, reg. 3 July 1850.

798. Finlayson, Alexander, storekeeper, in Charleston USA, heir to mo Elizabeth Mackay or Finlayson, in Aberdeen, reg. 3 July 1850.

799. Finlayson, James, millwright, in Payson Ut, heir to fa James Finlayson, farmer in Mainsbank Friockheim Angus, d. 29 Aug.1870, reg. 7 June 1871.

800. Finnie, Christina, in Mich, heir to mo Christina Fleming or Finnie, w of John Finnie powerloom dresser in Glasgow then Mich, reg. 20 Apr.1859.

801. Finnie or Drummond, Jane, w of Duncan Drummond engineer, in Chicago, heir to fa William Finnie, baker & spiritdealer in Linlithgow W Lothian, d. 13 May 1852, reg. 13 June 1881.

802. Finny, Alexander, minister, in Brandon Va, heir to fa William Finny, merchant in Aberdeen, reg. 1 Feb.1755.

803. Fisher, James Wauchope, in Jamaica, heir to fa Charles Fisher, SSC, d. 4 Aug.1850, reg. 22 Dec.1851.

804. Fisher, James Wauchope, in Hampstead Estate Trelawney Jamaica, heir to fa Charles Fisher, SSC in Edinburgh, d. 4 Aug.1850, reg. 12 May 1868.

805. Fisher, John, in Plympton Can, heir to grand-uncle John Hepburn, weaver in Perth, reg. 14 Apr.1846.

806. Fleck, Thomas, in Garrison House Benicia Cal, heir to bro Alexander Fleck, writer in Glasgow, d. 30 July 1845, reg. 15 Mar.1865.

807. Fleming or Thomson, Beatrice, wid of J Thomson, in Ga, heir to mo Margaret Boswell or Fleming, in Edinburgh, reg. 9 June 1806.

808. Fleming or Ford, Elizabeth, w of Andrew Joseph Ford, in Walcotville NA, heir to uncle John Barrowman, in Edinburgh, d. Oct.1850, reg. 10 Jan.1868.

809. Fleming, Helen, in Ga, heir to Margaret Boswell or Fleming, w of David Fleming currier in Edinburgh, reg. 9 June 1806.

810. Fleming, John Boyes, in NY, heir to fa Rev Dr Alexander Fleming, in Hamilton Lanarkshire, reg. 6 Aug.1830.

811. Fleming or McWhirter, Mary, w of David McWhirter builder, in Oh, heir to cousin John Fleming, teacher in Whithorn Wigtownshire, reg. 14 Dec.1852.

812. Fleming, Patrick, in NY, heir to fa Robert Fleming, ironmonger in Glasgow, d. 18 Dec.1848, reg. 25 Sep.1857.

813. Fletcher, James, miner, in Albion Mines NS, heir to bro Joseph Fletcher, collier in Crookedholm Kilmarnock Ayrshire, d. 20 Feb.1860, reg. 14 Sep.1861.

814. Flett or Ross, Elizabeth, wid of Alexander Ross merchant, in NE, heir to bro Alexander Flett, s of John Flett of Gruthay, reg. 10 Dec.1772.

815. Floyd, Margaret, w of Richard Floyd, in Christchurch Ga, heir to uncle James McIldoe, weaver in Glasgow, reg. 28 Jan.1774.

816. Fogo, David, merchant, in Antigua, heir to bro James Fogo yr of Roy, reg. 20 Jan.1749.

817. Forbes, Alexander, in Baltimore, heir to fa James Forbes, weaver in Dunshalt Fife, reg. 25 July 1842.

818. Forbes, Alexander, farmer, in PEI, heir to grand-aunt Mary Stewart, in Duntalich, reg. 8 Nov.1848.

819. Forbes, Duncan, in Little London Westmoreland Jamaica, heir to Mary Jameson or Forbes, wid of Benjamin Forbes physician in Dysart Fife, d. 22 July 1856, reg. 6 Dec.1871.

820. Forbes, Duncan, in Little London Westmoreland Jamaica, heir to bro Benjamin Forbes, physician in Dysart Fife, d. Oct.1855, reg. 7 Feb.1871.

821. Forbes, Duncan, minister, in Westmoreland Jamaica, heir to sis Jane Forbes or Johnston, w of James Johnston in Mains of Drumwhindle, d. 3 Sep.1873, reg. 26 Apr.1882.

822. Forbes, Helen, in Norfolk Va, heir to bro David Forbes, carver in Edinburgh, reg. 25 Oct.1815.

823. Forbes, Henry, in Nether Whindlemont, heir to bro William Forbes, merchant in Jamaica, reg. 19 July 1783.

824. Forbes, James, in NY, heir to aunt Euphame Forbes or Keith, wid of George Strachan Keith in Auchorsk, reg. 24 June 1825.

825. Forbes, James, in NY, heir to sis Euphame Forbes, reg. 24 June 1825.

826. Forbes, James, in America, heir to bro William Forbes, reg. 2 Nov.1869.

827. Forbes, James, in America, heir to sis Marianne Forbes, reg. 2 Nov.1869.
828. Forbes, James, in America, heir to bro Charles Scott Forbes, reg. 2 Nov.1869.
829. Forbes, John Murray, minister, in St Luke's NY, heir to grand-aunt Margaret Forbes or Paterson, in Newmill Keith Banffshire, reg. 15 July 1836.
830. Forbes, Philip Turpin, farmer, in Roseberry Tenn, heir to grandfa Robert Carmichael, in Newtown Hamilton Oh, d. 26 May 1849, reg. 1 Sep.1880.
831. Forbes, William, in Jamaica, heir to mo Jean Lumsden or Forbes, w of George Forbes merchant in Aberdeen, reg. 14 May 1814.
832. Ford or Dudgeon, Alison, in NY, heir to bro William Scott Ford, s of Peter Ford in Eyemouth Berwickshire, reg. 5 Mar.1855.
833. Ford or Dudgeon, Alison, in NY, heir to sis Mary Ford, da of Peter Ford in Eyemouth Berwickshire, reg. 5 Mar.1855.
834. Forrest, Joanna, in America, heir to mo Janet Irving or Forrest, wid of Peter Forrest in NA, d. 17 Sep.1857, reg. 12 Nov.1861.
835. Forrest, Robert Wilson, physician, in E Gwillimsburgh Ont, heir to cousin John Wilson, minister in Chelsea, d. 5 Feb.1880, reg. 21 Oct.1881.
836. Forrest, William, in Greenock Renfrewshire, heir to bro James Forrest, minister in USA, d. 18 Feb.1855, reg. 17 Mar.1859.
837. Forrester, Robert, in Rochester USA, heir to Robert Forrester, in S Badcur, reg. 14 Apr.1859.
838. Forret, Andrew, mason, in Chicago, heir to fa Thomas Forret, laborer in Blebo Craig Fife, d. 7 Aug.1870, reg. 16 Nov.1877.
839. Forsyth, James, solicitor, in Jamaica, heir to uncle Alexander Forsyth of Dunach, reg. 29 Apr.1833.
840. Fowler or Walker, Margaret, w of John Walker, in Montreal, heir to mo Rebecca Muir or Fowler, w of Thomas Fowler in Glasgow, d. 6 Nov.1835, reg. 1 Aug.1865.
841. Fowler or Walker, Margaret, w of John Walker, in Montreal, heir to mo Rebekah Muir or Fowler, w of Thomas Fowler in Glasgow, d. 6 Nov.1835, reg. 3 Sep.1872.
842. Fowlie, Robert, in St Catherine Ont, heir to uncle Joseph Fowlie, merchant in Banff, d. 17 Sep.1880, reg. 19 May 1881.
843. Fraser, Alexander, baker, in NY, heir to bro James Fraser, corn-dealer in Markinch Fife, d. 4 Sep.1851, reg. 22 Nov.1852.
844. Fraser, James, painter, in NY, heir to fa James Fraser, laborer in Inverness, d. Feb.1849, reg. 7 July 1870.
845. Fraser or Mackenzie, Joanna, w of Roderick Mackenzie, in Wisc, heir to mo Mary Joyner or Fraser, w of Donald Fraser in Invergordon Ross & Cromarty, reg. 10 May 1871.

846. Fraser, John Hutchison, barrister, in Jamaica, heir to fa Capt Simon Fraser of Fanellan, reg. 23 Oct.1793.

847. Fraser, John, in America, heir to fa Donald Fraser, heckler in Crieff Perthshire, reg. 1 Dec.1797.

848. Fraser, John, merchant, in St John Antigua, heir to cousin Elizabeth Mary Gregory, in Laurel Green Helensburgh Dunbartonshire, d. 16 July 1860, reg. 10 May 1861.

849. Fraser, John, merchant, in St Johns West Indies, heir to grandfa John McGregor, japanner in Glasgow, d. 5 Jan.1832, reg. 10 Feb.1862.

850. Fraser, John, in Salem Ont, heir to cousin James Donald, in Banchory Aberdeenshire, d. 4 May 1870, reg. 2 May 1871.

851. Fraser, Robert, in Minneapolis Minn, heir to gt grandfa William Oliver, dyer in Jedburgh Roxburghshire, reg. 18 Oct.1881.

852. Fraser, William, planter, in Va, heir to uncle Daniel Fraser, in Gorbals Glasgow, reg. 4 Oct.1826.

853. Fraser, William Johnston, in NY, heir to uncle John Fraser, painter in Perth, reg. 27 July 1841.

854. Fraser, William, minister, in Hampden NY, heir to fa John Fraser, wright in Dunning Perthshire, reg. 20 Feb.1852.

855. Fraser, William, in Can then Huntly Aberdeenshire, heir to bro John Fraser, merchant in Huntly, d. 24 May 1863, reg. 14 Sep.1863.

856. Fraser, William, in Ont, heir to bro Colin Fraser, merchant in Huntly Aberdeenshire, d. 26 Dec.1872, reg. 3 July 1873.

857. Frazer or Thompson, Elizabeth, w of William Sparrow Thompson, in NY, heir to fa George Alexander Frazer, Capt RN, d. 29 Apr.1866, reg. 1 July 1870.

858. Freebairn, Margaret Maxwell, in Hamilton Lanarkshire, heir to fa Charles Freebairn, wright in Jamaica then Hamilton, d. Jan.1791, reg. 28 Nov.1865.

859. Freebairn, Mary, in Hamilton Lanarkshire, heir to fa Charles Freebairn, wright in Jamaica then Hamilton, d. Jan.1791, reg. 28 Nov.1865.

860. Freeman, Thomas, heir to fa Thomas Freeman, in Antigua, reg. 20 Dec.1802.

861. French, Robert, in Can, heir to gt grandfa James French, laborer in E Kirkburn Edinburgh, d. 1811, reg. 11 Jan.1875.

862. Fry or Laing, Isabella Margaret, wid of Lt Oliver Fry 5th Infantry, heir to fa John Laing, in Dominica, reg. 20 Nov.1829.

863. Fullarton, James, ship carpenter, in St John NB, heir to Daniel McNaught, minister in Biggar Lanarkshire, reg. 24 Mar.1820.

864. Furman or Scrymgeour, Eliza, in Sumters SC, heir to grandfa George Scrymgeour of Thornhall, reg. 27 July 1835.

865. Gair, Alexander, in St Louis, heir to fa John Gair, farmer in Kilday Ross-shire, d. 9 June 1879, reg. 3 May 1883.

866. Gairdner, James, in Ga, heir to mo Rebecca Penman or Gairdner, wid of Andrew Gairdner merchant in Edinburgh, reg. 30 May 1826.
867. Gairdner, James Penman, in Shady Grove Ga, heir to fa James Gairdner, s of James Gairdner merchant in Edinburgh, reg. 6 Apr.1835.
868. Gairdner, James, in Port Gibson NA, heir to fa James Gairdner, Customs Office clerk in Edinburgh, d. 10 Jan.1836, reg. 11 Mar.1861.
869. Gairdner, Robert Hunter, advocate, in Quebec, heir to fa Robert Gairdner, solicitor in Edinburgh, reg. 31 Aug.1830.
870. Gairdner, Robert Hunter, advocate, in Quebec, heir to uncle George Gairdner, merchant in Va, reg. 28 June 1836.
871. Gairns, Robert, engineer, in Chicago, heir to mo Janet Johnston or Gairns, w of Andrew Gairns in Cupar Fife, reg. 27 Jan.1857.
872. Galbraith, James, tinsmith, in Glasgow then NY, heir to fa James Galbraith, tinsmith in Glasgow, reg. 1 Sep.1843.
873. Galbraith, James, tinsmith, in Glasgow then NY, heir to mo Mary Smith or Galbraith, in Glasgow, reg. 1 Sep.1843.
874. Gall or Campbell, Elizabeth Keiller, in Brooklyn, heir to mo Margaret Thomson or Templeman, in Dundee Angus, d. 14 Nov.1852, reg. 30 Sep.1876.
875. Gallie, James Boggs, in NS, heir to uncle Roderick Gallie, merchant in Invergordon Ross & Cromarty, reg. 9 July 1847.
876. Galloway, Jessie, in Andover Mass, heir to sis Mary Galloway, da of William Galloway baker in Brechin Angus, reg. 14 Nov.1851.
877. Galloway, Jessie, in Andover Mass, heir to grand-uncle John Strachan, feuar in Nether Tenements of Caldham Angus, reg. 15 Nov.1851.
878. Galloway or Middleton, Margaret, in Andover Mass, heir to sis Mary Galloway, da of William Galloway baker in Brechin Angus, reg. 14 Nov.1851.
879. Galloway or Middleton, Margaret, in Andover Mass, heir to grand-uncle John Strachan, farmer in Nether Tenements of Caldham Angus, reg. 15 Nov.1851.
880. Garden, John, sailor, in WI, heir to fa John Garden, smith in Newpark of Whitemyres, reg. 28 Nov.1800.
881. Gardiner, Andrew, in Douanville Jamaica, heir to bro John Gardiner, baker in Perth, reg. 17 Mar.1798.
882. Gardiner, Robert, in Muirend, heir to nephew John Gardiner, merchant in St Thomas WI, reg. 4 Dec.1835.
883. Gardiner, Thomas Jefferson, in Brooklyn NY, heir to grandmo Ann Robertson or Gardiner, w of Thomas Gardiner in Perth, d. 3 Dec.1857, reg. 23 Feb.1869.
884. Garvie, Joseph, in Owen Sound Ont, heir to fa William Garvie, manufacturer in Bankfoot Perthshire, d. July 1841, reg. 11 Oct.1869.

885. Gavin, William, in Drumlithie Kincardineshire, heir to bro John Gavin, in Grenada, reg. 30 May 1832.

886. Gay, Alexander, in Fredericton NB, heir to uncle William Gay, in Anstruther Easter Fife, d. 25 Apr.1853, reg. 12 Dec.1854.

887. Gay, William, merchant, in Va, heir to uncle John Gay, merchant in London, reg. 8 Oct.1772.

888. Gay or Rumgay, William, in Barbados then London, heir to gt grandfa John Rumgay, in Arncroach Fife, reg. 15 June 1844.

889. Gebbie, Alexander, MD, in Lowville NY, heir to fa Robert Gebbie, weaver in Darvel Ayrshire, d. 4 June 1863, reg. 8 Mar.1866.

890. Geddes, James, solicitor, in Can W, heir to grandfa James Geddes, flaxdresser in Gardenstown Banffshire, d. 1786, reg. 6 May 1873.

891. Geddes, James, civil engineer, in Nashville Tenn, heir to grandfa Alexander Geddes, in Portsoy Banffshire, d. 27 Mar.1810, reg. 14 Mar.1881.

892. Geekie, James Henry, in Ga, heir to fa William Geekie, merchant in Arbroath Angus, reg. 18 Oct.1809.

893. Gibb, David, painter, in Philadelphia, heir to fa Alexander Gibb, weaver in Dunikeir Fife, reg. 24 Feb.1842.

894. Gibb, William, mason, in San Francisco, heir to grandmo Elizabeth Reid or Gibb, w of William Gibb grocer in Westmuir, reg. 18 Jan.1872.

895. Gibbon, George Elmslie, in Muskoka Ont, heir to mo Jane Elmslie or Gibbon, w of John Gibbon in Elora, d. 23 Aug.1880, reg. 13 Dec.1881.

896. Gibbon, William, in Wellington Ont, heir to mo Jane Elmslie or Gibbon, w of John Gibbon in Elora, d. 23 Aug.1880, reg. 13 Dec.1881.

897. Gibson, Daniel, in Munro La, heir to mo Jean Henderson McCallum or Gibson, w of Hugh McCallum weaver in Glasgow, d. 4 July 1849, reg. 18 June 1872.

898. Gibson or Brown, Janet, w of John Brown, in Montreal, heir to bro William Gibson, farmer in Overburn Lamington Biggar Lanarkshire, reg. 31 Oct.1867.

899. Gibson or Brown, Janet, w of John Brown, in Montreal, heir to fa James Gibson, farmer in Overburn Lamington Biggar Lanarkshire, d. 6 Feb.1842, reg. 31 Oct.1867.

900. Gibson or Brown, Janet, w of John Brown, in Montreal, heir to bro Robert Gibson, 2nd s of James Gibson farmer in Overburn Lamington Biggar Lanarkshire, reg. 31 Oct.1867.

901. Gibson, John, merchant, in Va, heir to fa Robert Gibson, messenger in Kilmarnock Ayrshire, reg. 17 Aug.1791.

902. Gibson, John, tinsmith, in Can, heir to fa Richard Gibson, in Bankhouse Carlisle Cumberland, reg. 14 Dec.1841.

903. Gillies or Todd or Toddie, Rachael, w of John Todd or Toddie, in
　　　Edinburgh, heir to David Todd or Toddie, cotton planter in E Fla,
　　　reg. 10 Mar.1826.
904. Gilmore, John Morton, in Lancaster Va, heir to grandfa William
　　　Gilmore, candlemaker in Kilmarnock Ayrshire, reg. 6 Oct.1794.
905. Gilmore, John Morton, in Lancaster Va, heir to fa Robert Gilmore,
　　　merchant in Va, reg. 25 Mar.1795.
906. Gilmour, James, in Ozark Mo, heir to sis Mary Gillies, in Glasgow, d.
　　　28 Dec.1866, reg. 6 Dec.1875.
907. Gilmour, John, in Ramsay Up Can, heir to bro William Gilmour,
　　　merchant in Paisley Renfrewshire, reg. 12 Dec.1833.
908. Glen, David Corse, engineer, in Glasgow, heir to bro James Glen,
　　　merchant in San Francisco, d. Jan.1856, reg. 22 June 1865.
909. Glen, James, seaman, in Washington USA, heir to mo Elizabeth Weir or
　　　Glen, w of Walter Glen spirit dealer in Bonhill Dunbartonshire, d.
　　　15 Sep.1848, reg. 13 June 1882.
910. Glen, James, seaman, in Washington USA, heir to uncle James Weir,
　　　mason in Bonhill Dunbartonshire, d. 13 Sep.1857, reg. 13 June
　　　1882.
911. Glen, Walter, in Kirkliston W Lothian then Great Salt Lake City USA,
　　　heir to uncle Walter Glen, merchant in Linlithgow W Lothian, d.
　　　23 Oct.1855, reg. 30 July 1861.
912. Gloak or Steven, Agnes, w of John Steven confectioner, in Ont, heir to
　　　fa James Gloak, spirit dealer in Scouringburn Dundee Angus, d.
　　　Oct.1847, reg. 27 Feb.1880.
913. Gordon or McKay, Amelia Jane, in Mayville Chautauqua NY, heir to fa
　　　George Gordon, merchant in Aberdeen, d. 27 July 1850, reg. 30
　　　Sep.1880.
914. Gordon, Caroline Maria, in Mayville Chautauqua NY, heir to fa George
　　　Gordon, merchant in Aberdeen, d. 27 July 1850, reg. 30 Sep.1880.
915. Gordon, Elizabeth, da of George Gordon, in Jamaica, heir to uncle John
　　　Gordon of Auchanachy, in Aberdeenshire, reg. 15 Aug.1772.
916. Gordon, George, in Edenton NC, heir to sis Clementina Gordon, in
　　　Cairnfield Banff, reg. 14 June 1847.
917. Gordon, George, clerk, in Can W, heir to fa William Gordon, plasterer in
　　　Glasgow, reg. 28 Oct.1858.
918. Gordon or MacFarlane, Helen, w of John MacFarlane, in America, heir to
　　　bro Alexander Gordon, in Cairncry, d. 23 June 1847, reg. 22
　　　Nov.1861.
919. Gordon or Brebner, James, chief judge, in Grenada, heir to uncle James
　　　Gordon of Knockspeck, d. Apr.1768, reg. 7 Mar.1770.
920. Gordon or Livingstone, Jean, w of John Livingstone collier, in
　　　Bellahouston Glasgow, heir to uncle Thomas Gordon, wright in
　　　Jamaica, reg. 20 May 1799.

921. Gordon or Livingstone, Jean, w of John Livingstone collier, in Bellahouston Glasgow, heir to fa James Gordon, smith in Jamaica, reg. 30 May 1799.

922. Gordon, John, in Portland Surrey Jamaica, heir to fa George Gordon, merchant in Aberdeen, reg. 18 June 1772.

923. Gordon, John, in Providence Mission Chicago, heir to mo Margaret Bell or Gordon, w of Andrew Gordon weaver in Cupar Fife, reg. 4 Apr.1870.

924. Gordon, John, mill overseer, in Delaware Oh, heir to fa John Gordon, harbor weigher in Dundee Angus, d. 13 Oct.1870, reg. 12 Oct.1872.

925. Gordon of Kingsgrange, Alexander, customs collector, in Montserrat, heir to bro Patrick Gordon of Kingsgrange, Brig. Gen., d. Aug.1776, reg. 14 Oct.1777.

926. Gordon of Swiney, John Mackay, in America, heir to James Gordon of Swiney, Maj Gen in Wattin Caithness, d. 5 Apr.1867, reg. 13 Nov.1867.

927. Gordon, Robert Home, heir to fa Dr John Gordon, in Green Castle Jamaica, reg. 23 Aug.1776.

928. Gordon, Thomas, watchmaker, in NY, heir to fa James Gordon, merchant in Garmouth Morayshire, reg. 18 May 1770.

929. Gordon, William, s of John Gordon, in Carron Stirlingshire, heir to uncle William McDonald, Lt 79th Regiment in Jamaica, reg. 15 May 1797.

930. Gordon, William George, surgeon, in Jamaica, heir to grandmo Elizabeth Souter or Gordon, wid of Col Gordon 92nd Foot, reg. 20 Oct.1843.

931. Goudie, James, blacksmith, in Victoria Vancouver Is, heir to fa Peter Goudie, blacksmith in Stromness Orkney, d. 1815, reg. 12 June 1869.

932. Gould, John, carter, in Crieff Perthshire, heir to bro Thomas Gould, in Littlefalls NY, reg. 29 Apr.1836.

933. Gourlay or Harvey, Elizabeth, w of William Harvey, in Can, heir to mo Helen Sproat or Gourlay, w of Peter Gourlay weaver in Kirkcudbright, reg. 11 June 1857.

934. Gourlay, Peter, in Kirkcudbright then Lochgilphead Argyll, heir to bro Samuel Gourlay, in Jamaica, reg. 28 July 1851.

935. Gourlie, John, in Putnam NY, heir to bro William Gourlie, in Motherwell Lanarkshire, d. 21 Aug.1873, reg. 11 May 1881.

936. Govan or Paton, Jean, w of John Paton, in Hamilton Lanarkshire, heir to bro James Govan, wright in Jamaica, reg. 27 Nov.1789.

937. Gow, George, in Johnsonville NH, heir to uncle John Gow, builder in Kirkcaldy Fife, d. 2 Oct.1871, reg. 20 Jan.1872.

938. Gow, Neil, in Ceylon, heir to bro Alexander Cumings Gow, in BNA, d. 25 July 1871, reg. 22 Jan.1873.
939. Gowans, John, in Tenn, heir to mo Jean Clark or Gowans, w of Peter Gowans in Crieff Perthshire, reg. 29 May 1829.
940. Gracie, William, NP, in NY, heir to aunt Mary Gracie or Morison, in Va then Edinburgh, reg. 8 Feb.1830.
941. Graham, Agnes, heir to fa Duncan Graham, in Jamaica then Edinburgh, reg. 24 May 1787.
942. Graham, Alexander, in NY, heir to mo Grizel Grace McGlashan or Graham, d. 17 July 1865, reg. 30 Apr.1869.
943. Graham, Hugh, in Up Can, heir to fa Hugh Graham, in Antigua then Edinburgh, reg. 22 June 1846.
944. Graham, James, in Trinidad, heir to aunt Jean Paxton, sis of John Paxton in New Orchard, reg. 3 Nov.1804.
945. Graham, John, sailor, in WI, heir to aunt Jean Paxton, sis of John Paxton in New Orchard, reg. 3 Nov.1804.
946. Graham, John, in Kittochside Lanarkshire, heir to grand-uncle David McCulloch, surgeon in Jamaica, reg. 14 July 1851.
947. Graham, John, draper, in RI, heir to Janet Sneddon, in Lauriston Falkirk Stirlingshire, reg. 28 Apr.1852.
948. Graham, Walter, Lt, heir to bro William Graham of Glennie, in Antigua, reg. 14 Mar.1792.
949. Graham, William, in Baltimore, heir to bro Simon Graham of Glaisters, reg. 22 Jan.1803.
950. Graham, William, merchant, in Antigua, heir to fa William Graham of Lambhill, reg. 28 July 1830.
951. Grahame, William Richard, in The Moat Can, heir to grandfa Richard Graham of Blaatwood, reg. 8 Oct.1855.
952. Grainger or Johnson, Elizabeth, w of Henry Johnson banker, in Can W, heir to mo Margaret Stirrat or Grainger, w of Luke Grainger tailor in Paisley Renfrewshire, reg. 10 Nov.1871.
953. Grainger, Ellen, da of James Grainger MD, in St Kitts, heir to uncle William Grainger, writing master in Edinburgh, reg. 2 Feb.1781.
954. Grainger, James, MD, in St Kitts, heir to bro William Grainger, writing master in Edinburgh, reg. 8 Apr.1766.
955. Grant, Alexander, in Jamaica, heir to bro Robert Grant, Major 24th Foot, reg. 24 Feb.1780.
956. Grant or King, Ann, w of William Grant, in Philadelphia, heir to fa Hugh King, shipmaster in Philadelphia, reg. 3 Nov.1796.
957. Grant or Robertson, Barbara, wid of Alexander Robertson saddler, in America, heir to bro Robert Charles Grant, advocate in Aberdeen, reg. 23 Feb.1854.

958. Grant, Donald Fraser, in Cobourg Can W, heir to grandmo Christian
Munro or Grant, w of Duncan Grant cooper in Inverness, reg. 27
June 1864.

959. Grant, Donald Fraser, in Cobourg Can, heir to grand-aunt Ann Munro or
Hood, w of Adam Hood housewright in Inverness, d. 27 June
1843, reg. 27 June 1864.

960. Grant, Donald Fraser, in Ont, heir to grandmo Christian Munro or Grant,
w of Donald Grant cooper in Inverness, d. July 1838, reg. 27 June
1865.

961. Grant or Pillans, Elizabeth, w of Henry Grant, in SC, heir to fa William
Pillans, shipmaster in Leith Mid Lothian, reg. 9 Sep.1795.

962. Grant, Elizabeth, in Charleston SC, heir to grandfa William Pillans,
shipmaster in Leith Mid Lothian, reg. 23 Nov.1796.

963. Grant, Emilia, in Charleston SC, heir to grandfa William Pillans,
shipmaster in Leith Mid Lothian, reg. 23 Nov.1796.

964. Grant, Emily, da of H Grant US Consul, in London, heir to grandfa
William Pillans, in Leith Mid Lothian, reg. 21 June 1802.

965. Grant, Francis, in Jamaica, heir to bro John Grant of Kilgraston, Chief
Justice in Jamaica, reg. 4 Apr.1794.

966. Grant, Henry, merchant, in Charleston SC, heir to da Elizabeth Grant,
reg. 17 May 1804.

967. Grant, Henry, merchant, in Charleston SC, heir to da Emily Grant, reg.
17 May 1804.

968. Grant, James, in Vermont Va, heir to fa Alexander Grant, tenant farmer
in Kinmuckly, reg. 19 July 1786.

969. Grant or Maxwell, Jeannie, in Amherst Co Va, heir to grandmo Ann
Blair or Marshall, w of James Marshall carter in Glasgow, d. 15
Sep.1855, reg. 4 June 1883.

970. Grant or Maxwell, Jeannie, in Amherst Co Va, heir to grandfa James
Marshall, carter in Glasgow, d. 13 June 1865, reg. 4 June 1883.

971. Grant, William, in Woodlands Jamaica, heir to bro Hugh Grant,
tacksman in Wester Arr, reg. 30 Apr.1856.

972. Gray, Adam Whyte, in St Louis Mo, heir to bro Charles Gray, in
Adelaide Australia, d. 16 June 1855, reg. 12 Jan.1874.

973. Gray or White, Elizabeth, w of David White tailor, in Jamaica, heir to sis
Jean Gray, da of William Gray merchant in Aberdeen, reg. 23
Feb.1793.

974. Gray or White, Elizabeth, w of David Gray tailor, in Jamaica, heir to sis
Margaret Gray, da of William Gray merchant in Aberdeen, reg. 23
Feb.1793.

975. Gray or Pitt, Hannah, w of Jabez Pitt attorney, in Va, heir to fa William
Gray of Shirvadike, reg. 22 Mar.1786.

976. Gray, James, writer, in Edinburgh, heir to bro William Gray, customs
controller in Montserrat, reg. 10 Apr.1794.

977. Gray, James, in Buffalo NA, heir to grandfa David Gray, merchant in Grassmarket Edinburgh, d. 1800, reg. 2 June 1865.
978. Gray, James, in San Francisco, heir to aunt Mary Willox or Lyon, wid of David Lyon in Old Aberdeen, d. 18 July 1877, reg. 22 Oct.1878.
979. Gray, John William, in Tuchahoe USA, heir to uncle William Gray, merchant in Leith Mid Lothian, reg. 27 Mar.1847.
980. Gray, John William, in Tuchahoe USA, heir to fa Andrew Gray, in Tuchahoe USA, reg. 29 Mar.1847.
981. Gray, Mary, in Stirling, heir to uncle John Paton, in Jamaica, reg. 11 Sep.1832.
982. Gray, Robert, in Jamaica, heir to fa Hugh Gray, in Helmsdale Sutherland, reg. 9 Dec.1772.
983. Greenlaw or Black, Janet, w of David Black merchant, in NS, heir to fa John Greenlaw, merchant in Glasgow, reg. 20 Mar.1789.
984. Greenlaw or Black, Janet, w of David Black merchant, in NS, heir to fa John Greenlaw, merchant in Glasgow, reg. 20 Mar.1789.
985. Greig or Mitchell, Annie Davidson, in Nashville Tenn, heir to grandfa George Greig, reedmaker in Cupar Fife, d. Jan.1848, reg. 25 June 1879.
986. Greig, George, porter, in NY, heir to grandfa George Greig, reedmaker in Cupar Fife, d. Jan.1848, reg. 25 June 1879.
987. Greig, James, in Pattersson NY, heir to fa Simon Greig, farmer in Claydales Lanarkshire then East Wemyss Fife, d. 30 Nov.1851, reg. 9 May 1853.
988. Greig, James Fortune, bookseller, in Can, heir to Christian Burnett or Fortune, wid of James Fortune baker in Kirkcaldy Fife, d. 7 May 1833, reg. 9 Aug.1871.
989. Grieve or Turnbull, Margaret, wid of Rev Walter Turnbull, in Jamaica, heir to fa James Grieve, mason in Edinburgh, d. 6 June 1847, reg. 13 Aug.1856.
990. Guthrie, Ann, in Can, heir to Charles Winter, in Balgarrock then Craigends of Auldbar Angus, reg. 24 Mar.1824.
991. Guthrie, William, in Can, heir to Charles Winter, in Balgarrock then Craigends of Auldbar Angus, reg. 24 Mar.1824.
992. Guthrie, William, farmer, in Ryegate Vt, heir to cousin Elizabeth Lindsay, in Saltcoats Ayrshire, d. 20 June 1867, reg. 21 Sep.1867.
993. Haggart, James, in NY, heir to bro David Haggart, s of David Haggart carter in Dundee Angus, reg. 15 Oct.1834.
994. Haig or Moir, Barbara, wid of John Moir, in Maryhill, heir to sis Mary McDonald or Robinson, w of William Robinson in NY, d. Dec.1858, reg. 29 June 1882.

995. Halket or Wanless, Margaret, w of James Wanless farmer, in Varna Can W, heir to bro William Halket jr, manufacturer in Dundee Angus, d. 19 Jan.1848, reg. 4 Nov.1870.

996. Hall or Moffat, Alison, wid of George Moffat draper, in USA, heir to grandfa William Hall, smith in Kelso Roxburghshire, reg. 6 Apr.1850.

997. Hall, Donald, farmer, in Vt, heir to sis Mary Hall, da of Alexander Hall farmer in Dubbs, reg. 16 Jan.1857.

998. Hall or Bennet, Isabella, w of R Bennet, in NY, heir to grandfa William Hall, smith in Kelso Roxburghshire, reg. 6 Apr.1850.

999. Halley, Ebenezer, minister, in NY, heir to fa William Halley, in Glasgow, d. 5 Aug.1854, reg. 17 Mar.1856.

1000. Halliday, Edward Cairns, in NY, heir to mo Mary Cairns or Halliday, w of Robert Halliday merchant in NY, reg. 6 June 1860.

1001. Halliday or Forsyth, Elizabeth, w of John Forsyth, in Fort William Inverness-shire, heir to bro David Halliday, in Jamaica, reg. 24 July 1819.

1002. Halliday, George, blockcutter, in NY, heir to uncle Charles Liddell, smith in Barrhead Renfrewshire, reg. 13 Oct.1857.

1003. Halliday, James, cattledealer, in Clinton BC, heir to fa Hugh Halliday, nailer in Castle Douglas Kirkcudbrightshire, d. 16 Mar.1868, reg. 10 Aug.1882.

1004. Halliday or McMeiken, Janet, w of James McMeiken currier, in Whitehaven Cumberland, heir to bro David Halliday, in Jamaica, reg. 24 July 1819.

1005. Halliday or Hughes, Jean, w of Peter Hughes merchant, in Newton Stewart Wigtownshire, heir to bro David Halliday, in Jamaica, reg. 24 July 1819.

1006. Halliday, William Andrew, in Toronto, heir to grand-uncle Alexander Halliday, surgeon in Paris, d. 11 July 1851, reg. 16 Feb.1876.

1007. Hally, George, farmer, in Torwood Stirlingshire, heir to bro Charles Hally, in Me, reg. 10 Aug.1840.

1008. Halyburton, Thomas, merchant, in St Eustatia, heir to sis Ann Halyburton, reg. 3 July 1787.

1009. Hamilton, Alexander, in Can W, heir to bro James Hamilton, in Galston, reg. 19 Jan.1859.

1010. Hamilton, David, joiner, in Brantford Can, heir to fa Robert Hamilton, laborer in Muirmadzean Bellshill Can, d. 20 May 1832, reg. 14 Apr.1864.

1011. Hamilton, George, in Can W, heir to bro John Hamilton, in Constantinople, d. 28 Sep.1840, reg. 9 Feb.1858.

1012. Hamilton, George, in Can W, heir to sis Rebecca Hamilton or Innes, w of Col William Innes HEICS, d. 28 June 1842, reg. 8 Jan.1858.

1013. Hamilton, James, shoemaker, in Va, heir to cousin Helen Christie of Hill, reg. 3 Oct.1787.
1014. Hamilton, James, in Jamaica, heir to grandfa Lt James Hamilton of Dowan, reg. 14 Oct.1789.
1015. Hamilton, John, in Jamaica, heir to fa John Hamilton, clockmaker in Glasgow, reg. 10 Aug.1804.
1016. Hamilton, Robert, in Jamaica, heir to grandfa Lt James Hamilton of Dowan, reg. 14 Oct.1789.
1017. Hamilton, Robert, in Jamaica, heir to fa James Hamilton, Provost in Sanquhar Dumfries-shire, reg. 1 May 1820.
1018. Hamilton, Thomas, merchant, in Halifax NS, heir to grandfa Lt James Hamilton of Dowan, reg. 14 Oct.1789.
1019. Hannah or McQueen, Marion, w of A McQueen weaver, in Wigtown, heir to bro Peter Hannah, merchant in Petersburg Va, reg. 17 Nov.1829.
1020. Hardie, James, planter, in Jamaica, heir to grandfa James Hardie, carrier in Elgin Morayshire, reg. 6 Mar.1848.
1021. Harlaw, John, in Montserrat, heir to fa Alexander Harlaw, merchant in Fraserburgh Aberdeenshire, reg. 21 Jan.1789.
1022. Harley, Alexander, in USA, heir to fa Archibald Harley, tollkeeper in Beancross Falkirk Stirlingshire, reg. 30 Oct.1855.
1023. Harley, Alexander, in USA, heir to grandfa William Read, in Bainsford, reg. 30 Oct.1855.
1024. Harper or Cargill, Jane Smith, in Buffalo USA, heir to grandmo Jean Robertson or Smith, wid of John Smith in Aberdeen, d. 13 Nov.1854, reg. 5 Sep.1874.
1025. Harris or Miller, Ann, in Portsmouth USA, heir to aunt Agnes Miller or Thomson, wid of John Thomson shipmaster in Leith Mid Lothian, reg. 29 Nov.1830.
1026. Harris, Jeffrey, in Richibucto NA, heir to mo Jean Jeffrey or Johnstone, w of J Johnstone in Creetown Kirkcudbrightshire, reg. 29 Mar.1825.
1027. Hart, Janet, w of John Hart, in Glasgow, heir to uncle Coll Turner, merchant in Tobago, reg. 26 Feb.1817.
1028. Hartley or McFarlane, Eliza Harleston, in Blairnairn, heir to sis Mary Hartley, da of G H Hartley planter in SC, reg. 13 Jan.1813.
1029. Harvey, John, mason, in Kingston Up Can, heir to fa John Harvey, mason in Midlem, reg. 23 June 1827.
1030. Harvey, John, Central Railwayman, in Mich, heir to fa Charles Harvey, feuar in Huntly Aberdeenshire, d. 13 Dec.1861, reg. 30 Dec.1870.
1031. Harvie, John, in Toronto, heir to bro James Harvie, distiller in Campbelltown Argyll, d. 21 Oct.1880, reg. 31 Jan.1881.

1032. Hastie or Barnes, Helen, in Franklin Ind, heir to grandmo Helen Black or Hastie, wid of George Hastie grocer in Airdrie Lanarkshire, d. 24 May 1869, reg. 13 Nov.1873.

1033. Hatfield or Jones, Constance, w of A M Hatfield, in Argyle Shelbourne NS, heir to fa Anthony Hart Jones, in Argyle Shelbourne NS, reg. 30 Nov.1812.

1034. Hawkins, William, engineer, in Salem Oh, heir to Janet Hawkins or Bell, reg. 31 Jan.1872.

1035. Hawkins, William, engineer, in Salem Oh, heir to William Bell, in Sinclairburn, reg. 31 Jan.1872.

1036. Hawks, Nicholas, engineer, in NY & Erie Railroad, heir to fa Henry Hawks, Edinburgh, Perth & Dundee Railway Co in Edinburgh, d. 11 Aug.1858, reg. 12 Sep.1862.

1037. Hawley or Henderson, Isobella, in NY, heir to grandfa Daniel Manson, schoolmaster in Stirling, reg. 13 Oct.1834.

1038. Hay, Alexander George, in Montserrat, heir to grandmo Elizabeth Hay, w of Alexander Hay of Lickliehead in Aberdeenshire, reg. 23 Nov.1801.

1039. Hay, Alexander Balcarres, in Jamaica, heir to mo Agnes Ogilvy or Hay, w of John Hay of Pitfour, reg. 2 Feb.1807.

1040. Hay or Ferguson, Ann, w of Alexander Ferguson farmer, in Skillymarno, heir to uncle William Hay, in NA, d. 10 July 1850, reg. 24 Dec.1862.

1041. Hay, John, housecarpenter, in Cohoes Albany Co NA, heir to gt grandfa Andrew Hay, farmer in Garmouth Morayshire, d. 1788, reg. 19 Oct.1868.

1042. Hays or Howat, Janet, in Newport Ky, heir to mo Janet Boyd or Howat, w of James Howat in Cincinnati, d. 16 Oct.1876, reg. 18 Sep.1877.

1043. Heddle or Peattie, Mary, w of Rev William Peattie, in Can W, heir to bro Hugh Leask Heddle, d. Aug.1856, reg. 8 Oct.1863.

1044. Heddle, Thomas James, in Ottawa, heir to grandfa William Heddle of Quildon, d. 14 May 1849, reg. 20 Mar.1879.

1045. Heddle, Thomas James, in Ottawa, heir to fa William Heddle, in America, d. 1854, reg. 30 Apr.1879.

1046. Hempsed, John, sailor, in Charleston SC, heir to fa John Hempsed, shipowner in Charleston SC, reg. 28 May 1817.

1047. Henderson, Balfour, planter, in Jamaica, heir to bro Daniel Henderson, writer in Edinburgh, reg. 13 Mar.1820.

1048. Henderson or Snyder, Elizabeth, in NY, heir to grandfa Daniel Manson, schoolmaster in Stirling, reg. 13 Oct.1834.

1049. Henderson or Roach, Jane, in NY, heir to grandfa Daniel Manson, schoolmaster in Stirling, reg. 13 Oct.1834.

1050. Henderson, John, surgeon, in Antigua, heir to fa John Henderson of
Cleughbrae, reg. 23 Sep.1797.
1051. Henderson, John, in USA, heir to mo Grizel Henderson, w of John
Henderson in Kinghorn Fife, d. 12 July 1853, reg. 23 Dec.1873.
1052. Henderson or Tower, Mary, w of Col G Henderson, heir to fa John
Tower, in St Croix, reg. 20 Jan.1830.
1053. Henderson, Peter, in St Johns Newfoundland, heir to fa James Henderson
of Rosebank, writer in Falkirk Stirlingshire, reg. 15 June 1818.
1054. Henderson, Peter, in St Johns Newfoundland, heir to grandmo Robina
MacCraire or Henderson, in Falkirk Stirlingshire, reg. 7 June
1819.
1055. Henderson, Peter, merchant, in St Johns Newfoundland, heir to fa James
Henderson, writer in Falkirk Stirlingshire, reg. 30 Oct.1820.
1056. Henderson, Robert, weaver, in Hamilton Lanarkshire, heir to mo Anna
Perrie or Henderson, w of J Henderson mason in NY, reg. 15
Apr.1824.
1057. Henderson, Robert, in Carlton Pl Beckwith Can W, heir to fa John
Henderson, weaver in Cambusbarron Stirlingshire, d. 14 July
1841, reg. 17 Mar.1870.
1058. Henderson, Thomas Rattray, in Oakland Md, heir to grand-uncle James
Banks, farmer in E Lundie Angus, d. 1 June 1851, reg. 10
Nov.1871.
1059. Henderson, Walter, MD, in Arthur Can, heir to cousin Jessie Henderson,
in Inverness, d. 15 Mar.1872, reg. 23 Nov.1872.
1060. Henderson, William Forsyth, MD, in London, heir to mo Jean Reid or
Henderson, wid of William Henderson in Jamaica, reg. 22
Apr.1843.
1061. Hendry, Alexander, in Buffalo America, heir to grand-aunt Elizabeth
Hendry or Nicol, in Forres Morayshire, d. 2 Apr.1873, reg. 5
Feb.1876.
1062. Hendry, Daniel, in Va, heir to uncle Duncan Hendry, shipmaster in
Campbelltown Argyll, d. 1767, reg. 22 May 1786.
1063. Hendry jr, Alexander, in Buffalo America, heir to grand-uncle Alexander
Hendry jr, merchant in Forres Morayshire, d. 30 July 1873, reg. 5
Feb.1876.
1064. Henry or Allison, Catherine, wife of Edward Allison merchant, in St
John NB, heir to uncle George Henry, merchant in Aberdeen, d. 3
Mar.1867, reg. 2 Oct.1867.
1065. Henry, James, heir to aunt Elizabeth Cross Henry, in Schaw Park St
Anne's Jamaica, reg. 17 June 1823.
1066. Henry, John, joiner & cartwright, in Chicago, heir to fa John Henry,
cabinetmaker in Greenock Renfrewshire, d. 1 Oct.1848, reg. 26
Oct.1878.

1067. Heron, George, in Detroit, heir to William Simpson, nurseyman in Falkirk Stirlingshire, d. 19 Oct.1850, reg. 15 July 1852.

1068. Hewat, Richard, in Australia then Toronto, heir to grandmo Margaret Walker or MacEwan, wid of A MacEwan bootmaker in Edinburgh, reg. 11 Apr.1864.

1069. Hewitson, Judith, w of C Hewitson merchant, in Antigua, heir to grandfa William Wand, portioner of Pitgober, reg. 26 Mar.1794.

1070. Hill, Robert Armour, in Can, heir to sis Margaret Hill or Simpson, w of Capt D Simpson HEICS, reg. 9 Dec.1839.

1071. Hislop, Alexander, in Ont, heir to fa Robert Hislop sr, in Innerleithen Peebles-shire, d. 14 May 1873, reg. 17 June 1881.

1072. Hitt, Frederick, builder, in Baltimore, heir to bro John Hitt, s of Walter Hitt manufacturer in Kirkcaldy Fife, d. 16 July 1873, reg. 7 July 1880.

1073. Hodge, James, farmer, in Cramond Mid Lothian, heir to uncle David Hodge, in New Orleans, reg. 23 Apr.1819.

1074. Hodgson, John, bookseller, in Boston NE, heir to fa William Hodgson, merchant in Glasgow, reg. 20 Jan.1772.

1075. Hogg, Andrew Gordon, minister, in New Broughton Jamaica, heir to bro William Gordon Hogg, in Perth, d. 27 Apr.1875, reg. 11 June 1880.

1076. Hogg, Robert, brass-finisher, in NY, heir to grandfa Robert Hogg, seaman in Cromarty Ross & Cromarty, reg. 27 Apr.1854.

1077. Holywell or Clinkscales, Elizabeth, in Dunbar E Lothian, heir to bro John Holywell, engineer in Dunbar then NY, d. 25 Aug.1849, reg. 18 Feb.1863.

1078. Holywell or Dempster, Helen, w of Robert Dempster flaxspinner, in Newmylne, heir to bro John Holywell, in NY, d. 25 Aug.1849, reg. 18 Feb.1863.

1079. Holywell or Palmer, Jessie, w of David Palmer meal-dealer, in Edinburgh, heir to bro John Holywell, engineer in Dunbar then NY, d. 25 Aug.1849, reg. 18 Feb.1863.

1080. Holywell or Farquhar, Joan, w of William Farquhar gardener, in Pittenweem Fife, heir to bro John Holywell, engineer in Dunbar then NY, d. 25 Aug.1849, reg. 18 Feb.1863.

1081. Holywell or Knox, Margaret, in Innerwick E Lothian, heir to bro John Holywell, engineer in Dunbar then NY, d. 25 Aug.1849, reg. 18 Feb.1863.

1082. Hood, Adam, in Can, heir to grandmo Alison Paterson or Hood, w of Adam Hood wright in Dalkeith Mid Lothian, d. 3 Apr.1831, reg. 15 July 1861.

1083. Hood or Galston, Helen, w of Duncan T Galston machinist, in Detroit Mich, heir to grandfa John Hood, in Tarbolton Ayrshire, d. 1804, reg. 22 June 1875.

1084. Hood or Jewell, Margaret, w of Ralph J Jewell merchant, in Adrian USA, heir to grandfa John Hood, in Tarbolton Ayrshire, d. 1804, reg. 22 June 1875.

1085. Hopkirk, James, in Kingston Can W, heir to fa James Hopkirk, advocate in Woodstone Can, reg. 8 Nov.1864.

1086. Horn, John, in Mich, heir to fa John Horn, merchant in Dunfermline Fife, d. 24 June 1832, reg. 17 Mar.1873.

1087. Hourston, Thomas, farmer, in Firth Orkney, heir to bro John Hourston, in Halifax NS, reg. 16 Dec.1829.

1088. Houston, Helen, w of Alexander Houston merchant, in Grenada, heir to grandfa Patrick Mackie of Barmore, merchant in Wigtown, d. 27 Dec.1764, reg. 26 Apr.1784.

1089. Houston, Lady Ann, in Ga, heir to grandfa John Mackenzie, shipmaster in North Berwick E Lothian, reg. 14 Sep.1818.

1090. How, Robert, s of Job How planter, in NC, heir to grandfa Alexander Goodlet, s of James Goodlet of Abbotshaugh in Fife, reg. 28 Dec.1743.

1091. Howard or Wilson, Margaret, in Chicago, heir to fa William Wilson, in Rochford Ill, d. 12 Sep.1873, reg. 3 May 1883.

1092. Howat, George, in Newport Ky, heir to mo Janet Boyd or Howat, w of James Howat in Cincinnati, d. 16 Oct.1876, reg. 18 Oct.1877.

1093. Howat, Hugh, engineer, in New Orleans, heir to mo Janet Boyd or Howat, w of James Howat in Cincinnati, d. 16 Oct.1876, reg. 18 Sep.1877.

1094. Howat, John, in Wabashaw America, heir to cousin John Howat, farmer in Kincuichland Banffshire, reg. 22 June 1860.

1095. Howat, John, in Newport Ky, heir to mo Janet Boyd or Howat, w of James Howat in Cincinnati, d. 16 Oct.1876, reg. 18 Sep.1877.

1096. Howat, Mary Isabella, heir to grand-aunt Isabella Howat or Jarrett, w of R Jarrett in Hobokken USA, d. 10 Mar.1862, reg. 21 Sep.1875.

1097. Howat, Robert, in Newport Ky, heir to mo Janet Boyd or Howat, w of James Howat in Cincinnati, d. 16 Oct.1876, reg. 18 Sep.1877.

1098. Howatson, Andrew Smith, storekeeper, in Pittston Pa, heir to grandmo Janet Cowan or Smith, wid of Andrew Smith in Longmyre Kirkcudbrightshire, d. 1825, reg. 4 Apr.1866.

1099. Howie, Samuel, in Greenock Renfrewshire then Roscoe NA, heir to sis Isabella Howie or Alexander, wid of John Alexander feuar in Greenock Renfrewshire, reg. 9 Apr.1863.

1100. Howison, William, in Clyde Grove, heir to sis Jane Howison or Wilson, wid of John Wilson in Trinidad, reg. 14 Nov.1845.

1101. Hoyes, James, in Jamaica, heir to fa James Hoyes, tacksman in Newton of Dalvey, reg. 30 May 1846.

1102. Hume, David, in Tenn, heir to fa George Hume, shoemaker in Lauder Berwickshire, reg. 31 Aug.1838.

1103. Hume, Walter, in America, heir to fa James Hume, in Southdean, reg. 5 Sep.1849.
1104. Humphreys, Dorothea, wid of Rev William Humphreys, in Antigua, heir to uncle Robert Ferguson of Finart, reg. 4 Jan.1813.
1105. Hunter or McClelland, Agnes, w of Robert McClelland, in Sudsbury Pa, heir to fa Patrick Hunter, in America, reg. 26 Apr.1784.
1106. Hunter, Alexander, in NB, heir to mo Catherine Fotheringham or Hunter, w of J Hunter in Deafknows, reg. 23 June 1830.
1107. Hunter, Alexander, in Brighton Mass, heir to fa Peter Hunter, mason in Burntisland Fife, d. 25 Apr.1877, reg. 9 July 1878.
1108. Hunter, Andrew Halley, in Newcastle Can W, heir to fa John Hunter, teacher in Greenock Renfrewshire, reg. 10 Aug.1860.
1109. Hunter, David Gilmore, in Antis Pa, heir to fa David Hunter, farmer in Thornyflat Ayrshire, reg. 13 June 1820.
1110. Hunter, Hector Alexander, farmer & smith, in Lower Can, heir to grandfa John Hunter, smith in Linlithgow W Lothian, d. pre 1810, reg. 12 May 1863.
1111. Hunter, James, merchant, in Fredericksburg Va, heir to uncle Alexander Hunter, merchant in Duns Berwickshire, reg. 29 July 1756.
1112. Hunter, James, in NA, heir to aunt Jane Hunter or Amos, in Melrose Roxburghshire, reg. 8 Nov.1839.
1113. Hunter, James Arnott, in Ingersoll Oxford Can, heir to fa Andrew Halley Hunter, in Newcastle Can, d. 4 Apr.1872, reg. 22 June 1877.
1114. Hunter, John, moulder, in Can, heir to fa Hugh Hunter, in Newton-on-Ayr Ayrshire, reg. 10 Oct.1855.
1115. Hunter, John, moulder, in Can, heir to uncle Charles Hunter, shipmaster in *The Enterprise of Ayr*, reg. 10 Oct.1855.
1116. Hunter, Robert, merchant, in Philadelphia, heir to fa William Hunter, merchant in Glasgow, reg. 15 May 1806.
1117. Hunter or McCulloch, Sarah, w of George McCulloch, in Philadelphia, heir to bro James Hunter, printer in England, reg. 2 Mar.1857.
1118. Hunter or mcCulloch, Sarah, w of George McCulloch, in Philadelphia, heir to bro Hugh Hunter, soldier, reg. 2 Apr.1857.
1119. Husband, Thomas Blair, counsellor-at-law, in Rochester USA, heir to grandfa Thomas Blair, merchant in Alyth Perthshire, d. 3 Jan.1810, reg. 31 Aug.1855.
1120. Hutcheon, John, in Edinburgh then NY, heir to fa David Hutcheon, fisherman in Edinburgh, d. 20 Aug.1850, reg. 24 Apr.1862.
1121. Hutcheson, William, joiner, in Toronto, heir to cousin Ann Ogilvie, in Scouringburn Dundee Angus, d. 26 Mar.1861, reg. 7 Oct.1871.
1122. Hutchison, George, in Can W, heir to fa Robert Hutchison, flesher in Loanhead, d. 9 May 1864, reg. 8 Mar.1865.
1123. Hutchison, Henry, shipowner, in Philadelphia, heir to nephew John McFarlane, innkeeper in Glasgow, reg. 23 Oct.1837.

1124. Hutchison, Hugh, in Morrison Whiteside Ill, heir to uncle William Thomson, minister in Old Monkland Ayrshire, d. 16 Aug.1841, reg. 4 Jan.1868.

1125. Hutchison, Jane, in Morrison Whiteside Ill, heir to uncle William Thomson, minister in Old Monkland Ayrshire, d. 16 Aug.1841, reg. 4 Jan.1868.

1126. Hutchison, Matthew, in America, heir to sis Isabella Black or Hutchison, wid of Archibald Black cooper in Rothesay Bute, reg. 19 Dec.1839.

1127. Hutchison, Robert, in Morrison Whiteside Ill, heir to uncle William Thomson, minister in Old Monkland Ayrshire, d. 16 Aug.1841, reg. 4 Jan.1868.

1128. Hutton or Cumstock, Elizabeth, w of George Cumstock, in NJ, heir to mo Janet Stevens or Hutton, w of George Hutton in NY, d. 18 Apr.1851, reg. 18 Dec.1867.

1129. Hynd or Hall, Margaret, in Va, heir to gt grandmo Helen Lowson or Morrison, w of G Morrison in Dundee Angus, reg. 30 June 1847.

1130. Hyslop, Hamilton Douglas, farmer, in Tower, heir to bro Thomas Logan Hyslop, mercantile clerk in NY, reg. 5 Apr.1866.

1131. Hyslop or Graham, Janet, w of Robert Graham, in Cleveland Oh, heir to aunt Helen Ballantine or Davis, in Maxwelltown Kirkcudbrightshire, d. 26 Nov.1875, reg. 9 Dec.1876.

1132. Imrie, John, ship carpenter, in St Augustine E Fla, heir to s Duncan Imrie, in America, reg. 22 Aug.1782.

1133. Inglis, George, in Kingsmills, heir to bro John Inglis, merchant in America, reg. 20 Aug.1821.

1134. Inglis, Thomas, MD & surgeon, in Glasgow, heir to bro James Inglis, in Barrataria La, reg. 22 July 1836.

1135. Ingram, George, smith, in Banff then Trinidad, heir to uncle George Ingram, feuar in MacDuff Banffshire, reg. 22 Mar.1842.

1136. Innes, George, customs inspector, in NY, heir to sis Margaret Innes, da of George Innes wright in Edinburgh, reg. 14 May 1827.

1137. Innes or Boxil, Helen Eliza, w of William Boxil, in Barbados, heir to mo Isabelle Lumsden or Innes, in Aberdeen, reg. 7 Dec.1816.

1138. Ireland, William Wotherspoon, in India, heir to uncle James Dundas Wotherspoon, in NY, reg. 8 June 1857.

1139. Irvine, James, druggist, in Tollesboro Ky, heir to fa James Irvine, schooner owner in Perth, reg. 23 Aug.1871.

1140. Irvine, William, in Jamaica, heir to uncle Andrew Irvine, in Edinburgh, reg. 3 June 1806.

1141. Irving, James, in Jamaica & London, heir to fa James Irving of Ironshore, in Jamaica, reg. 14 July 1841.

1142. Irving, James, in Jamaica & London, heir to grandfa James Irving, in St James Jamaica, reg. 14 July 1841.

1143. Irving or Robertson, Mary, w of Thomas Robertson weaver, in Ecclefechan Dumfries-shire, heir to uncle Walter Paisley, in Jamaica, reg. 7 May 1831.

1144. Isbister, Samuel, seaman RN, heir to fa Samuel Isbister, Hudson Bay Co, d. 22 May 1809, reg. 4 Oct.1854.

1145. Jack, Robert, machinist, in Jersey City NA, heir to fa Robert Jack, thread manufacturer in Paisley Renfrewshire, d. 4 Mar.1860, reg. 5 May 1863.

1146. Jacket, Robert, in Up Can, heir to sis Agnes Jacket, in Hagelbank, reg. 18 May 1858.

1147. Jackson or Cram, Agnes, in USA, heir to fa George Jackson, in Tormorden then Stockton-on-Tees England, reg. 13 Apr.1853.

1148. Jackson, Georgina Bell, heir to fa George Jackson jr, in Charleston SC, d. 10 Aug.1860, reg. 2 Dec.1867.

1149. Jackson, Georgina Bell, heir to grandfa George Jackson, tinplateworker in Charleston SC, d. 30 July 1861, reg. 2 Dec.1867.

1150. Jackson, James, in Fort Valley Ga, heir to bro Allan Jackson, s of George Jackson tinplateworker in Charleston SC, d. 9 Jan.1863, reg. 6 Nov.1867.

1151. Jackson, James, in Fort Valley Ga, heir to bro Wallace Jackson, d. 11 Jan.1861, reg. 6 Nov.1867.

1152. Jackson, John, in Shrewsbury then Hamilton Ont, heir to fa Edward Jackson, in Paulsland Dumfries-shire, d. 4 July 1845, reg. 14 Jan.1876.

1153. Jackson, Susanna, in Jamaica, heir to grandfa Alexander Campbell, merchant in Glasgow, reg. 24 Nov.1817.

1154. Jaffray, Robert, in NY, heir to fa Robert Jaffray, minister in Kilmarnock Ayrshire, reg. 7 Dec.1825.

1155. James, A H, in Kingston Jamaica, heir to uncle Robert Mein, Lt 1st Regt Infantry, reg. 15 Dec.1815.

1156. James, Margaret, in Jamaica, heir to fa William John James, attorney in Jamaica, reg. 1 July 1823.

1157. James, Margaret, in Jamaica, heir to gt grand-uncle David Mackie, merchant in Edinburgh, reg. 13 Feb.1826.

1158. James, Margaret, in Jamaica, heir to gt grandmo Marion Mackie or Mein, w of W Mein merchant in Edinburgh, reg. 13 Feb.1826.

1159. James, Thomas, in Halifax NS, heir to bro William James, in Stranraer Wigtownshire, d. 20 Aug.1843, reg. 16 Sep.1876.

1160. James, Thomas, in Halifax NS, heir to sis Agnes James, in Stranraer Wigtownshire, d. 11 Apr.1875, reg. 16 Sep.1876.

1161. James, William John, in Kingston Jamaica, heir to uncle Andrew Mein, merchant in Edinburgh, reg. 15 Dec.1815.

1162. James, William, in Kinlough Kinloss Ont, heir to fa William James, seaman in Arbroath Angus, d. 11 Mar.1848, reg. 10 Nov.1882.

1163. Jamieson, James, brassfounder, in Greenock Renfrewshire, heir to mo Christiana Steel or Jamieson, wid of John Jamieson surgeon in Charleston America, d. 10 Sep.1849, reg. 29 May 1861.

1164. Jamieson, Janet, in Ind, heir to grandfa Daniel Jamieson, in Greenock Renfrewshire, d. 1805, reg. 8 Sep.1854.

1165. Jamieson, John Coutts, in Goshen Jamaica, heir to fa Andrew Jamieson, merchant in Turriff Aberdeenshire, reg. 19 Apr.1850.

1166. Jamieson, John William, in NB, heir to grand-uncle Thomas Patterson, paymaster 22nd Foot Regt in Dalserf, d. July 1823, reg. 26 Sep.1876.

1167. Jamieson or Stirrat, Nancy Lee, w of J Stirrat, in Baltimore, heir to grandfa Daniel Jamieson, in Greenock Renfrewshire, d. 1805, reg. 8 Sep.1854.

1168. Jardine or Nicholson, Mary, w of William Nicholson, in Can, heir to fa Thomas Nicholson, weaver in Dornoch Ross & Cromarty, reg. 16 Jan.1856.

1169. Jeans, William Duthie, in Montreal, heir to grandfa John Baxter, Customs House boatman in Aberdeen, d. 4 Dec.1847, reg. 6 Aug.1861.

1170. Jeffey, Jean, heir to fa William Jeffrey, s of James Jeffrey merchant in Philadelphia, reg. 30 Sep.1758.

1171. Jemkinson, John, florist, in Philadelphia, heir to fa John Jenkinson, contractor in Leith Mid Lothian, d. 23 May 1861, reg. 1 Mar.1872.

1172. Jenkieson, Robert, printer, in Cincinnati, heir to grandfa Robert Jenkieson, in Edinburgh, reg. 21 Dec.1858.

1173. Johnston, Agnes, in Glasgow, heir to mo Euphemia Cheyne or Johnston, w of James Johnston in Boston USA, reg. 26 June 1846.

1174. Johnston, Andrew, merchant, in NY, heir to sis Agnes Dempster or Johnston, da of Michael Johnston merchant in Glasgow, reg. 17 Mar.1856.

1175. Johnston, Andrew, confectioner, in America, heir to fa George Johnston, hotelkeeper in Edinburgh, reg. 3 May 1860.

1176. Johnston or Mitchell, Ann, in America, heir to bro Thomas Mitchell, in Phillan's Well Ayrshire, reg. 20 Aug.1842.

1177. Johnston, David, bank clerk, in Boston, heir to grandfa David Johnston , shipmaster in E Wemyss Fife, d. 27 July 1812, reg. 2 Aug.1861.

1178. Johnston or Ferguson, Elizabeth, wid of N Ferguson attorney, in Jamaica, heir to fa Richard Johnston, wine merchant in Edinburgh, reg. 28 June 1765.

1179. Johnston or Brown, Elizabeth, in Hamilton Can, heir to bro James Johnston, in Burntisland Fife, d. 6 Sep.1875, reg. 10 Jan.1876.

1180. Johnston, George, in Philadelphia, heir to sis Grace Johnston or Yates, w of James Yates gentleman's servant in Edinburgh, reg. 20 Apr.1825.

1181. Johnston, George Lovie, in Downie Can W, heir to grandfa George Lovie, shipmaster in Banff then Whitehills, reg. 9 Mar.1867.

1182. Johnston, James, in Franklinville NY, heir to grandmo Janet Johnston, in Crocketford, reg. 29 June 1838.

1183. Johnston, James, surgeon, in Newfoundland, heir to James Johnston, spirit dealer in Edinburgh, d. June 1850, reg. 29 Mar.1854.

1184. Johnston, James, in Montreal, heir to fa James Johnston, spirit merchant in Glasgow, d. 3 Apr.1854, reg. 7 Apr.1869.

1185. Johnston, Joseph, in Lockerbie Dumfriesshire then Jamaica, heir to grandmo Mary Stewart or Thomson, in Annan Dumfriesshire, reg. 31 Mar.1837.

1186. Johnston, Lewis, merchant, in St Kitts, heir to fa James Johnston, merchant in Edinburgh, reg. 27 Apr.1756.

1187. Johnston or Kincaid, Margaret, wid of Thomas Kincaid, in NY, heir to sis Ann Balderstone or Johnston, reg. 19 Apr.1864.

1188. Johnston or Mathison, Mary, in Can, heir to aunt Janet Mathison, reg. 18 Oct.1851.

1189. Johnston or Mathison, Mary, in Can, heir to aunt Helen Mathison, reg. 18 Oct.1851.

1190. Johnston or Mathison, Mary, in Can, heir to uncle James Mathison, reg. 18 Oct.1851.

1191. Johnston or Mathison, Mary, in Can, heir to mo Mary Ledgerwood or Mathison, reg. 18 Oct.1851.

1192. Johnston, Quintin, in Chicago, heir to fa Quintin Johnston of Trolorg, writer in Ayr, d. 21 Nov.1847, reg. 3 Nov.1869.

1193. Johnston, Robert, physician, in Grenada, heir to fa Robert Johnston, baillie in Annan Dumfriesshire, reg. 15 Jan.1783.

1194. Johnston, Robert Henry, in Boston USA, heir to bro Ebenezer Cheyne Johnston, s of James Johnston in Boston, reg. 26 June 1846.

1195. Johnston, Robert Henry, in Boston USA, heir to mo Euphemia Cheyne or Johnston, w of James Johnston in Boston, reg. 26 June 1846.

1196. Johnston, Thomas, in Quebec, heir to fa Archibald Johnston, bookseller in Falkirk Stirlingshire, d. 18 June 1877, reg. 29 July 1878.

1197. Johnstone or Anderson, Elizabeth, w of W Anderson, in PEI, heir to bro John Johnstone, in Annan Dumfriesshire, reg. 30 Aug.1854.

1198. Johnstone or Wiepert, Esther, w of Theodore Wiepert, in NY, heir to grandfa Douglas Johnstone, joiner in Annan Dumfries-shire, d. 13 Mar.1858, reg. 19 Jan.1867.

1199. Johnstone, James, in NY, heir to uncle Capt A Johnstone, in Portobello Mid Lothian, reg. 26 Feb.1849.

1200. Johnstone, Jeffrey, in Richibucto NA, heir to mo Jean Johnstone, w of J Johnstone in Creetown Kirkcudbrightshire, reg. 25 Mar.1825.

1201. Johnstone, Robert, smith, in Can, heir to bro John Johnstone, mariner in Annan Dumfriesshire, reg. 30 Aug.1854.

1202. Jones or Larkin, Ann, w of Reuben Larkin, in Argyle Shelbourne NS, heir to fa Anthony Hart Jones, in Shelbourne NS, reg. 30 Nov.1813.

1203. Jones, Anthony Hart, in Argyle NS, heir to bro William Jones, shipmaster in Leith Mid Lothian, reg. 1 Oct.1798.

1204. Jones or Hetfield, Constance, w of A M Hetfield, in Argyle Shelbourne NS, heir to fa Anthony Hart Jones, in Shelbourne NS, reg. 30 Nov.1813.

1205. Jones or Seallie, Margaret, w of Henry Seallie, in Argyle Shelbourne NS, heir to fa Anthony Hart Jones, in Shelbourne NS, reg. 30 Nov.1813.

1206. Jopp, Charles Mitchell, in Keith Hall Jamaica, heir to aunt Jean Jopp or Young, wid of Gavin Young merchant in Aberdeen, reg. 8 Dec.1837.

1207. Joyner or Masson, Elizabeth, wid of James Masson, in Aberdeen, heir to bro Robert Joyner, in Baltimore, reg. 12 May 1810.

1208. Joyner, Hugh, in Glassville NB, heir to uncle John Joyner, grocer in Tain Ross & Cromarty, d. 28 Mar.1846, reg. 31 May 1876.

1209. Junor, John, in Seymour Can W, heir to fa John Junor, farmer in Balmungy Ross-shire, d. 22 June 1876, reg. 21 June 1877.

1210. Kay, David, in Kinsman Township Oh, heir to mo Margaret Murray or Kay, w of David Kay merchant in Leith Mid Lothian then Glasgow, d. 7 Feb.1854, reg. 31 Dec.1862.

1211. Kay, David, in Kinsman Township Oh, heir to uncle John Murray, Capt HEICS, d. 18 May 1832, reg. 18 Feb.1863.

1212. Kay, John, merchant, in Montreal, heir to bro Robert Kay, writer in Kilmarnock Ayrshire, reg. 29 June 1853.

1213. Kay, Robert, in Jamaica, heir to sis Isabella Kay, da of John Kay feuar in Duns Berwickshire, reg. 21 Oct.1841.

1214. Kay, William, s of William Kay, in Montreal, heir to granduncle Alexander Hutchison, wine merchant in Edinburgh, reg. 14 Nov.1793.

1215. Kedglie or Kervand, Ann Elizabeth, in America, heir to fa John Kedglie, slater in Tranent E Lothian then Washington, reg. 12 Jan.1846.

1216. Kedglie, Henry Turnbull, in Tranent E Lothian, heir to bro John Kedglie, in Washington USA, d. 14 July 1847, reg. 5 June 1850.

1217. Keir, Robert, mill overseer, in Montrose Angus, heir to uncle George Simson, mariner in Arbroath Angus then NA, reg. 3 Dec.1863.

1218. Keith, Alexander, in Halifax NS, heir to fa Donald Keith, in Halkirk Caithness, d. 21 Sep.1847, reg. 17 Dec.1868.

1219. Keith, George, in Aberdeen, heir to bro James Keith, in Lachine Can then Aberdeen, d. 27 Jan.1851, reg. 26 Sep.1851.

1220. Keith or Steele, Helen, w of William Keith wright, in America, heir to grandfa James Steele, brewer in Forfar Angus, reg. 6 Mar.1843.

1221. Kellock, James, in NY, heir to fa John Kellock, mason in Coatbridge Lanarkshire, d. 1 Jan.1863, reg. 9 Apr.1875.

1222. Kemp or Edwards, Euphemia, w of Charles Francis Edwards, in Can, heir to mo Mary Gibson or Kemp, w of David Kemp chemist in Portobello Mid Lothian, d. 24 June 1875, reg. 16 Dec.1875.

1223. Kemp, Henry, in NY, heir to bro Archibald Kemp, in Musselburgh Mid Lothian, d. 2 July 1880, reg. 10 Aug.1881.

1224. Kemp, John, merchant, in New Orleans, heir to uncle William Kemp, victualler & feuar in Crieff Perthshire, reg. 1 Oct.1847.

1225. Kennedy or Miller, Elizabeth, in Pequay Pa, heir to grandfa Alexander Baillie of Meikle Dunragget, reg. 16 June 1775.

1226. Kennedy or Rintoul, Helen, in NY, heir to bro Thomas Rintoul, sailor in Perth, reg. 24 Dec.1833.

1227. Kennedy, John, surgeon, in RN Hospital Bermuda, heir to bro William Kennedy, reg. 17 Jan.1838.

1228. Kennedy, Louisa, w of William Davidson, in Ind, heir to bro Benjamin Kennedy, publisher in Arbroath Angus, reg. 7 Feb.1868.

1229. Kennedy, Robert Lenox, in NY, heir to fa David Sproat Kennedy, in NY, reg. 18 Oct.1855.

1230. Keppie, William, in Pittsburg, heir to fa John Keppie, damask manufacturer in Low Blair Wigtownshire, d. 5 Dec.1838, reg. 8 Aug.1867.

1231. Keppie, William, in Pittsburg, heir to mo Mary Walker or Keppie, wid of John Keppie damask manufacturer in Low Blair Wigtownshire, d. 5 Dec.1838, reg. 8 Aug.1867.

1232. Kermack or White, Susan, w of D White, in SC, heir to mo Florence Fullerton or Kermack, w of Peter Kermack in Greenock Renfrewshire, reg. 21 Jan.1813.

1233. Kerr or Wilson, Agnes Anne, w of William Wilson, in NY, heir to bro George B Kerr, merchant in Norfolk America, reg. 8 Apr.1816.

1234. Kerr or Wilson, Agnes Ann, in NY, heir to grandfa James Corbet sr of Kenmuir, reg. 1 June 1830.

1235. Kerr, Alexander, in W Boyleston NA, heir to fa James Kerr, weaver in Dysart Fife, d. 2 Dec.1859, reg. 8 Apr.1861.

1236. Kerr, David, in Jamaica, heir to cousin James Ballingall, merchant in Dundee Angus, reg. 15 Jan.1807.

1237. Kerr, David, in Jamaica, heir to cousin John Ballingall of Denoon, writer in Dundee Angus, d. Jan.1788, reg. 13 Apr.1807.

1238. Kerr, David, painter, in Quebec, heir to bro Walter Kerr, shoemaker in Cupar Fife, d. 25 Mar.1861, reg. 10 Aug.1871.

1239. Kerr, George Brown, in Va, heir to uncle James Corbett yr of Kenmuir, reg. 6 Sep.1810.

1240. Kerr, James, heir to cousin Sir James Henry Craig, Governor General in Can, reg. 26 May 1812.

1241. Kerr, James Lee, in St Thomas Jamaica, heir to fa Alexander Kerr, merchant in Edinburgh, reg. 26 Oct.1853.

1242. Kerr, James Lee, in St Thomas Jamaica, heir to sis Grace Kerr or Grant, w of James Fitzgerald Grant in Edinburgh, reg. 26 Oct.1853.

1243. Kerr, James Lee, in St Thomas Jamaica, heir to bro Alexander Kerr, in Jamaica then S America, reg. 14 Nov.1853.

1244. Kerr, John Campbell, saddler, in Can, heir to bro William Kerr, nephew of Peter Kerr innkeeper in Cupar Fife, reg. 25 Apr.1836.

1245. Kerr, John Campbell, saddler, in Can, heir to bro George Kerr, writer in Edinburgh, reg. 19 Aug.1839.

1246. Kerr, John, in Three Rivers Can, heir to aunt Mary Learmount, in Edinburgh, reg. 10 Dec.1855.

1247. Kerr, John, merchant, in Toronto then Cal, heir to fa James Kerr, engraver in Glasgow, d. 26 Oct.1841, reg. 30 Nov.1867.

1248. Kerr, John, merchant, in Toronto then Cal, heir to sis Isabella Margaret Kerr, in Glasgow, d. 8 Dec.1862, reg. 30 Nov.1867.

1249. Kerr or Lamb, Margaret Stewart, w of W B Lamb, in Va, heir to bro George Brown Kerr, merchant in Norfolk America, reg. 8 Apr.1816.

1250. Kerr or Lamb, Margaret Stewart, in Va, heir to grandfa James Corbet sr of Kenmuir, reg. 1 June 1830.

1251. Kerr or Halkett, Margaret, w of Col James Halkett, in London, heir to fa Dr William Kerr, in St Croix, d. 8 Dec.1837, reg. 22 Sep.1865.

1252. Kerr, Mary, in Norfolk America, heir to bro George Brown Kerr, merchant in Norfolk America, reg. 8 Apr.1816.

1253. Kerr, Mary, in Norfolk America, heir to grandfa James Corbet sr of Kenmuir, reg. 1 June 1830.

1254. Key, William Inglis, merchant, in New Orleans, heir to grandfa James Key, in Crail Fife, reg. 25 Oct.1856.

1255. Kidd or Toddie or Tod, Janet, in Edinburgh, heir to Lindsay Toddie or Tod, cotton planter in America, reg. 25 Mar.1833.

1256. Kincaid, James, in USA, heir to aunt Elizabeth Kincaid, da of John Kincaid of Gartcows, reg. 16 Feb.1835.

1257. King, Agnes, in Paisley Renfrewshire then SC, heir to uncle John King, in NY, reg. 7 Feb.1820.

1258. King or Grant, Ann, w of William Grant, in Philadelphia, heir to fa Hugh King, ship carpenter in Philadelphia, reg. 3 Nov.1796.

1259. King, James, in Montreal, heir to fa John King, portioner in Windmillhill, reg. 16 Oct.1850.

1260. King, John, farmer, in Stamford NY, heir to bro William King, stocking maker in Denholm Roxburghshire, reg. 5 May 1847.

1261. King, John Robert, in Jasper City Ia, heir to fa John King, innkeeper in Arbroath Angus, d. 20 May 1858, reg. 9 Jan.1872.

1262. King, John, in Del, heir to bro James King, in Denholm Roxburghshire, d. 24 Feb.1872, reg. 19 Mar.1873.

1263. King, Sarah, in Paisley Renfrewshire then SC, heir to uncle John King, in NY, reg. 7 Feb.1820.

1264. King or Stanfield, Susan, w of Thomas Stanfield, in Philadelphia, heir to fa Hugh King, ship carpenter in Philadelphia, reg. 3 Nov.1796.

1265. Kinghorn, William, miller, in Schenectady NY, heir to grandfa Robert McLarne, tailor in Chirnside Berwickshire, reg. 13 Nov.1851.

1266. Kinloch of Rosemount, George Oliphant, heir to bro John Kinloch of Blacklaws, in Westmoreland Jamaica, reg. 1 Nov.1770.

1267. Kinmond, William Leighton, in Dundee Angus then Belleville Can, heir to fa Peter Kinmond, merchant in Dundee , d. 12 Oct.1856, reg. 24 Sep.1862.

1268. Kinninburgh, John, wright, in Glasgow then Va, heir to bro Robert Kinninburgh, merchant in Glasgow, reg. 8 June 1751.

1269. Kinninmont, William, miller, in Albion Orleans Co NY, heir to grandfa William Kinninmont, in Rothesay Bute, d. 9 Nov.1856, reg. 9 July 1868.

1270. Kippen, James, in Salt Lake City, heir to bro Duncan Kippen, spirit merchant in Edinburgh, d. 24 Apr.1879, reg. 16 June 1880.

1271. Kirk, Thomas, in St John Antigua, heir to uncle Andrew Kirk, in Gatehouse Kirkcudbrightshire, d. 9 June 1865, reg. 7 Jan.1867.

1272. Kirkcaldy or Dove, Jean, wid of James Dove, in Kingston Jamaica, heir to bro John Kirkcaldy, landwaiter in Limekilns Fife, reg. 16 Aug.1805.

1273. Kirkpatrick, Jane Watson, in NA, heir to grandfa Watson Kirkpatrick, in High Kelton, reg. 11 June 1831.

1274. Kirkpatrick, Thomas, in Kingston Jamaica, heir to fa Watson Kirkpatrick, in High Kelton, reg. 16 Feb.1828.

1275. Kissock or Gillies, Helen, w of J Gillies, in USA, heir to mo Marion Swan or Kissock, reg. 14 Mar.1859.

1276. Knight, Robert, minister, in Can, heir to aunt Elizabeth Knight, in Portsoy Banffshire, reg. 26 Apr.1842.

1277. Knox, David, in Beverly Ont, heir to bro Robert Knox, merchant in New Byth King Edward Aberdeenshire, d. 20 July 1875, reg. 31 May 1876.

1278. Knox, James, minister, in St Kitts, heir to fa Henry Knox, minister in Bowden Roxburghshire, reg. 30 July 1719.

1279. Knox, John, in NY, heir to fa David Knox, surgeon in Edinburgh, reg. 27 July 1750.

1280. Knox, Robert Dade, in Ga, heir to fa Robert Knox, merchant in Va, reg. 8 Mar.1819.

1281. Knox, Robert Dade, in Wilkes Co Ga, heir to gt grandfa John Knox, ship carpenter in Renfrew, reg. 8 July 1820.

1282. Kyd, John, weaver, in Arbroath Angus then Washington USA, heir to fa George Kyd, weaver in Muirlands Arbroath, d. 15 June 1831, reg. 17 Oct.1851.

1283. Kyd, John, weaver, in Arbroath Angus then Washington USA, heir to bro George Kyd, manufacturer in Arbroath, d. 9 June 1850, reg. 17 Oct.1851.

1284. Kyle, Matthew, in Tobago, heir to fa Andrew Kyle, farmer in Crookston Renfrewshire, reg. 9 Sep.1813.

1285. Laing or Rule, Agnes, w of Thomas Rule, in Lisbon NY, heir to Cecilia Laing or Lauder, wid of John Lauder victual dealer in Canongate Edinburgh, d. 30 Sep.1863, reg. 9 Feb.1865.

1286. Laing, James McGregor, surgeon, in USA, heir to fa William Laing, physician in Aberdeen, d. 22 Aug.1862, reg. 12 Mar.1874.

1287. Laing, Robert, in St Thomas Jamaica, heir to fa William Laing, merchant in Glasgow, reg. 21 July 1789.

1288. Laing, Susan, in Stonehouse Lanarkshire, heir to fa John Laing, in Dominica, d. 30 Aug.1808, reg. 20 Nov.1829.

1289. Laird, Helen Jane, in Newfoundland, heir to fa James Laird, cooper in Demerara, d. Dec.1837, reg. 13 Oct.1869.

1290. Lamb, Eloise, in Fredericton NB, heir to grandfa Robert Lamb of Templehall, reg. 16 Oct.1829.

1291. Lamb, James, in Cleveland Oh, heir to cousin Peter Douglas jr, in Edinburgh, d. 15 Jan.1878, reg. 1 May 1878.

1292. Lamb, Robert Boyd, in St Thomas, heir to bro William McCormack Lamb, mercantile clerk in Calcutta, reg. 1 Dec.1847.

1293. Lamb, Robert Henry, in Annawan Ill, heir to fa William Lamb jr, nurseyman in Galashiels Selkirkshire, d. 9 Oct.1856, reg. 1 Feb.1881.

1294. Lambert, Alexander, sailor, heir to grandfa Alexander MacKenzie, tailor in SC, reg. 27 Oct.1818.

1295. Lambert, Margaret, da of Robert Lambert, in Trinidad, heir to grandfa William Lambert, in Barshagra, reg. 5 Nov.1847.

1296. Lamont or Bishop, Barbara, wid of Dwight Bishop, in Stratford Ct, heir to aunt Margaret Lamont, in Aberdeen, d. Jan.1833, reg. 16 Feb.1878.

1297. Lamont, Colin Daniel, bank accountant, in Greenock Renfrewshire, heir to uncle Duncan Lamont, merchant in NY, d. 13 Feb.1865, reg. 28 Nov.1881.

1298. Lamont or McGrath, Helen, w of William McGrath, in Bridgeport Ct, heir to aunt Margaret Lamont, in Aberdeen, d. Jan.1833, reg. 16 Feb.1878.

1299. Lancefield, William Adams, in Edinburgh then America, heir to bro Alfred Henry Lancefield, s of Alfred Lancefield civil engineer in London, reg. 11 May 1870.

1300. Lancefield, William Adams, in Edinburgh then America, heir to bro James Brown Lancefield, s of Alfred Lancefield civil engineer in London, reg. 11 May 1870.

1301. Landell, William, in Dalkeith Mid Lothian, heir to bro Robert Landell, in Kingston Jamaica, d. 1 Apr.1866, reg. 25 May 1868.

1302. Landrum, Thomas Keith, heir to fa Thomas Landrum, in Port Royal Va, reg. 3 Jan.1784.

1303. Lang, William, merchant, in Glasgow, heir to bro John Lang, merchant in Glasgow then Jamaica, reg. 14 Aug.1761.

1304. Lapsley, Sarah Ogden, da of William Lapsley, in Montreal, heir to grandfa William Lapsley, grocer in Glasgow, reg. 12 Feb.1819.

1305. Lauder or Sutherland, Mary, wid of Rev F Lauder, in Fredericton USA, heir to aunt Marjory Stuart, in Canongate Edinburgh, reg. 23 Dec.1795.

1306. Laurie, Richard, sergeant 2nd NY Artillery, heir to fa James Laurie, merchant in London, d. 28 Aug.1854, reg. 20 July 1865.

1307. Lawrie or Hogg, Barbara, w of James Hogg, in Can W, heir to fa David Lawrie, comb manufacturer in Aberdeen, d. 8 Nov.1858, reg. 8 Sep.1859.

1308. Lawrie, James, tailor, in Milwaukee USA, heir to gt grandfa Matthew Lawrie, in Corseflat, d. 1812, reg. 20 Jan.1863.

1309. Lawrie or Parker, Jean, in Glasgow then Can, heir to fa Robert Lawrie of Isles, in Kilmarnock Ayrshire, reg. 28 Dec.1853.

1310. Lawson or Brodie, Charlotte, w of Rev George Brodie, in Port of Spain Trinidad, heir to fa George Lawson, minister in Selkirk, d. 15 Dec.1849, reg. 19 Apr.1869.

1311. Lawson, James, underwriter & insurance broker, in NY, heir to fa John Lawson, merchant in Glasgow, reg. 29 Nov.1851.

1312. Lawson, John, in Can, heir to mo Mary Wright, w of William Wright in Glasgow, reg. 2 Dec.1825.

1313. Lawson, Robert, in Sacramento Cal, heir to grandfa George Lawson of Knockhornock, d. 2 July 1845, reg. 5 Dec.1870.

1314. Lawson, William, in Ind, heir to fa George Lawson of Cuparhead, in Lanarkshire, d. Nov.1829, reg. 16 Apr.1849.

1315. Layton, Napier, in Selkirk Man, heir to grandmo Sarah Stark or Layton, w of Thomas Layton in Kinross, d. 1 Mar.1857, reg. 4 May 1881.

1316. Layton, Napier, in Selkirk Man, heir to aunt Margaret Anne Layton, w of David Syme of Warroch, d. 3 Jan.1875, reg. 4 May 1881.

1317. Learmont, John, in Ga, heir to mo Marion Martin or Learmont, w of John Learmont in Welldale of Troquier, d. 8 Sep.1848, reg. 14 Aug.1873.

1318. Leask, William, in NY, heir to grand uncle John Leask, merchant in Macduff Banffshire, d. 4 May 1844, reg. 20 Mar.1872.

1319. Leckie or Hatton, Emmeline, w of John Goodrick Hatton, in Portsmouth Va, heir to Ralph Foster, in Drummoyne Lanarkshire, d. Feb.1810, reg. 8 Nov.1853.

1320. Leckie, William, in Commercial Bank, heir to bro John Leckie, teacher in NY, reg. 29 Apr.1845.

1321. Lees jr, Alexander, weaver, in Glasgow then NY, heir to grandfa Charles Patterson, portioner in Glasgow, d. 6 Oct.1823, reg. 4 Mar.1865.

1322. Lees, William, teacher, in Wishaw Lanarkshire, heir to John Lees, in San Francisco, reg. 21 Jan.1875.

1323. Leggat or Buol, Janet, w of Charles Buol, in Philadelphia, heir to gt grandfa Andrew Leggat, in Howdenburn Hawick Roxburghshire, d. 29 Jan.1826, reg. 28 Apr.1870.

1324. Leighton or Bowman, Elizabeth, w of George Bowman baker, in NY, heir to fa Francis Leighton, in Edinburgh, d. 10 Nov.1843, reg. 7 Dec.1869.

1325. Leitch, Christina, in Belleville Can W, heir to mo Margaret Brown or Leitch, w of John Leitch merchant in Greenock Renfrewshire, d. July 1828, reg. 19 Oct.1866.

1326. Leitch or McGibbons, Janet, w of Malcolm McGibbons, in Manchester NA, heir to fa Andrew Leitch, engineer in Lochgelly Fife, d. 11 Jan.1863, reg. 31 July 1867.

1327. Leith, John, in Annotto Bay Jamaica, heir to grandfa John Leith of Blair, reg. 17 Sep.1790.

1328. Leithan, Sarah, in Philadelphia, heir to uncle David Sproat of Portmary, reg. 3 Dec.1799.

1329. Lennox, James, in NY, heir to uncle James Lennox of Dalscairth, in Kirkcudbright, reg. 14 Apr.1840.

1330. Lennox, Matthew, farmer, in Sacramento Co Cal, heir to fa James Lennox, sawyer in Kilmarnock Ayrshire, d. 14 Feb.1862, reg. 4 Dec.1872.

1331. Lenox, Robert, heir to bro David Lenox, in Port May Kirkcudbrightshire then Philadelphia, reg. 25 Aug.1829.

1332. Lenox, Robert, in NY, heir to bro James Lenox of Dalscairth, in Kirkcudbrightshire, reg. 20 Dec.1839.

1333. Lerrie, Hugh, in NA, heir to fa James Lerrie, in Anderston Glasgow, d. 17 Jan.1848, reg. 9 July 1863.

1334. Leslie, George, in NY, heir to gt grand uncle George Willox, in Perth Amboy NJ, reg. 25 Mar.1786.

1335. Leslie, Hugh Fraser, in Jamaica, heir to bro John Leslie of Powis, in Aberdeen, d. 27 Nov.1847, reg. 21 Aug.1848.

1336. Leslie, Hugh Fraser, in Jamaica, heir to fa Hugh Leslie of Powis, in Aberdeen, d. 8 Apr.1812, reg. 21 Aug.1848.

1337. Leslie, John Alexander, accountant, in Bank of B N A Toronto, heir to sis Arabella Leslie, in Edinburgh, d. 18 Dec.1868, reg. 24 Jan.1873.

1338. Lewars, James, in Hanover Oh, heir to mo Helen Lithgow or Lewars, w of John Lewars weaver in Lanark, reg. 18 Jan.1853.

1339. Liddell, David James, in Collingwood Ont, heir to cousin Robert Liddell, in Milton of Auchtertool Fife, d. 25 Dec.1842, reg. 21 July 1879.

1340. Liddle, Elspeth, in South Gray's Close Edinburgh, heir to mo Janet Liddle, w of Thomas Liddle in NY, reg. 8 May 1860.

1341. Lilburn, Robert, in America, heir to mo Margaret Laurie or Lilburn, da of William Laurie of Drunzie, reg. 4 Apr.1860.

1342. Lillie, John, limeburner, in Fort Wayne Ind, heir to fa John Lillie, feuar in Greenlaw Berwickshire, d. 1 Apr.1858, reg. 6 May 1870.

1343. Lillie or Strother, Margaret, in Petty Inverness-shire, heir to sis Jess Lillie, in Forres Morayshire then Kingston Jamaica, d. 6 Jan.1832, reg. 12 Nov.1861.

1344. Lillie, Mary, in Inverness, heir to sis Jess Lillie, in Forres Morayshire then Kingston Jamaica, d. 6 Jan.1832, reg. 12 Nov.1861.

1345. Lindsay, George, surgeon, in NY, heir to mo Margaret Stalker or Lindsay, in Edinburgh, reg. 27 Dec.1841.

1346. Lindsay, George, surgeon, in NY, heir to grandfa James Stalker, teacher in Edinburgh, reg. 27 Dec.1841.

1347. Lindsay, Thomas, wright, in Dunbarton, heir to bro Alexander Lindsay, in Jamaica, reg. 11 Nov.1836.

1348. Linn, George, machinist, in Belleville Ont, heir to Margaret Waldie or Linn, w of Henry Linn in Edinburgh, d. 1 Dec.1868, reg. 17 Jan.1882.

1349. Linn, Walter, in Peel Wellington Co Can W, heir to uncle John Fleming, in St James Rd Glasgow, d. 19 Aug.1854, reg. 1 Mar.1875.

1350. Linn, Walter, in Peel Wellington Co Can W, heir to uncle Daniel Fleming, in Glasgow, d. 14 Aug.1854, reg. 1 Mar.1875.

1351. Lithgow, Alexander, in Va, heir to sis Mary Lithgow or Wilson, w of James Wilson innkeeper in Douglas Lanarkshire, reg. 3 May 1793.

1352. Little, William, in Tenn, heir to uncle Bryce Little, minister in Covington Lanarkshire, reg. 20 Dec.1822.

1353. Littlejohn, Thomas, storekeeper, in St John NB, heir to fa John Littlejohn, shoemaker in Torry Aberdeenshire, d. 20 Nov.1856, reg. 13 Feb.1863.

1354. Livingston, Jean, w of John Livingston collier, in Bellahouston Glasgow, heir to uncle Thomas Gordon, wright in Jamaica, reg. 20 May 1799.

1355. Livingstone or Thomas, Elizabeth, w of I Thomas cottonspinner, in Portsmouth NA, heir to uncle Archibald Livingstone, in Glasgow, reg. 23 Mar.1864.

1356. Livingstone or Thomas, Elizabeth, w of I Thomas cottonspinner, in Portsmouth NA, heir to fa James Livingstone, cottondresser in Ashton-under-Lyme England, d. 1 June 1859, reg. 11 Apr.1864.

1357. Livingstone, James, soldier, in USA, heir to uncle Archibald Livingstone, in Glasgow, d. 1 Jan.1841, reg. 3 Feb.1864.

1358. Livingstone, James, soldier, in USA, heir to fa James Livingstone, in Ashton-under-Lyme England, d. 1 June 1859, reg. 11 Apr.1864.

1359. Lockerbie, Andrew, engineer, in Can, heir to aunt Jean Lockerbie or Vallance, w of Andrew Vallance surgeon in Liverpool, d. 1836, reg. 13 Mar.1883.

1360. Lockerbie, Andrew, engineer, in Can, heir to fa William Lockerbie, in Colchester Can, d. 27 Dec.1856, reg. 13 Mar.1883.

1361. Lockhart, Alexander, heir to cousin Janet Wright or Bogle, w of Lachlan Bogle in Jamaica, reg. 1808.

1362. Lockhart, Alexander Macdonald, in Can W, heir to fa Norman Lockhart of Tarbrax, in Lanarkshire, d. 5 Mar.1853, reg. 2 Apr.1855.

1363. Lockhart, Laurence Archibald, in Col, heir to mo Katherine Anne Russell, w of Lt Col L W M Lockhart, d. 11 Feb.1870, reg. 17 July 1873.

1364. Lockhart, Samuel, in Del, heir to fa Samuel Lockhart, in Pearhill Tarbolton Ayrshire, reg. 24 Oct.1860.

1365. Logan, Henry, dyer, in PEI, heir to fa John Logan, dealer in Kilmarnock Ayrshire, d. 20 Oct.1859, reg. 7 Jan.1864.

1366. Logan, Isobel, wid of George Logan, in Va, heir to Mary Campbell or White, w of James White merchant in Jamaica, reg. 20 Dec.1799.

1367. Logan, James, in Montreal, heir to fa William Logan, in Clarkstone Stirlingshire, reg. 13 Nov.1844.

1368. Logan, John, saddler, in America, heir to fa William Logan, in Lanark, d. 1 Sep.1858, reg. 19 Feb.1861.

1369. Longmoor, William, printer, in Toronto, heir to mo Mainie Reid or Longmoor, wid of James Reid printer in Toronto, d. 12 June 1863, reg. 7 Mar.1871.

1370. Loudon, Robert, in Boston, heir to William Aitchison, quarrier in Airdrie Lanarkshire, reg. 23 Sep.1875.

1371. Loudon, Robert, in Boston, heir to Daniel Rankin, shoemaker in Airdrie Lanarkshire, reg. 23 Sep.1875.

1372. Loudon, William, in La, heir to cousin Agnes Loudon, in Helensburgh Dunbartonshire, d. 19 Sep.1847, reg. 8 July 1850.

1373. Love jr, Thomas, ironfounder, in Chicago, heir to William Clark, weigher in Calderbank Lanarkshire, reg. 4 Mar.1876.

1374. Lovell, John, in Lee NA, heir to bro James Lovell, papermaker in Penecuik Mid Lothian, d. 16 Feb.1848, reg. 12 Mar.1862.

1375. Low, Andrew, in Savanna Ga then Liverpool, heir to fa William Low, merchant in Brechin Angus, reg. 18 Aug.1857.

1376. Low, James, minister, in Miramachi, heir to fa James Low, slater in Dundee Angus, reg. 12 Dec.1816.

1377. Low, John Park, in NY, heir to fa John Low, china merchant in Edinburgh, reg. 19 July 1854.

1378. Lumgair, David, in Trinidad, heir to mo Ann Henderson or Lumgair, w of James Lumgair mason in Arbroath Angus, d. 25 Sep.1855, reg. 15 Dec.1856.

1379. Lumgair, James, in San Fernando Trinidad, heir to fa James Lumgair, mason in Curend Angus, d. 21 Dec.1863, reg. 16 Aug.1867.

1380. Lumsden, Jean, wid of David Lumsden, in Strathmore, heir to bro David Lumsden, merchant in Aberdeen then Kingston Jamaica, reg. 26 Feb.1763.

1381. Lumsden, Rachel, wid of William Lumsden , in Mid Clova Aberdeenshire, heir to bro David Lumsden, merchant in Aberdeen then Kingston Jamaica, reg. 26 Feb.1763.

1382. Lundie, Archibald, in Kingston Jamaica, heir to grandfa Archibald Ballantyne of Kelly, d. 1712, reg. 9 June 1794.

1383. Lyall, James Gibson, in Gallery Angus then Jamaica, heir to uncle David Lyall of Gallery, reg. 18 Apr.1816.

1384. Lyle, Ann, in Houston Renfrewshire, heir to bro Robert Lyle, in Jamaica, reg. 26 Aug.1839.

1385. Lyle, Elizabeth, in Houston Renfrewshire, heir to bro Robert Lyle, in Jamaica, reg. 26 Aug.1839.

1386. Lyle or Barbour, Margaret, in Houston Renfrewshire, heir to bro Robert Lyle, in Lottery Jamaica, reg. 26 Aug.1839.

1387. Lynch, Mary Ann, da of W H Lynch, in Clarendon Jamaica, heir to uncle Alexander Skene of Marcus, RN, reg. 20 Nov.1829.

1388. Lyon, Alexander, farmer, in Can, heir to fa James Lyon, sawyer in Douglastown NB, reg. 19 Apr.1843.

1389. Lyon, Andrew Mann, in Ottawa, heir to grandmo Sarah Cowie or Mann, w of Andrew Mann in Ottawa, d. 19 Oct.1849, reg. 8 Apr.1878.

1390. Lyon, Andrew Mann, in Ottawa, heir to gt grandmo Sarah Watts or Cowie, wid of William Cowie in Aberdeen, d. 28 Mar.1851, reg. 22 Apr.1879.

1391. Lyon, George, in Up Can, heir to cousin Janet Lyon or Park, in Inverurie Aberdeenshire, reg. 13 Oct.1838.

1392. McAdie, William, in Belleville Ont, heir to fa David McAdie, merchant in W Watten Caithness then Belleville, d. 9 Mar.1860, reg. 27 July 1877.

1393. Macalister, Alexander, in Can, heir to grand-uncle Robert Patison, in Paisley Renfrewshire, reg. 3 Jan.1854.

1394. Macalister, Henry Bowie, clerk, in Can, heir to bro Robert Macalister, in Paisley Renfrewshire, reg. 13 Aug.1856.

1395. Macalister, Henry Bowie, clerk, in Can, heir to bro John Macalister, in Pictou NS, reg. 13 Aug.1856.

1396. McAllister, William, combmaker, in America, heir to fa Patrick McAllister, candlemaker in Glasgow, reg. 17 June 1785.

1397. MacAlpine, Jane, da of R MacAlpine surgeon, in Norfolk NA, heir to uncle John MacAlpine, surgeon in Glasgow, reg. 7 Nov.1827.

1398. MacAlpine, Margaret, da of R MacAlpine surgeon, in Norfolk NA, heir to uncle John MacAlpine, surgeon in Glasgow, reg. 7 Nov.1827.

1399. McArthur, John, in Johnstown Center Wisc, heir to sis Mary McArthur, spirit-dealer in Torrance, d. 26 Aug.1871, reg. 10 June 1872.

1400. McArthur, Robert, in Tucksmith Rodgerville Can W, heir to grandfa Robert McArthur, dyer in Callendar Stirlingshire, d. 13 Sep.1832, reg. 2 Dec.1873.

1401. Macartney, George, surgeon, in Jamaica, heir to mo Margaret Grierson or Macartney, in Castle Douglas, reg. 8 Oct.1847.

1402. McAskell, Donald, in Ebest Skye Inverness-shire, heir to grandfa Allan McAskell, in Barbados, reg. 2 July 1702.

1403. McAulay or Ewing, Elizabeth, wid of William Ewing clerk, in Glasgow then Montreal, heir to bro Henry McAulay, weaver in Glasgow, d. 22 Dec.1849, reg. 28 Nov.1853.

1404. McBeath or Wright, Helen, gardener, in Stirling, heir to s James McBeath, in NY, reg. 7 Feb.1834.

1405. McBeath or Watson, Helen, in Ont, heir to mo Ann Watson, w of David Watson in Dundee Angus, d. 13 Jan.1840, reg. 5 May 1879.

1406. McCall or Goudie, Janet, in Montreal, heir to mo Janet Bone or McCall, w of James McCall mason in Content, reg. 26 Feb.1851.

1407. McCandlish, Peter, yeoman, in Elmsley Can, heir to sis Elizabeth McCandlish, spinster in Wigtown, d. 29 Jan.1855, reg. 3 June 1862.

1408. McCandlish, Peter, yeoman, in Elmsley Can, heir to sis Blair McCandlish or Irvine, w of John Irvine plasterer in Wigtown, d. 31 July 1835, reg. 3 June 1862.

1409. McClelland or Hunter, Agnes, w of Robert McClelland, in Sudsbury Pa, heir to fa Patrick Hunter, in America, reg. 26 Apr.1784.

1410. McClune, James, merchant, in Liverpool, heir to uncle James Carson, merchant in Charleston NA, reg. 24 Nov.1812.

1411. McClune, James, heir to cousin James Carson or Porter, s of J Carson merchant in Charleston NA, reg. 24 Nov.1812.

1412. McClure, William, minister, in Nassau New Providence Bahamas, heir to cousin James McClure, in Crosshill Ayrshire, reg. 4 Apr.1861.

1413. McClure, William Malcolm, MD, in Bahamas, heir to fa William McClure, minister in Bahamas, d. 10 May 1863, reg. 27 Sep.1864.

1414. McClusky or McKnight, Jane, w of James McKnight laborer, in Creetown Kirkcudbrightshire, heir to nephew Alexander McClusky, in New Orleans, d. 18 Sep.1861, reg. 4 July 1865.

1415. McCormick, Emmeline Leckie, in Pa, heir to Ralph Foster of Drummoyne, in Lanarkshire, d. Feb.1810, reg. 21 Aug.1856.

1416. McCoull, John, in Va, heir to Christiana McCoull, da of James McCoull merchant in Glasgow, reg. 7 Dec.1810.

1417. McCredie, John Kevan, in Portage City NA, heir to mo Grace Kevan or McCredie, w of Hugh McCredie in Portage City, reg. 1 Nov.1867.

1418. McCredie, John Kevan, in Portage City NA, heir to fa Hugh McCredie, in Portage City, reg. 1 Nov.1867.

1419. McCrorie, William, tailor, in Warrenton NC, heir to sis Grizel McCrorie, in Argyle St Glasgow, reg. 21 Nov.1827.

1420. McCulloch, Alexander, farmer, in Cairndoon Glasserton Wigtownshire, heir to cousin James McCulloch, in Cal, d. 16 Dec.1841, reg. 5 Dec.1865.

1421. McCulloch, Alexander, farmer, in Cairndoon Glasserton Wigtownshire, heir to uncle Andrew McCulloch, in Cal, d. 12 Mar.1855, reg. 5 Dec.1865.

1422. McCulloch, Ann, in Kilbirnie Ayrshire then Can, heir to fa Archibald McCulloch, bleacher in Blackland Miln, reg. 8 Sep.1828.

1423. McCulloch, John, clerk, in Sagua la Grande Cuba, heir to uncle John McCulloch jr, in Sagua la Grande, d. 14 Sep.1868, reg. 24 Feb.1882.

1424. McDiarmid, Finlay, in Aldborough Can, heir to cousin John McDiarmid, Captain Rifle Brigade in Edinburgh, reg. 6 Mar.1847.

1425. McDonald, Alexander, in Golden Spring Jamaica, heir to bro Ronald McDonald, Capt 44th Regt in Irvine Ayrshire, reg. 5 Oct.1829.

1426. MacDonald, Allan, in PEI, heir to remote cousin John MacDonald, s of Allan More MacDonald of Morar, reg. 4 July 1825.

1427. McDonald, Angus, farmer, in NS, heir to bro Hugh McDonald, merchant in Aberdeen, reg. 17 Oct.1812.

1428. McDonald, James, in Edinburgh, heir to fa Daniel McDonald, smith in Edinburgh then America, reg. 27 Apr.1835.

1429. MacDonald, John, in Sand Point Can, heir to grandfa John MacDonald, in Scothouse Knoydart Inverness-shire, reg. 28 Oct.1853.

1430. McDonald, John, in Toronto, heir to aunt Isabella Huie or Alexander, wid of John Alexander feuar in Greenock Renfrewshire, d. 12 Apr.1860, reg. 9 Apr.1863.

1431. MacDonald, Ranald, in Girinish Can, heir to uncle Allan MacDonald, in Edinburgh then PEI, reg. 15 June 1853.

1432. MacDonald, Ranald, in Girinish Can, heir to cousin Major Simon MacDonald of Morar Inverness-shire, reg. 2 Aug.1854.

1433. McDonald, William, engineer, in NA, heir to bro John McDonald, millwright & builder in Newtonhill Kincardineshire, reg. 10 Nov.1865.

1434. McDougall or Ronald, Agnes, w of George Ronald warehouseman, in NY, heir to fa William McDougall, minister in Paisley Renfrewshire, d. 20 Feb.1867, reg. 11 June 1868.

1435. McDougall, Alexander Edward, in Jersey USA, heir to grand-uncle Robert McDougall, tailor in Glasgow, d. 21 Apr.1860, reg. 11 July 1883.

1436. McDougall, Peter, in Cal, heir to aunt Christian Duff or McLeary, in Bridge of Allan Stirlingshire, d. 18 May 1877, reg. 11 Nov.1878.

1437. McDougall, Thomas, butcher, in Kingston Can, heir to grandfa William McDougall, weaver in Kelso Roxburghshire, d. 6 Jan.1851, reg. 27 May 1873.

1438. McDougall, William, in Can, heir to fa Alexander McDougall, feuar in Hill of Fortrose, d. 11 Jan.1872, reg. 16 Oct.1873.

1439. McDowall, Patrick, merchant, in Onancocktown America, heir to bro Robert McDowall, physician in Marlborough, reg. 22 Feb.1758.

1440. McEwan or Ross, Jean, in Port Patrick Wigtownshire, heir to bro Alexander Ross, ship carpenter in Jamaica, reg. 15 June 1835.

1441. McEwan or McTaggart, Mary, w of John McTaggart merchant, in Whithorn Kirkcudbrightshire, heir to bro William McEwan, physician in Jamaica, reg. 25 July 1791.

1442. McEwan, William, physician, in Jamaica, heir to bro John McEwan, writer in Edinburgh, reg. 29 June 1785.

1443. McFarlane, Helen, in America, heir to mo Janet Anderson or McFarlane, in Can, reg. 24 Nov.1845.

1444. McFarlane, James, in America, heir to mo Janet Anderson or McFarlane, in Can, reg. 24 Nov.1845.

1445. McFarlane, James, in Mitchellville Palk Ia, heir to uncle Peter McFarlane, farmer in Balmacolly, d. 24 Sep.1852, reg. 11 July 1871.

1446. McFarlane or Wilkie, Janet, in America, heir to mo Janet Anderson or McFarlane, in Can, reg. 24 Nov.1845.

1447. McFarlane, John, heir to aunt Mary Campbell or White, wid of James White merchant in Jamaica, reg. 1806.

1448. McFarlane jr, Daniel, farmer, in Front River Elgin Lower Can, heir to mo Margaret Lyon or McFarlane, w of Daniel McFarlane in Front River, d. 8 July 1863, reg. 31 Aug.1864.

1449. McFarlane, Mary Stewart, in London, heir to fa Duncan McFarlane, planter in Jamaica, reg. 28 Nov.1794.

1450. McFarlane, Matthew, in America, heir to mo Janet Anderson or McFarlane, in Can, reg. 24 Nov.1845.

1451. McFarlane, Robert, in America, heir to mo Janet Anderson or McFarlane, in Can, reg. 24 Nov.1845.

1452. McFarlane, Thomas, in America, heir to mo Janet Anderson or McFarlane, in Can, reg. 24 Nov.1845.

1453. McGeachy, Alexander, in NB, heir to bro Duncan McGeachy, chemist in Glasgow, d. 9 Jan.1855, reg. 18 Apr.1855.

1454. McGibbon, John, in NB, heir to cousin Donald McGregor of Balholdie, d. 30 Dec.1854, reg. 10 Jan.1856.

1455. McGill, James, joiner, in Mobile Ala, heir to sis Jean McGill or Bryde, in Carseduchan Mochrum, d. 25 Nov.1874, reg. 14 Dec.1876.

1456. McGillivray, John, in Glengarry Can, heir to fa Farquhar McGillivray of Dalcrombie, in Inverness-shire, reg. 21 Oct.1852.

1457. McGillivray, Neil John, in Can W, heir to remote cousin John McGillivray of Dunmaglass, in Inverness-shire, d. 6 Feb.1852, reg. 12 Jan.1858.

1458. McGlashan, Charles, s of Alexander McGlashan merchant, in Dundee Angus, heir to uncle Nicholas McIntosh, merchant in Jamaica, reg. Mar.1770.

1459. McGlashan, John, in Ga, heir to fa James McGlashan, grocer in Edinburgh, d. 23 Apr.1849, reg. 13 July 1857.

1460. McGlashan, John, in Feliz Valley Cal, heir to fa William McGlashan, vintner in Edinburgh, d. 26 May 1831, reg. 12 Jan.1863.

1461. McGlashan, William, merchant, in Cromarty Ross & Cromarty, heir to uncle A McGlashan, merchant in Newfoundland, reg. 29 May 1832.

1462. McGlashan, William, in NY, heir to grand-uncle James McGlashan, in Strathbraan, reg. 25 Dec.1855.

1463. MacGoun, Archibald, in Mexico, heir to uncle Robert MacGoun, merchant in Greenock Renfrewshire, d. 28 Feb.1846, reg. 22 Mar.1871.

1464. MacGoun, Duncan, in Dunedin NZ, heir to fa Duncan MacGoun, in Rio Seco Tex, d. 1850, reg. 23 Jan.1871.

1465. MacGoun, Duncan, in Dunedin NZ, heir to uncle John MacGoun, in Mexico, d. 1851, reg. 23 Jan.1871.

1466. MacGoun, Lauchlan Campbell, in Guan Axuhato Mexico, heir to bro Duncan MacGoun, in Plaistow Essex England, reg. 14 Dec.1870.

1467. MacGoun, Lauchlan Campbell, in Mexico, heir to uncle Robert
MacGoun, merchant in Greenock Renfrewshire, d. 28 Feb.1846,
reg. 22 Mar.1871.
1468. MacGoun, Margaret Fraser, wid of Donald Campbell attorney, in
Jamaica, heir to uncle Robert MacGoun, merchant in Greenock
Renfrewshire, reg. 22 Mar.1871.
1469. McGowan or Gordon, Catherine C, in Alman Town Kingston Jamaica,
heir to grandfa John McGowan, in Garliestown, d. 1818, reg. 21
Mar.1877.
1470. McGowan, John, in Garliestown, heir to uncle Andrew McGowan,
shipmaster in NC, reg. 10 Oct.1811.
1471. McGowan or Sproull, Margaret Jane, in Washington Ia, heir to aunt
Elizabeth McGowan, innkeeper in Sorbie, d. 2 Apr.1881, reg. 6
Oct.1881.
1472. McGregor or Stewart, Catherine, w of Rev Murdoch Stewart, in Cape
Breton NS, heir to sis Mary McGregor, in Braemar Aberdeenshire,
d. 28 July 1880, reg. 26 Feb.1881.
1473. MacGregor, Donald, painter, in Philadelphia, heir to bro David
MacGregor, bookseller in Edinburgh, reg. 9 Dec.1857.
1474. MacGregor, Donald, painter, in Philadelphia, heir to sis Margaret
MacGregor, in Edinburgh, reg. 9 Dec.1857.
1475. McGregor, James, baker, in Crieff Perthshire then Galt Ont, heir to fa
Peter McGregor, baker in Crieff, d. 17 Nov.1872, reg. 14
Feb.1874.
1476. MacGregor, John, in Can, heir to James MacGregor, schoolmaster in
Arbroath Angus, reg. 28 May 1855.
1477. McGregor, Robert, in Cincinnati, heir to bro John McGregor, in Ind, reg.
19 July 1852.
1478. McGregor, Robert Coll, in Can W, heir to fa William McGregor, in Can
W, reg. 5 Apr.1854.
1479. MacGrigor, James, commission agent, in Cincinnati, heir to fa Robert
MacGrigor, weaver in Stanley Perthshire, reg. 13 June 1860.
1480. McHoull, Hugh, merchant, in Oshawa Can, heir to fa William McHoull,
merchant in Galston, reg. 19 Mar.1851.
1481. McIndoe, Walter, merchant, in Petersburg Va, heir to uncle James
McIndoe, in Carbeth Strathblane, reg. 13 Dec.1822.
1482. McInnes, John Taylor, lime merchant, in Philadelphia, heir to mo
Martha Hunter or McInnes, w of John McInnes weaver in Paisley
Renfrewshire then Philadelphia, reg. 2 Mar.1857.
1483. McInnes, John Taylor, lime merchant, in Philadelphia, heir to uncle
James Hunter, printer in England, reg. 2 Mar.1857.
1484. McInnes, John Taylor, lime merchant, in Philadelphia, heir to uncle
Hugh Hunter, soldier in Stewart's Raes, reg. 2 Apr.1857.

1485. McIntosh, John, wright, in Can, heir to uncle James McIntosh, gamekeeper in Culloden Inverness-shire, reg. 6 Mar.1843.

1486. McIntosh, Thomas, farmer, in St Vincent Can W, heir to grandfa John Kinross, vintner in Dunblane Perthshire, d. 31 May 1827, reg. 8 Aug.1870.

1487. McIntosh, Zilia Cecilia, in New Orleans, heir to grandmo Jean Keay or McIntosh, wid of Alexander McIntosh plasterer in Dundee Angus, d. 14 Mar.1874, reg. 12 Apr.1880.

1488. McIver, John, merchant, in Alexandria Potomac River Va, heir to bro Colin McIver, merchant in Alexandria, reg. 26 June 1789.

1489. McIver, John, merchant, in Columbia SC, heir to grand-uncle Thomas Agnew, tenant farmer in Clanny, reg. 6 Mar.1829.

1490. McJannet, John, in Clifford Minto Can W, heir to bro Samuel Watkinson McJannet, in Melbourne, d. 14 Sep.1853, reg. 18 Aug.1864.

1491. Mack, John, farmer, in Payson Ill, heir to fa Hamilton Mack, farmer in Westinghouse Carluke Lanarkshire, d. 25 Oct.1842, reg. 5 Jan.1880.

1492. Mack, William, in Dunloskin Lower Can, heir to grandfa William Mack, writer in Airdrie Lanarkshire, reg. 24 Oct.1838.

1493. Mack, William, advocate, in Montreal, heir to grandfa William Mack, writer in Airdrie Lanarkshire, reg. 24 Oct.1849.

1494. McKarchar, Duncan, farmer, in Can W, heir to bro John McKarchar, leather merchant in Perth, d. 4 Aug.1863, reg. 1 Mar.1864.

1495. Mackay, Alexander, in Kidcan Hall Can W, heir to fa Thomas Mackay, in Kidcan Hall, d. 9 Oct.1855, reg. 7 Oct.1856.

1496. Mackay, Donald, in Vancouver Is, heir to fa William Mackay, merchant in Portnalick, d. 1857, reg. 2 Apr.1867.

1497. Mackay or Kyd, Isabella, wid of H Kyd engineer, in USA then Arbroath Angus, heir to bro Peter Mackay, builder in Arbroath, d. 1 Apr.1854, reg. 2 Aug.1854.

1498. Mackay or Kyd, Isabella, wid of G Mackay engineer, in USA then Arbroath Angus, heir to bro William Mackay, in Arbroath, reg. 4 Oct.1854.

1499. Mackay or Kyd, Isabella, wid of G Kyd engineer, in USA then Arbroath Angus, heir to bro John Mackay, mason in Jamaica, reg. 4 Oct.1854.

1500. Mackay, James, farmer, in Wester Ballat Stirlingshire, heir to gt grand-uncle Charles McKay, planter in Jamaica, reg. 24 Sep.1860.

1501. Mackay, Jessie, in NY, heir to grandmo Elizabeth Stevenson or Giffen, w of Alexander Giffen in Sanquhar Dumfries-shire, d. 3 Apr.1876, reg. 5 Dec.1882.

1502. McKay, William, merchant & planter, in Tobago, heir to fa Hugh McKay, tacksman in Glengally, reg. 22 Feb.1817.

1503. McKean, John, candlemaker, in Dunbarton, heir to bro James McKean, in Jamaica, reg. 15 Dec.1813.

1504. McKean, William, merchant, in NY, heir to mo Jean Kerr or McKean, w of Robert McKean in Kilmarnock Ayrshire, d. 23 June 1826, reg. 6 July 1826.

1505. McKechnie, Archibald, weaver, in Eaglesham Renfrewshire, heir to bro Peter McKechnie, merchant in Chambly Montreal, reg. 1 June 1827.

1506. McKen, Adam John, in St Mary's Newfoundland, heir to fa Thomas McKen, surgeon in Newfoundland, d. 26 Nov.1869, reg. 22 May 1872.

1507. Mackenzie, Alexander, in Hudson Bay Co, heir to bro Daniel Mackenzie, in Inverness, reg. 8 June 1840.

1508. Mackenzie, Alexander, coachpainter, in USA, heir to aunt Hannah McDonald or Dick, wid of James Dick cabinetmaker in Edinburgh, reg. 18 Apr.1859.

1509. McKenzie, Duncan Roderick, in Brooklyn NY, heir to fa Roderick Mackenzie, sheriff substitute in Stornaway Ross & Cromarty, d. 1 Apr.1853, reg. 30 Jan.1868.

1510. McKenzie, George, merchant, in Barbados, heir to mo Bethia Law or McKenzie, wid of George McKenzie writer in Edinburgh, reg. 20 Apr.1704.

1511. Mackenzie, George, in Cumberland Hill Dundas PEI, heir to mo Ann Mackenzie, d. 23 Aug.1851, reg. 23 Oct.1868.

1512. Mackenzie, George, in Cumberland Hill Dundas PEI, heir to fa Kenneth Mackenzie, in Invergordon Ross & Cromarty, d. 14 May 1868, reg. 23 Oct.1868.

1513. Mackenzie, James George, Lt Gov, in St Kitts & Nevis, heir to nephew James Mackenzie of Forret, reg. 1 Nov.1867.

1514. McKenzie, John, in Jamaica, heir to grandfa John Hossack, minister in Inverness, reg. 13 Feb.1788.

1515. Mackenzie, John, baker, in Columbia USA, heir to grandmo Mary Stewart or Mackenzie, reg. 4 Nov.1850.

1516. McKenzie, John, in St John Can E, heir to fa Alexander McKenzie, deer forester in Deanie Inverness-shire, d. 22 Sep.1851, reg. 13 Jan.1872.

1517. McKenzie or Campsie, Mary, w of Thomas Campsie carpenter, in NY, heir to aunt Hannah McDonald or Dick, wid of James Dick in Edinburgh, reg. 18 Apr.1859.

1518. Mackenzie, Simon, surgeon, in Jamaica, heir to fa John Mackenzie, surgeon in Fortrose, reg. 22 Oct.1773.

1519. Mackenzie, William Rattray, in Can, heir to sis Jemima Mackenzie, in Aberdeen, reg. 25 June 1847.

1520. McKenzie, William Mason, in Charleston USA, heir to grand-aunt Jane Mavor or Grant, ww of John Grant in Birchfield Aberdeen, d. 28 Jan.1846, reg. 7 Nov.1874.

1521. MacKid, Alexander, minister, in Goderick Can W, heir to uncle Anstruther Taylor, minister in Carnbee Fife, d. 28 Oct.1863, reg. 12 Oct.1864.

1522. Mackie, Elizabeth, in Dunjarg, heir to uncle Peter Sloane, in New Orleans, d. 18 May 1842, reg. 14 Oct.1861.

1523. Mackie, Elizabeth, in Dunjarg, heir to uncle Anthony Sloane, in New Orleans, d. 3 Jan.1844, reg. 14 Oct.1861.

1524. Mackie, Elizabeth, in Dunjarg, heir to uncle Alexander Sloane, in New Orleans then Whithorn Wigtownshire, d. 13 Dec.1835, reg. 22 Oct.1861.

1525. Mackie, James, in USA, heir to fa Charles Mackie, shoemaker in Forfar Angus, reg. 25 July 1854.

1526. Mackie or Robertson, Jane, in Manchester, heir to uncle Peter Sloane, in New Orleans, d. 18 May 1842, reg. 14 Oct.1861.

1527. Mackie or Robertson, Jane, in Manchester, heir to uncle Anthony Sloane, in New Orleans, d. 13 Jan.1844, reg. 14 Oct.1861.

1528. Mackie or Robertson, Jane, in Manchester, heir to uncle Alexander Sloane, in New Orleans then Whithorn Wigtownshire, d. 13 Dec.1835, reg. 22 Oct.1861.

1529. Mackie, John, heir to cousin Quintin Alexander of Drumnachrim, planter in Jamaica, reg. 11 Apr.1804.

1530. Mackie, Margaret, in Dunjarg, heir to uncle Alexander Sloane, in New Orleans then Whithorn Wigtownshire, d. 13 Dec.1835, reg. 22 Oct.1861.

1531. Mackie, Margaret, in Dunjarg, heir to uncle Peter Sloane, in New Orleans, d. 18 May 1842, reg. 14 Oct.1861.

1532. Mackie, Margaret, in Dunjarg, heir to uncle Anthony Sloane, in New Orleans, d. 3 Jan.1844, reg. 14 Oct.1861.

1533. Mackie, Thomas, saddler, in Tonquier Va, heir to bro Robert Mackie, merchant in Forres Morayshire, reg. 31 Jan.1767.

1534. Mackie, William, jeweller, in Edinburgh then Cuba, heir to fa Charles Mackie, jeweller in London, reg. 22 Mar.1826.

1535. Mackinlay, William, in Can W, heir to fa Matthew Mackinlay, collier in Tranent E Lothian, reg. 19 Jan.1859.

1536. McKinnon, Archibald, in Winnipeg, heir to mo Christina MacLean or McKinnon, in Kenyon Can, d. 28 Sep.1871, reg. 28 Jan.1881.

1537. Mackirdy, John Lachlan, in Quebec, heir to fa John Mackirdy, writer in Greenock Renfrewshire, reg. 6 Oct.1834.

1538. MacKnaight or Hannay, Margaret, in Newton Stewart Wigtownshire, heir to bro Thomas MacKnaight, in Grenada, reg. 10 July 1827.

1539. McLachlan, Cuthbert, s of Allan McLachlan bookseller, in Dumfries, heir to bro Allan McLachlan, in Tobago, reg. 27 Nov.1813.

1540. McLachlan, John Clark, Edinburgh Militia, heir to uncle Allan McLachlan, in Tobago, reg. 24 May 1814.

1541. McLachlan, Margaret, heir to fa Hugh McLachlan of Cameron, merchant in Glasgow then Kingston Jamaica, reg. 10 Sep.1756.

1542. McLachlan, William, farmer, in NS, heir to bro James McLachlan, farmer in Sauchiemill Stirlingshire then Torbrex, reg. 22 Mar.1848.

1543. McLaren or Smith, Catherine, w of R Smith, in Can, heir to grandmo Catherine Paton or Fulton, in Dollar, reg. 4 Oct.1854.

1544. McLaren, Catherine, in Smith Falls Lanark Ont, heir to cousin Donald McLaren, merchant in Callendar Stirlingshire, d. 7 Feb.1880, reg. 20 Aug.1881.

1545. McLaren, Duncan, merchant, in St John's Newfoundland, heir to fa Alexander McLaren, in Gilmerton Crieff Perthshire, d. 25 Dec.1871, reg. 12 Mar.1872.

1546. McLaren, Ellen, in Smith Falls Lanark Ont, heir to cousin Donald McLaren, merchant in Callendar Stirlingshire, d. 7 Feb.1880, reg. 20 Aug.1881.

1547. McLaren or McGregor, Margaret Ann, in Smith Falls Lanark Ont, heir to cousin Donald McLaren, merchant in Callendar Stirlingshire, d. 7 Feb.1880, reg. 20 Aug.1881.

1548. McLaren or Johnston, Mary, in Smith's Falls Lanark Ont, heir to cousin Donald McLaren, merchant in Callendar Stirlingshire, d. 7 Feb.1880, reg. 20 Aug.1881.

1549. McLaren, Peter, in Hamden Dello NY, heir to cousin William McLaren, in Muthil Perthshire, d. 18 Dec.1870, reg. 22 July 1871.

1550. McLaughlan, Andrew, in NY, heir to fa George McLaughlan, in Edinburgh, d. 1836, reg. 8 Jan.1862.

1551. McLea, Archibald, merchant, in NY, heir to bro Robert McLea, merchant & cooper in Greenock Renfrewshire, reg. 18 Apr.1817.

1552. McLean, Archibald, farmer, in NB, heir to mo Susan Drummond or McLean, w of Capt Archibald McLean in NY Volunteers, d. 17 Feb.1858, reg. 25 May 1858.

1553. MacLean, John, in Halifax NS, heir to mo Margaret Reid or MacLean, w of John MacLean, reg. 30 June 1823.

1554. MacLean, Mary, in Pennycross Mull Argyll then Edinburgh, heir to nephew James MacLean, in St Mary's Jamaica, reg. 26 Aug.1826.

1555. McLean, Robert, merchant, in Mobile, heir to mo Helen Chisholm or McLean, in Parkhill Ross-shire, d. 4 Dec.1857, reg. 28 Dec.1878.

1556. McLean, Thomas Annan, in Moncton NB, heir to mo Mary Alexander or McLean, in Cambus Alloa Clackmannanshire, d. 29 Aug.1878, reg. 14 May 1880.

83

1557. McLeary, John, miner, in Buena Vista NA, heir to fa Samuel McLeary, collier in Crookedholm Kilmarnock Ayrshire, d. Dec.1863, reg. 16 June 1864.

1558. McLehose, James, maltster, in Glasgow, heir to bro John McLehose, merchant in Jamaica, reg. 23 Dec.1782.

1559. McLeish or Sharpe, Isabella, w of T E Sharpe, in Boston, heir to fa David McLeish, cooper in Edinburgh, d. Feb.1849, reg. 8 Jan.1875.

1560. McLellan, Archibald Leitch, solicitor, in Chancery Can W, heir to grandmo Margaret Brown or Leitch, w of John Leitch merchant in Greenock Renfrewshire, reg. 19 Oct.1866.

1561. McLennan, Thomas, in Collingwood Ont, heir to cousin Thomas McLennan, in Chirnside Berwickshire, d. 15 Feb.1877, reg. 9 May 1878.

1562. McLeod, John, postal worker, in Washington USA, heir to bro George McLeod, surgeon in Glasgow, reg. 10 Jan.1834.

1563. McLeod, Thomas, in New Baltimore America, heir to fa George McLeod, printer in Edinburgh, d. 7 June 1852, reg. 11 Jan.1861.

1564. McLeod, Thomas, in Houghton Portage Lake NA, heir to fa George McLeod, printer in Drummond St Edinburgh, d. 7 June 1862, reg. 25 Nov.1863.

1565. MacLure, Alexander, in New Harmony USA, heir to sis Margaret MacLure, reg. 16 July 1840.

1566. McMillan or McConnell, Margaret, w of John McConnell, in Can, heir to sis Marion McMillan or Mundell, in Wallacehall, reg. 19 Mar.1852.

1567. McMillan, William, minister, in Holybush Alleghany Pa, heir to fa George McMillan, mason in Kirkcudbright then Pittsburg, reg. 12 Dec.1853.

1568. McMillan, William, in Stewarton Ayrshire then America, heir to Gilbert McMillan, gardener in Kair House, d. 5 June 1855, reg. 10 July 1862.

1569. McNab, Archibald, in McNab Township Can, heir to Lillias Millar, da of Richard Millar of Braeandarn, reg. 19 Dec.1831.

1570. MacNab or Millie, Jean, w of G Millie, in Dovan, heir to bro John MacNab, surgeon in Hudson Bay Co, reg. 16 Oct.1820.

1571. McNaughton or Adams, Elizabeth, w of Robert Adams merchant, in Montreal, heir to fa Daniel McNaughton, in Montreal, reg. 6 Aug.1849.

1572. McNaughton, James Henry, minister, in Kirkoswald then Can, heir to fa John McNaughton, carter in Dundee Angus, d. 17 Jan.1848, reg. 9 Jan.1855.

1573. McNeill, Alicia Margaret, heir to mo Alicia Clunie or McNeill, da of John Clunie in NY, reg. 6 July 1824.

1574. McNeill, Donald, in Sunnidale Can, heir to uncle James Stewart, in Auchnaba, reg. 13 Aug.1856.
1575. McNeill, Donald, in Woodville Can, heir to uncle James Stewart, in Auchnaba, reg. 13 Aug.1856.
1576. McNicol or Nicol, James Hunter, in Cal then Glasgow, heir to sis Mary Nicol, in Troon Ayrshire then Glasgow, d. 7 Dec.1859, reg. 5 Nov.1863.
1577. McNicol or Nicol, James Hunter, in Cal then Glasgow, heir to bro Robert McNicol or Nicol, seaman HEICS, d. 9 Jan.1855, reg. 5 Nov.1863.
1578. McNicol or Nairn, Magdalene, w of Peter McNicol, in Murraybay Can, heir to bro Thomas Nairn, Capt 49th Regt, reg. 28 Apr.1815.
1579. McNicol or Nicol, Magdalene, w of P McNicol, in Murraybay Can, heir to sis Christian Nairn, in Murraybay, reg. 7 Nov.1821.
1580. McNiven, William, in Schnectady College NY, heir to uncle Alexander McNiven, in Bowerswell Rd Perth, reg. 1 Apr.1848.
1581. McOmish, Peter, in Wanganui NZ, heir to bro John McOmish, in New Orleans, d. 19 Aug.1830, reg. 5 June 1871.
1582. McOwan or Oswald, Catherine, w of John Oswald, in Can, heir to cousin John Clark, in Arnfinlay, reg. 16 July 1857.
1583. McOwan or Bayne, Mary, in Muthil Perthshire, heir to bro Peter McOwan, in Comrie Perthshire then Can, reg. 18 June 1849.
1584. McPherson, Henry William, in America, heir to uncle George McPherson, mason in Westmuir Lanarkshire , d. 18 Dec.1839, reg. 4 Sep.1848.
1585. McPherson, Hugh, in Buckhorn Can, heir to fa Duncan McPherson, innkeeper in Easdale, reg. 11 Jan.1860.
1586. McQuhae, John, clerk, in Mono Can, heir to aunt Janet Hutton, in Millhouse of Kelton Kirkcudbrightshire, d. 25 Mar.1860, reg. 18 Feb.1863.
1587. McQuhae, John, storekeeper, in Camilla Mona Can W, heir to gt grandfa Nathaniel Morison, wright in Rhonehouse Kirkcudbrightshire, reg. 15 Nov.1864.
1588. McRitchie, George, baker, in NY, heir to fa David McRitchie, in NY, d. Aug.1853, reg. 12 May 1866.
1589. McRonald, Alexander, carpenter, in Toronto, heir to fa Thomas McRonald, clerk of works in Edinburgh, d. 27 Apr.1870, reg. 29 Nov.1876.
1590. McRoul, John, in Va, heir to James Laurie, s of Thomas Laurie merchant in Glasgow, reg. 2 Nov.1811.
1591. Mactavish, William, in Hudson Bay Co, heir to fa Dugald Mactavish, WS in Campbelltown Argyll, reg. 8 Mar.1858.
1592. McVicar, David, in Spanish Town Jamaica, heir to sis Elizabeth McVicar, da of Nigel McVicar of Fergushill, reg. 25 July 1825.

1593. McVittie, James, in Downie Can, heir to grandfa James McVity, tailor in Langholm Dumfries-shire, reg. 13 July 1864.

1594. McWhan, Thomas, merchant, in New Orleans, heir to mo Jane Haining or McWhan, w of James McWhan mason in Liverpool, reg. 8 May 1849.

1595. McWhirter, William McCargow, in Can W, heir to aunt Janet Alexander or Wilson, w of David Wilson in Wallacetown, d. 27 Mar.1864, reg. 15 Nov.1866.

1596. McWilliam or Gunnian, Elizabeth, w of John Gunnian, in Kirkbean, heir to bro John McWilliam, planter in Grenada, reg. 16 May 1829.

1597. MacWilliam, James, in Drummelzier Haugh, heir to fa James MacWilliam, in Jamaica, d. 17 Dec.1843, reg. 20 Nov.1852.

1598. Maguire, John, merchant, in Toronto, heir to fa John Maguire, merchant in Stranraer Wigtownshire, reg. 20 July 1868.

1599. Maguire, John, merchant, in Toronto, heir to mo Margaret O'Neil or Maguire, w of John Maguire merchant in Stranraer Wigtownshire, reg. 20 July 1868.

1600. Maiklem, Elizabeth, w of Finlay Maiklem, in Glasgow, heir to cousin John Williamson, planter in Va, reg. 17 Sep.1785.

1601. Mailer, Andrew, shoemaker, in Depere Wisc, heir to fa Andrew Mailer, mason in Edinburgh, d. 31 Dec.1830, reg. 25 June 1877.

1602. Main, David, in New Galloway NA, heir to bro James Main, in Longtown Cumberland, reg. 4 Sep.1830.

1603. Main, William Dick, merchant, in Amherst NS, heir to bro James Main, baker in Maybole Ayrshire, d. 12 Feb.1868, reg. 22 Aug.1873.

1604. Mair, Thomas, in Can W, heir to bro James Mair, advocate in Aberdeen, reg. 6 Sep.1848.

1605. Maitland, David, merchant, in NY, heir to sis Lillias Maitland, reg. 14 May 1794.

1606. Malcolm, Samuel Smythe, merchant, in Glasgow, heir to Elizabeth Wignal or Smythe, w of Samuel Smythe in USA, d. 9 May 1848, reg. 19 Apr.1858.

1607. Malcolm, William, merchant, in Glasgow, heir to Elizabeth Wignal or Smythe, w of Samuel Smythe in USA, d. 9 May 1848, reg. 19 Apr.1858.

1608. Malloch, James Chrystal, in Chisham Sq NY, heir to fa Andrew Malloch, writer in Dunblane Perthshire, d. 4 Feb.1838, reg. 20 Feb.1872.

1609. Maltman, James, stonecutter, in Perth then NY, heir to fa John Maltman, mason & wright in Auchterarder Perthshire, reg. 30 Apr.1824.

1610. Mann, Jane Rainie, in Quebec, heir to mo Sarah Cowie or Mann, reg. 14 June 1852.

1611. Manuel, Simon, smith, in NY, heir to grandfa John Swanston, mason in Bowden, reg. 27 May 1843.

1612. Mark or Anderson, Sara F, w of P Anderson, in Halifax NS, heir to bro Alexander Mark, writer in Edinburgh, d. 4 Apr.1823, reg. 20 Mar.1871.

1613. Marke, William, heir to cousin Quintin Alexander of Drumnachrim, planter in Jamaica, reg. 11 Apr.1804.

1614. Marquis, Alexander, in Milwaukee Wisc, heir to fa John Marquis, victualler in Glasgow, d. 14 Feb.1832, reg. 7 Nov.1881.

1615. Marshall or Valk, Anne, in Carolina, heir to bro James Marshall, painter in Edinburgh, reg. 13 June 1831.

1616. Marshall, James, farmer, in Vienna Ont, heir to bro David Marshall, in Roughhaugh Polmont Stirlingshire, d. Nov.1863, reg. 16 Oct.1878.

1617. Marshall, Jean, in Dundee Angus, heir to bro George Marshall, wright in Dunshalt Fife then New Orleans, reg. 13 Feb.1843.

1618. Marshall, John, in Edinburgh, heir to bro Joseph Marshall, merchant in Jamaica, reg. 22 Feb.1836.

1619. Marshall, John, in SC, heir to aunt Catherine Thomson, reg. 3 Nov.1857.

1620. Marshall, John, merchant, in NY, heir to fa William Marshall, merchant in Garlieston Wigtownshire, d. 15 Mar.1865, reg. 3 Aug.1878.

1621. Marshall, Mary C, in Philadelphia, heir to grandfa Francis Marshall, merchant in Edinburgh, reg. 21 July 1806.

1622. Marshall of Starrieshaw, Robert, heir to bro John Marshall, s of John Marshall of Starrieshaw in Carolina, reg. 15 July 1699.

1623. Marshall, William, in West Portown of Erskine Renfrewshire, heir to bro John Marshall, in Antigua, reg. 6 Feb.1786.

1624. Martin, Alexander, clerk, in Boston USA, heir to mo Helen Miller or Martin, w of Robert Martin mason in Dunblane Perthshire, d. 28 Apr.1883, reg. 23 June 1883.

1625. Martin, Catherine, in St John NB, heir to fa James Martin, stationer in Edinburgh, d. 14 Mar.1868, reg. 12 Sep.1878.

1626. Martin or Kilner, Christina, w of T Kilner clerk, in Bank of England, heir to bro William A Martin, in Tobago, d. 24 Jan.1850, reg. 16 Sep.1850.

1627. Martin or Johnstone, Elizabeth, in Chiccanoggo USA, heir to bro George Martin, mason in Edinburgh, reg. 30 Oct.1833.

1628. Martin or Nelson, Helen, in San Francisco, heir to mo Mary Bryce or Martin, wid of William Bryce in Garlieston Wigtownshire, d. 19 Oct.1868, reg. 10 Dec.1879.

1629. Martin or Denniston, Jane, w of Samuel Martin, in Paisley Renfrewshire, heir to fa John Denniston, skinner in Can, d. 1826, reg. 5 Dec.1883.

1630. Martin, John, in Can, heir to cousin John Gillies, surgeon in Edinburgh, d. 24 Nov.1834, reg. 5 July 1866.

1631. Martin or Loft, Margaret Boswell, wid of Lt T C Loft 92nd Foot Regt, heir to bro William A Martin, in Tobago, d. 24 Jan.1850, reg. 16 Sep.1850.

1632. Martin, Margaret Johnston, in Grey Ont, heir to mo Margaret Johnston or Martin, w of William Martin in Grey Ont, d. 24 Jan.1855, reg. 10 Mar.1877.

1633. Martin or Tweed, Margaret, w of James Tweed fireman, in Patterson NJ, heir to fa Robert Martin, laborer in Wishawtown Lanarkshire, reg. 19 Mar.1877.

1634. Martin or Tweed, Margaret, wid of James Tweed fireman, in Patterson NJ, heir to Jean Selkirk or Martin, w of Robert Martin in Wishawtown Lanarkshire, reg. 19 Mar.1877.

1635. Martin, Thomas, smith, in Dumfries Can, heir to fa James Martin, smith in Lochgelly Fife, reg. 29 June 1852.

1636. Martin, William, in Miramachi NB, heir to fa Alexander Martin, in Hardgate of Ferryhill, reg. 20 Feb.1808.

1637. Martin, William Alexander, in Tobago, heir to gt grandfa William Alexander, wright in Edinburgh, reg. 17 Dec.1838.

1638. Martin, William Alexander, in King's Bay Estate Tobago, heir to bro Peter Martin, HEICS, reg. 17 Oct.1849.

1639. Mason, Robert, baker, in Rockford Ill, heir to fa Robert Mason, shoemaker in S Queensferry W Lothian, d. 17 Mar.1853, reg. 10 Dec.1877.

1640. Masson, James, minister, in Pembroke Can W, heir to uncle Joseph Duncan, in Elgin Morayshire, d. 30 Mar.1829, reg. 9 Dec.1862.

1641. Masson or Lovemore, Mary, wid of Charles Lovemore, in Jamaica, heir to sis Elizabeth Masson, da of William Masson in Edinburgh, reg. 23 Feb.1791.

1642. Matheson, Allan Frederick, in Ont, heir to mo Annabella Russell or Matheson, w of Roderick Matheson in Perth Ont, d. 10 Nov.1854, reg. 8 Dec.1876.

1643. Matheson, Anna, in Ont, heir to mo Annabella Russell or Matheson, w of Roderick Matheson in Perth Ont, d. 10 Nov.1854, reg. 8 Dec.1876.

1644. Matheson, Arthur James, in Ont, heir to mo Annabella Russell or Matheson, w of Roderick Matheson in Perth Ont, d. 10 Nov.1854, reg. 8 Dec.1876.

1645. Matheson, Charles Albert, in Ont, heir to mo Annabella Russell or Matheson, w of Roderick Matheson in Perth Ont, d. 10 Nov.1854, reg. 8 Dec.1876.

1646. Matheson, Eliza Jean, in Ont, heir to mo Annabella Russell or Matheson, w of Roderick Matheson in Perth Ont, d. 10 Nov.1854, reg. 8 Dec.1876.

1647. Matheson or Shaw, Flora Madelina, in Ont, heir to mo Annabella Russell or Matheson, w of Roderick Matheson in Perth Ont, d. 10 Nov.1854, reg. 8 Dec.1876.

1648. Matheson, Isabella Russell, in Ont, heir to mo Annabella Russell or Matheson, w of Roderick Matheson in Perth Ont, d. 10 Nov.1854, reg. 8 Dec.1876.

1649. Matheson, Joanna, in Ont, heir to mo Annabella Russell or Matheson, w of Roderick Matheson in Perth Ont, d. 10 Nov.1854, reg. 8 Dec.1876.

1650. Matheson, Robert, in Ont, heir to mo Annabella Russell or Matheson, w of Roderick Matheson in Perth Ont, d. 10 Nov.1854, reg. 8 Dec.1876.

1651. Matheson, Rose Thyne, in Ont, heir to mo Annabella Russell or Matheson, w of Roderick Matheson in Perth Ont, d. 10 Nov.1854, reg. 8 Dec.1876.

1652. Matheson, William, plasterer, in Ga, heir to uncle George Smith, in Ga, reg. 6 Nov.1850.

1653. Matheson, William Marshall, in Ont, heir to mo Annabella Russell or Matheson, w of Roderick Matheson in Perth Ont, d. 10 Nov.1854, reg. 8 Dec.1876.

1654. Matthews, John Edward, in NY, heir to fa Alexander Matthews, in NY, d. 5 Dec.1864, reg. 11 Dec.1876.

1655. Matthewson, Donald, in Johnstown USA, heir to fa John Matthewson, feuar in Stanley Perthshire, reg. 10 Jan.1843.

1656. Maull, Catherine, heir to fa James Maull, minister in Antigua, reg. 8 May 1697.

1657. Maurice, James, tinworker, in Troy USA, heir to uncle Alexander Maurice, merchant in Turriff Aberdeenshire, d. 6 Feb.1860, reg. 31 Mar.1862.

1658. Maxwell, David, weaver, in Philadelphia, heir to fa Alexander Maxwell, weaver in Glasgow, d. 15 Dec.1867, reg. 27 Oct.1871.

1659. Maxwell, Helen F, in Elvira NY, heir to grandfa Charles Maxwell, dyer in Minnyhive, d. 13 Nov.1859, reg. 18 Mar.1871.

1660. Maxwell, James, surgeon, in Jamaica, heir to fa James Maxwell, manufacturer in Dundee Angus, reg. 28 Nov.1838.

1661. Maxwell, John, in NY, heir to bro William Maxwell, in W Nisbet Berwickshire, reg. 5 Jan.1842.

1662. Maxwell, John Strange, in Toronto, heir to cousin James Warrach, brewer in Anderston Glasgow then Prestonpans E Lothian, d. 27 Jan.1814, reg. 1 Nov.1866.

1663. Maxwell or Malony, Mary Ann, w of Thomas Malony, in Williamsburgh NY, heir to grandfa Charles Maxwell, dyker in Minnyhive, d. 13 Nov.1859, reg. 18 Mar.1871.

1664. Maxwell, William Strange, in Kingston Can W, heir to fa John Strange Maxwell, in Caledonia Springs Can, d. 14 Oct.1840, reg. 7 June 1866.

1665. Meikle or McHoull, Mary, w of Robert McHoull, in Can, heir to grandfa James McClune, in Galston Ayrshire, d. 24 Mar.1837, reg. 17 June 1857.

1666. Meikle or Martin, Mary, w of William Martin, in Ont, heir to fa James Meikle, in Galston Ayrshire, d. 29 July 1872, reg. 15 Feb.1873.

1667. Meldrum, Elizabeth, in Vankleck Hill Ont, heir to grandfa Andrew Meldrum, laborer in Limekilns Fife, d. 22 Jan.1857, reg. 23 July 1879.

1668. Meldrum, Isabella, in Vankleck Hill Ont, heir to grandfa Andrew Meldrum, laborer in Limekilns Fife, d. 22 Jan.1857, reg. 23 July 1879.

1669. Meldrum or Stewart, Peterichia, in Vankleck Hill Ont, heir to grandfa Andrew Meldrum, laborer in Limekilns Fife, d. 22 Jan.1857, reg. 23 July 1879.

1670. Melrose, Robert, joiner, in St John NB, heir to fa Robert Melrose, dairyman in Galashiels Selkirkshire, d. 12 Dec.1868, reg. 7 June 1870.

1671. Melville, Andrew, merchant, in Mexico, heir to uncle Andrew Melville, in Surinam, reg. 8 May 1844.

1672. Menmuir, Charles, cabinetmaker, in Philadelphia, heir to mo Sarah Marnie or Menmuir, w of James Menmuir tinsmith in Dundee Angus, d. 4 Nov.1853, reg. 16 Nov.1872.

1673. Menzies, Thomas, merchant, in Peterboro Can, heir to fa James Menzies, shoemaker in Comrie Perthshire, d. 14 Feb.1849, reg. 1 Sep.1877.

1674. Mercer, James, joiner, in Dundas Can, heir to grandfa James Mercer, laborer in Catacraig Bannockburn Stirlingshire, d. 9 Aug.1853, reg. 15 Oct.1877.

1675. Merrilees, William, in Bellafonteine Logan Co USA, heir to bro Fletcher Merrilees, in Jock's Lodge Edinburgh, d. 2 Feb.1883, reg. 8 Aug.1883.

1676. Meservey or Wilkie, Elizabeth S, in SC, heir to grandfa Peter Wilkie, grocer in Glasgow, reg. 9 Sep.1844.

1677. Metcalfe, William, traveller, in Waterloo Can W, heir to sis Penelope Metcalfe, in Aberdeen, d. 8 Feb.1862, reg. 26 Apr.1862.

1678. Methven or Whyte, Isobel, wid of John Whyte weaver, in USA, heir to sis Margaret Methven or Whyte, wid of Robert Whyte in Leslie Fife, reg. 6 Nov.1856.

1679. Millar, Alexander, heir to fa Alexander Millar, merchant in Dundee
        Angus then Lewisham USA, reg. 13 May 1835.
1680. Millar, David , heir to fa Alexander Millar, merchant in Dundee Angus
        then Lewisham USA, reg. 13 May 1835.
1681. Millar, Elizabeth, heir to fa Alexander Millar, merchant in Dundee Angus
        then Lewisham USA, reg. 13 May 1835.
1682. Millar, Frederick, heir to fa Alexander Millar, merchant in Dundee Angus
        then Lewisham USA, reg. 13 May 1835.
1683. Millar, George, in Strawberryhill Bahamas, heir to fa James Millar, baker
        in Canongate Edinburgh, reg. 23 Nov.1794.
1684. Millar, George, bricklayer, in Codnor Park Derbyshire, heir to cousin
        John Millar, in Columbus Col, d. 2 July 1863, reg. 1 Oct.1868.
1685. Millar, James, in Bahamas, heir to bro Archibald Millar, coachbuilder in
        Canongate Edinburgh, reg. 17 May 1791.
1686. Millar, Jane, heir to fa Alexander Millar, merchant in Dundee Angus then
        Lewisham USA, reg. 13 May 1835.
1687. Millar, Janet, heir to fa Alexander Millar, merchant in Dundee Angus
        then Lewisham USA, reg. 13 May 1835.
1688. Millar or Stark, Jean, in Can, heir to fa Joseph Millar, ex RN in
        Lauriston Kirkcudbrightshire, reg. 4 Jan.1833.
1689. Millar or Whyte, Jessie, in Drayton Ont, heir to fa John Millar, farmer in
        Howick Ont, d. 20 Feb.1880, reg. 14 Oct.1881.
1690. Millar, John, heir to fa Alexander Millar, merchant in Dundee Angus
        then Lewisham USA, reg. 13 May 1835.
1691. Millar, Lilly, heir to fa Alexander Millar, merchant in Dundee Angus
        then Lewisham USA, reg. 13 May 1835.
1692. Millar, Robert, grain miller, in Clinton Ont, heir to fa John Millar, in
        Howick Ont, d. 20 Feb.1880, reg. 14 Oct.1881.
1693. Millar, William, heir to fa Alexander Millar, merchant in Dundee Angus
        then Lewisham USA, reg. 13 May 1835.
1694. Millar, William, mason, in Dunoon Argyll then NY, heir to bro David
        Millar, in Milton Mill, d. 2 Aug.1865, reg. 5 Apr.1866.
1695. Miller, David, surgeon, in Jamaica, heir to bro James Miller, reg. 8
        Nov.1768.
1696. Miller, David, surgeon, in Westmoreland Jamaica, heir to uncle William
        Hill, writer in Edinburgh, reg. 3 May 1770.
1697. Miller, Elizabeth, wid, in Pequay Pa, heir to grandfa Alexander Baillie of
        Meikle Dunragget, reg. 16 June 1775.
1698. Miller, George, teacher, in Montego Bay Jamaica, heir to bro James
        Miller, merchant in Musselburgh Mid Lothian, reg. 5 June 1850.
1699. Miller, George, bricklayer, in Codnor Park Derbyshire, heir to cousin
        Agnes Janet Nicholson, in Columbus Col, d. 9 Feb.1857, reg. 1
        Oct.1868.

1700. Miller or Pierrepoint, Harriot, in Portsmouth USA, heir to aunt Agnes Miller or Thomson, wid of John Thomson shipmaster in Leith Mid Lothian, reg. 29 Oct.1830.

1701. Miller, Isabella, in Mordstone Can W, heir to fa George Miller, in Murrayshall Perthshire, d. 1834, reg. 9 May 1851.

1702. Miller, James, in Brighton England, heir to bro Philip Miller, in Edington USA, reg. 24 Jan.1831.

1703. Miller or Ferrel, James, in Jamaica, heir to sis Ann Miller or Tilley, da of James Miller merchant in Glasgow, reg. 27 May 1835.

1704. Miller, James Scott, merchant, in NA, heir to grandfa James Scott, master mariner RN in Inverkeithing Fife, d. 26 Mar.1850, reg. 20 Feb.1861.

1705. Miller or Bowie, Jane, in Kingston Can W, heir to bro Thomas Miller, in Darvel Ayrshire, d. Aug.1854, reg. 5 Mar.1862.

1706. Miller, John, in Saltcoats Ayrshire, heir to fa Joseph Miller, farmer in Mountfodd then Montreal, reg. 12 Jan.1829.

1707. Miller, John, in St Vincent, heir to fa James Miller, carter in Banff, reg. 14 Feb.1840.

1708. Miller, John Watson, in Cookshire Quebec, heir to mo Elizabeth Watson or Miller, w of William Cleugh Miller clerk in Edinburgh, d. 27 Jan.1851, reg. 18 Oct.1876.

1709. Miller or Grieve, Marion, w of John Grieve shoemaker, in Edinburgh then America, heir to bro Daniel Miller, tailor in Edinburgh, reg. 6 Apr.1807.

1710. Miller or Hunt, Mary Ann, in Mardstone Can W, heir to fa George Miller, in Murrayshall Perthshire, d. 1834, reg. May 1851.

1711. Miller, Mary Jane, in Bradford Miami, heir to grandfa Matthew Beveridge, shoemaker in Strathmiglo Fife, d. 23 May 1859, reg. 21 June 1878.

1712. Miller, William, in Mardstone Can W, heir to fa George Miller, in Murrayshall Perthshire, d. 1834, reg. 9 May 1851.

1713. Miller, William Gillies, in Frenton Clinton Co Ill, heir to mo Isabella Cowden or Miller, wid of William Miller carter in Glencaple, reg. 17 July 1869.

1714. Miller, William, commission agent, in London, heir to bro Alexander Crumm Miller, clerk in Ottawa, d. 24 Feb.1839, reg. 20 Nov.1877.

1715. Milln, James, banker, in Glasgow, heir to bro John Milln, storekeeper in Dundee Angus then Montreal, d. 21 Sep.1843, reg. 27 June 1863.

1716. Mills, Peter Drummond, in Ponce Porto Rico, heir to fa John Miln or Mills, wheelwright in Perth, d. 31 Jan.1861, reg. 15 Aug.1863.

1717. Milne, Alexander, in NY then Banff, heir to fa John Milne, carter in Banff, reg. 14 Feb.1840.

1718. Milne, Alexander Panton, in Toronto, heir to uncle Francis Milne, baker in Turriff Aberdeenshire, d. 13 Oct.1860, reg. 2 May 1877.

1719. Milne or Fairbairn, Helen, w of Robert Fairbairn joiner, in Edinburgh then Can, heir to bro Charles Milne, baker in Edinburgh, reg. 25 Sep.1851.

1720. Milne or Louttit, Johanna, w of James Louttit MD, in Hartlepool England, heir to bro William Milne, in Barbados, d. 21 June 1854, reg. 11 Sep.1866.

1721. Milne, Nicol, in Westminster Can, heir to s Robert Milne, in Wellington Pl Leith Mid Lothian, d. 13 July 1871, reg. 28 May 1872.

1722. Milne, William, tailor, in NY, heir to fa William Milne, in Kirriemuir Angus, reg. 12 June 1856.

1723. Mitchell, Charles, in Cincinnati, heir to fa Robert Mitchell, shipowner in Aberdeen, d. 19 Feb.1862, reg. 13 May 1863.

1724. Mitchell, David, in Can, heir to mo Elizabeth Anderson or Mitchell, w of Andrew Anderson manufacturer in Livingstone W Lothian, reg. 1 Nov.1802.

1725. Mitchell, David, in Can, heir to uncle James Anderson, Physician General in India, reg. 28 Nov.1810.

1726. Mitchell, David, in Can, heir to uncle Andrew Anderson, staff surgeon in Dominica, reg. 28 Nov.1810.

1727. Mitchell or Atchison, Isabell, w of W Atchison machinist, in Jersey USA, heir to mo Ann Gunn or Young, wid of J Mitchell machinist in Jersey, reg. 7 Dec.1871.

1728. Mitchell, James, postmaster, in Port Union Can, heir to uncle David Mitchell, clothier in Dundee Angus, d. 25 Dec.1852, reg. 5 June 1866.

1729. Mitchell, James Ritchie, farmer, in Tarr Pa, heir to sis Jessie Mitchell, in 28 Dundas St Edinburgh, d. 18 Mar.1867, reg. 31 Oct.1867.

1730. Mitchell, James, in America, heir to mo Marion Lang or Mitchell, wid of John Mitchell in Easterton Gartshore, d. 24 Dec.1879, reg. 31 Oct.1882.

1731. Mitchell, John, in Parkhill Can W, heir to Janet Eston or Sutherland, in Arbroath Angus, reg. 26 July 1878.

1732. Mitchell, John James, in Welsford Mills Pictou NS, heir to grandfa James Mitchell sr, in Gargunnock Stirlingshire, d. 25 Dec.1855, reg. 9 Oct.1879.

1733. Mitchell or Meudell, Margaret, w of William Fabian Meudell, in Belleville Up Can, heir to fa George Mitchell, wright in Edinburgh, d. 12 May 1831, reg. 22 Mar.1867.

1734. Mitchell or Meudell, Margaret, w of William Fabian Meudell, in Belleville Up Can, heir to mo Helen Anderson or Mitchell, w of

George Mitchell wright in Edinburgh, d. 19 June 1847, reg. 22 Mar.1867.

1735. Mitchell of Blairgetts, William, in Jamaica, heir to bro James Mitchell of Blairgetts, reg. 2 Mar.1764.

1736. Mitchell, Thomas Reeves, in Miss, heir to cousin Euphemia Moffat, in Grangehill then Kinghorn Fife, reg. 16 Nov.1846.

1737. Mitchell, William, in Toronto, heir to bro Young Mitchell, minister in Nelson NZ, d. 7 Feb.1882, reg. 14 Sep.1882.

1738. Mitchell, William, in Toronto, heir to fa Young Mitchell, in Sheffield School of Design, d. 2 May 1865, reg. 9 Jan.1883.

1739. Moar, Jonathan, in Souvies Is Ore, heir to bro Peter Clouston Moar, s of Jonathan Moar blacksmith in Stromness Orkney, d. 1838, reg. 2 Dec.1862.

1740. Moffat or Polwarth, Isabella, w of Thomas Polwarth butcher, in Leitholm Berwickshire, heir to mo Margaret Dods or Moffat, w of Robert Moffat in Can, reg. 17 Oct.1870.

1741. Moffat, James, blacksmith, in Can, heir to mo Margaret Dods or Moffat, w of Robert Moffat in Can, d. 14 Oct.1861, reg. 17 Oct.1870.

1742. Moffat, John, in Garrapaxa Can, heir to bro George Moffat, tailor in Almerieclose Arbroath Angus, reg. 14 July 1841.

1743. Moffat, John, in Can W, heir to fa John Moffat, merchant in Kilmarnock Ayrshire, d. 11 Dec.1848, reg. 16 Oct.1850.

1744. Moffat, Robert, store clerk, in Can, heir to mo Margaret Dods or Moffat, w of Robert Moffat in Can, d. 14 Oct.1861, reg. 17 Oct.1870.

1745. Moir, George, engineer, in Detroit, heir to aunt Mary Morrison, in Turriff Aberdeenshire, d. 22 Jan.1863, reg. 27 Apr.1878.

1746. Monach, Andrew Buchanan, in Philadelphia, heir to bro James Monach, s of A Monach hatter in Glasgow then Philadelphia, reg. 18 Jan.1826.

1747. Monach, Andrew Buchanan, in Philadelphia, heir to sis Margaret Monach, da of A Monach hatter in Glasgow then Philadelphia, reg. 19 Apr.1826.

1748. Monach, Andrew Buchanan, in Philadelphia, heir to sis Janet Monach, da of A Monach hatter in Glasgow then Philadelphia, reg. 4 Oct.1826.

1749. Monro, John Campbell, MD, in S Finch Can, heir to aunt Catherine Monro, in Edinburgh, d. 29 May 1866, reg. 11 Sep.1878.

1750. Monteath, Amilia, wid of Thomas Monteath, in Jamaica, heir to grandfa John Schaw, merchant in Edinburgh, reg. 10 Apr.1799.

1751. Monteath, Thomas, in Bridgetown Barbados, heir to aunt Margaret Monteath, da of Thomas Monteath tenant farmer in Carnock Fife, reg. 18 Mar.1791.

1752. Montgomery or Donaldson, Barbara H, w of John L Donaldson, in NY, heir to mo Agnes Greenfield or Montgomery, wid of George Montgomery confectioner in Edinburgh, reg. 7 Aug.1856.

1753. Montgomery, George Henderson, in Columbia USA, heir to mo Agnes Greenfield or Montgomery, wid of George Montgomery confectioner in Edinburgh, reg. 7 Aug.1856.

1754. Montgomery, Robert, in Winton NC, heir to fa John Montgomery of Nettlehurst & Mosshead, in Ayrshire, reg. 4 Aug.1795.

1755. Moodie, Lady Ann, in Ga, heir to grandfa John McKenzie, shipmaster in N Berwick E Lothian, reg. 14 Sep.1818.

1756. Moodie or Affleck, Margaret, wid of John Affleck farmer, in Columbus Oh, heir to fa James Moodie, portioner in Nungate Haddington E Lothian, d. 5 Mar.1827, reg. 3 Aug.1871.

1757. Moodie or Affleck, Margaret, wid of John Affleck farmer, in Columbus Oh, heir to bro James Moodie, boot & shoe maker in Haddington E Lothian, d. 26 Oct.1869, reg. 3 Aug.1871.

1758. Moody or Hynd, Helen, in Va, heir to gt grandmo Helen Lowson or Morrison, w of George Morrison in Dundee Angus, reg. 30 June 1847.

1759. Moor, Benjamin, in NJ, heir to grandmo Elizabeth Archibald or Moor, w of John Moor wright in Canongate Edinburgh, reg. May 1762.

1760. Morin, Jean Baptiste, smith, in Quebec, heir to fa John Morin of Morintown, in Dumfries-shire, reg. 15 July 1799.

1761. Morin, Jean Baptiste, smith, in Quebec, heir to uncle William Morin of Morintown, in Dumfries-shire, reg. 15 July 1799.

1762. Morison, John, in Chicago, heir to fa John Morison, shipmaster in Stornaway Ross & Cromarty , d. 4 Oct.1859, reg. 19 June 1874.

1763. Morison, Joseph John, in Banff, heir to fa John Morison, in Real del Monte Mexico, d. July 1853, reg. 4 June 1863.

1764. Morison, Maria Cleophas, in Banff, heir to fa John Morison, in Real del Monte Mexico, d. July 1853, reg. 4 June 1863.

1765. Morison, Robert, merchant, in Havanna then Edinburgh, heir to fa Robert Morison, painter in Perth, reg. 28 Sep.1853.

1766. Morison, William, farmer, in Can W, heir to bro John Gray-Morison of Craigend, in Lanarkshire, d. 30 July 1855, reg. 28 Apr.1859.

1767. Morris, Agnes, in Glasgow, heir to bro Alexander Morris, planter in Jamaica, reg. 12 June 1795.

1768. Morris, David, smith, in Ill, heir to bro James Morris, in Dalry, reg. 6 July 1859.

1769. Morris, David, blacksmith, in Ill, heir to fa Thomas Morris, grocer in Dalry Ayrshire, d. 9 Apr.1862, reg. 3 Feb.1863.

1770. Morris, Harvey, in Glasgow, heir to bro Alexander Morris, planter in Jamaica, reg. 12 June 1795.

1771. Morris, Margaret, in Glasgow, heir to bro Alexander Morris, planter in Jamaica, reg. 12 June 1795.

1772. Morris of Auldmuir or Baxter, Hugh, in Hamilton Can W, heir to Archibald McKerrell or Morris of Auldmuir, d. 24 Mar.1861, reg. 29 May 1861.

1773. Morrison, Benjamin, in Jamaica, heir to mo Isobel Leslie or Morrison, wid of Benjamin Morrison in Muirtown of Forgue, d. 10 July 1810, reg. 20 Jan.1813.

1774. Morrison, Thomas, cabinetmaker, in America, heir to fa Thomas Morrison, wright in Anstruther Fife, reg. 7 Dec.1848.

1775. Morrison, William, carter, in Paisley Renfrewshire, heir to uncle Peter Paterson, in Port Rothesay NA, reg. 24 Nov.1826.

1776. Morrison, William, engineer, in Jersey City NA, heir to mo Margaret Campbell or Morrison, w of George Morrison in Paisley Renfrewshire, d. 16 Jan.1867, reg. 13 June 1867.

1777. Morrison, William Gray, farmer, in Elgin Huntingdon Can, heir to fa William Morrison of Craighead, in Glasgow, d. 24 July 1879, reg. 21 July 1880.

1778. Mouat, Alexander Henderson, in Guelph Ont, heir to bro Peter Mouat of Wadbister, in Shetland, d. Mar.1855, reg. 30 July 1877.

1779. Mowbray or Anderson, Margaret, w of John Anderson, in Chicago, heir to cousin Elizabeth Mowbray, in Airth Stirlingshire, d. Sep.1854, reg. 15 Dec.1870.

1780. Mowbray, Seymour, in Killearny Ireland, heir to bro Richard Mowbray, farmer in Edinburgh then Ottoway Can, reg. 12 Nov.1860.

1781. Mudie, Alexander, in Jamaica then Edinburgh, heir to bro William Mudie, in Montrose Angus, reg. 23 Apr.1835.

1782. Mudie, Margaret, in Douglas NS, heir to mo Christian Robertson or Mudie, in Dunning Perthshire, reg. 11 Nov.1825.

1783. Muir, Robert, in Jamaica, heir to fa James Muir, surgeon in Glasgow, reg. 30 Oct.1811.

1784. Muir, Robert, in Jamaica, heir to mo Elizabeth Wardrope or Niven, wid of James Niven surgeon in Glasgow, reg. 9 June 1820.

1785. Muir, Thomas, in Alexandria America, heir to fa John Muir, portioner in Newstead Roxburghshire, reg. 29 Sep.1802.

1786. Muirhead, John, truckman, in Lubec America, heir to fa John Muirhead, in Bankhead Denny Stirlingshire, d. Dec.1839, reg. 5 Feb.1868.

1787. Muirhead, John, in Lubec Washington Co Me, heir to grandfa John Muirhead, in Bankhead Denny Stirlingshire, d. Dec.1839, reg. 21 Oct.1874.

1788. Muirhead, Peter, planter, in Jamaica, heir to Alexander Muirhead of Linhouse, reg. 1 Apr.1801.

1789. Mulholland, Bernard John, in Rondout NY, heir to mo Janet Webster or Mulholland, wid of John Mulholland innkeeper in Maghera Londonderry Ireland, d. 25 July 1865, reg. 9 June 1876.

1790. Mullion, Charles, in Louisville Ky, heir to grandfa James Finlay, brewer in Coupar Angus Perthshire, reg. 30 Jan.1835.

1791. Mundell, Robert, tobacconist, in Dumfries, heir to bro Joseph Mundell, planter in Clarendon Jamaica, reg. 1 May 1824.

1792. Munro, Hugh, in Green Is Jamaica, heir to fa George Munro, in Tain Ross & Cromarty, reg. 13 Nov.1832.

1793. Munro, Sutherland Shaw, in America, heir to grandfa Sutherland Munro, joiner in Pultneytown Wick Caithness, d. 24 Aug.1855, reg. 13 Mar.1879.

1794. Murdoch, Alexander, in San Francisco, heir to mo Margaret Grant or Murdoch, wid of A Murdoch shipmaster in London, d. 12 May 1864, reg. 19 Dec.1873.

1795. Murdoch, James, in Mass, heir to bro John Murdoch, in Springs Coylton, reg. 27 July 1842.

1796. Murdoch, William, in Halifax NS, heir to Agnes Cuming, in Hawick Roxburghshire, reg. 10 Nov.1852.

1797. Mure, Robert, merchant, in Charleston America, heir to mo Elizabeth Carson or Mure, w of Robert Mure in Kirkcudbright, reg. 1 Oct.1867.

1798. Mure, Robert, merchant, in Charleston America, heir to aunt Grace Carson, in Kirkcudbright, reg. 1 Oct.1867.

1799. Mure, Robert, merchant, in Charleston America, heir to aunt Mary Carson, in Kirkcudbright, reg. 1 Oct.1867.

1800. Murison, William Alexander, clerk, in New Orleans, heir to fa John Murison, cotton factor & merchant in New Orleans, d. 22 Aug.1870, reg. 19 June 1872.

1801. Murray, Alexander, merchant, in Charleston SC, heir to fa Charles Murray, clerk of the Bailliary of Lauderdale, reg. 17 Dec.1737.

1802. Murray, Alexander McGrigor, in Md, heir to mo Frances McGrigor or Murray, w of Patrick Murray writer in Glasgow, d. 24 Dec.1848, reg. 3 Nov.1851.

1803. Murray, Alexander McGrigor, in Md, heir to fa Patrick Murray, writer in Glasgow, d. 31 July 1836, reg. 22 Dec.1851.

1804. Murray, Amelia, da of William Murray, in Quebec, heir to grandfa William Murray, in Buckhaven Fife, reg. 9 Sep.1805.

1805. Murray, Archibald, in Up Can, heir to grandfa John Murray of Kinloch, in Glenquaich Perthshire, reg. 12 Sep.1848.

1806. Murray, Elizabeth, da of William Murray, in Quebec, heir to grandfa William Murray, in Buckhaven Fife, reg. 9 Sep.1805.

1807. Murray, George Ferguson, merchant, in Racine Wisc, heir to fa John Murray, in Ballus Mintlaw Aberdeenshire, d. 7 May 1856, reg. 8 Aug.1868.

1808. Murray, Gordon H, in Cal, heir to aunt Alie Murray or Moffat, in Dumfries, reg. 8 Nov.1854.

1809. Murray or Shepherd, Grizel, in Montreal, heir to bro Richard Murray, reg. 23 Nov.1838.

1810. Murray, James, in Md, heir to bro John Murray, writer in Glasgow, d. 13 Aug.1862, reg. 21 Dec.1865.

1811. Murray, James, in Joppa Md, heir to bro John Murray, writer in Glasgow, d. 13 Aug.1862, reg. 16 Dec.1875.

1812. Murray or Schawfield, Jane, w of Alexander Schawfield physician, in Va, heir to grandfa John Schawfield, merchant in Edinburgh, reg. 10 Apr.1799.

1813. Murray or Stevenson, Joan, w of Hamilton Stevenson, in Jamaica, heir to grandfa William Bell, cooper in Leith Mid Lothian, reg. 25 June 1782.

1814. Murray, John, in St Kitts, heir to fa William Murray, merchant in Aberdeen, reg. 4 July 1792.

1815. Murray, John, accountant, in Edinburgh, heir to bro Gilbert Murray, in Jamaica, reg. 7 July 1837.

1816. Murray, John, accountant, in Edinburgh, heir to bro Andrew Murray, in Jamaica, reg. 7 July 1837.

1817. Murray, John, slater, in Auchtermuchty Fife, heir to bro James Murray, slater in Charleston SC, d. 27 June 1857, reg. 25 Jan.1866.

1818. Murray, John, plasterer, in Maddiston NA, heir to sis Margaret Murray, in Moffat Dumfries-shire, d. 2 June 1868, reg. 1 May 1869.

1819. Murray, John, in Auburn NY, heir to fa James Murray, in Glenside of Badrochwood, d. 6 Apr.1862, reg. 6 July 1874.

1820. Murray, Lewis Wilmot, in St Louis, heir to fa Peter Findlator Murray, in Perry Co Oh, d. 20 June 1855, reg. 8 Aug.1873.

1821. Murray, William, farmer, in NY, heir to fa John Murray, baker in Edinburgh, reg. 2 Apr.1857.

1822. Murray, William, farmer, in Wisc, heir to sis Margaret Murray, in Moffat Dumfries-shire, d. 2 June 1868, reg. 1 May 1869.

1823. Murray, William, in Bearsbrook Ottawa, heir to grand-uncle Alexander Minnoch jr, in Blackcraig, d. 6 Mar.1847, reg. 18 Mar.1879.

1824. Muschett, Robert, in Jamaica, heir to aunt Eleanora Bethune, reg. 29 Jan.1799.

1825. Myles, Alexander, in America, heir to bro John Myles, in Hillbank Dundee Angus, reg. 8 Sep.1789.

1826. Myles, James, mechanic, in NY, heir to fa James Myles, weaver in Dundee Angus, reg. 24 June 1859.

1827. Nairn, Christiana, in Murraybay Can, heir to bro Thomas Nairn, Capt 49th Regt, reg. 28 Apr.1815.
1828. Nairn, John, carpenter, in Goderich Can, heir to James McDonald, gardener, reg. 7 July 1856.
1829. Nairne or Blackburn, Mary, w of A Blackburn, in Murraybay Can, heir to bro Thomas Nairn, Capt 49th Regt, reg. 28 Apr.1815.
1830. Napier, James, goldsmith, in Glasgow, heir to bro William Napier, surgeon in Charleston SC, reg. 30 May 1735.
1831. Napier, Sir James, Surgeon General, in America, heir to nephew James Robertson, in Montrose Angus, reg. 15 Mar.1787.
1832. Neilson, William, in Valcartier Quebec, heir to uncle William Neilson, in Gatehouse Kirkcudbrightshire, d. 8 Sep.1857, reg. 8 Nov.1861.
1833. Nelson, William Ball, sailmaker, in NY, heir to grand-aunt Jean Corner or Murray, in Leven Fife, reg. 19 Dec.1842.
1834. Ness, Ida Malvina, in NY, heir to grand-uncle Benjamin Bell, in Rosebank Dumfries-shire, d. 3 May 1872, reg. 2 Dec.1873.
1835. Newlands or Chalmers, Margaret, w of John Chalmers laborer, in Edinburgh, heir to bro John Newlands, in Jamaica, reg. 17 Aug.1812.
1836. Nichol, John, in La Salle Ill, heir to bro Henry Nichol, in Ayr, d. May 1851, reg. 19 Nov.1867.
1837. Nicholson, Francis, surveyor, in NY, heir to bro James Nicholson, surgeon in Mauchline Ayrshire, reg. 25 June 1850.
1838. Nicholson, Richard, in Brooklyn NY, heir to mo Mary Fawcett or Nicholson, wid of John Nicholson tailor in Edinburgh then NY, d. 6 Dec.1865, reg. 6 Dec.1869.
1839. Nicol or Richardson, Christina, w of Matthew Richardson, in Ill, heir to fa Andrew Nicol, farmer in Cleughhead, reg. 22 Jan.1867.
1840. Nicol, James, in Grenada, heir to fa Benjamin Nicol, wheelwright in Falkirk Stirlingshire, reg. 13 Jan.1837.
1841. Nicol or Jefferson, Janet, w of Martin Jefferson, in Ownes Ill, heir to fa Andrew Nicol, farmer in Cleughhead, reg. 22 Jan.1867.
1842. Nicol, Robert, ship carpenter, in America, heir to mo Frances Morton or Nicol, in Falkirk Stirlingshire, d. 1 July 1855, reg. 11 May 1861.
1843. Nicol, Robert, in St Thomas Up Can, heir to fa William Nicol, brazier in Fountainbridge Edinburgh, d. 12 Mar.1830, reg. 17 Feb.1874.
1844. Nicol, William, farmer, in Can W, heir to fa Andrew Nicol, farmer in Cleughhead, reg. 22 Jan.1867.
1845. Nicoll, James Brydon, heir to fa Thomas Nicoll, shipowner in Jamaica then Dundee Angus, reg. 19 June 1839.
1846. Nicoll, John, bridge inspector, in Palmerston Ont, heir to bro Robert Nicoll, painter in New Rattray, d. 1 Jan.1881, reg. 9 Feb.1882.
1847. Nimmo, Robert, in Falkirk Stirlingshire, heir to fa William Nimmo, merchant in Va, reg. 26 Sep.1817.

1848. Nisbet or Fraser, Elizabeth Isabella, w of Andrew Fraser, in Ill, heir to nephew Thomas Nisbet, in 5 Gayfield Sq Edinburgh, d. 11 July 1862, reg. 7 May 1863.

1849. Niven, George, police officer, in NY, heir to fa George Niven, grocer in NY, reg. 17 Mar.1859.

1850. Noble or Campbell, Isabella Jane, w of W D Campbell NP, in Quebec, heir to mo Geils Donald or Noble, wid of Lt George Noble RN in Greenock Renfrewshire, reg. 10 Aug.1863.

1851. Norflect, Nathaniel, in Va, heir to mo Janet Wilson or Norflect, w of Thomas Norflect tobacco overseer in Va, reg. 28 Oct.1790.

1852. Normand, Joseph, in Worcester Mass, heir to grandfa Joseph Normand, wright in Edinburgh then America, d. Oct.1852, reg. 9 Jan.1871.

1853. Norval or French, Agnes, in Davenport Ia, heir to mo Isabella Lockerby or Norval, w of James Norval ironfounder in Davenport, d. 1835, reg. 30 Nov.1882.

1854. Norval, John, in Can, heir to nephew William Norval, brushmaker in Glasgow then Can, reg. 19 May 1841.

1855. Notman, George, in Can W, heir to grandfa George Notman, in Ecclefechan Dumfries-shire, d. 29 Nov.1833, reg. 6 Oct.1858.

1856. O'Neill, Charles Henry, sailmaker, in Portsmouth America, heir to grandmo Elizabeth Lovie or O'Neill, w of Charles O'Neill cabinetmaker in St Ivox Ayrshire, d. 1817, reg. 16 Jan.1861.

1857. O'Neill, John, in Roxbury Boston , heir to uncle Anthony O'Neill, statuarymaker in Edinburgh, d. 7 Sep.1849, reg. 13 Feb.1851.

1858. Officer, William Walker, in Muirkirk Ayrshire, heir to bro James Officer, in Jamaica, d. 15 Nov.1828, reg. 27 June 1865.

1859. Ogilvie, Elizabeth, in Aberdeen, heir to bro James Ogilvie, in America then London, reg. 8 Dec.1832.

1860. Ogilvie, Jane, in Montrose Angus, heir to uncle Robert Ogilvie, wright in Heatherwick Angus then Jamaica, reg. 22 Feb.1827.

1861. Ogilvie, Jean Fletcher, in Aberdeen, heir to bro James Ogilvie, in America then London, reg. 8 Dec.1832.

1862. Ogilvie, Margaret, in Aberdeen, heir to bro James Ogilvie, in America then London, reg. 8 Dec.1832.

1863. Ogilvie, William, doctor, in Va, heir to mo Janet Webster or Ogilvie, wid of William Ogilvie in Shielhill, reg. 27 Apr.1713.

1864. Oliphant, David, in Jamaica, heir to uncle John Oliphant, merchant in Leith Mid Lothian, reg. 7 Dec.1809.

1865. Oliphant, David, in Jamaica, heir to fa David Oliphant, merchant in Edinburgh, reg. 7 Dec.1809.

1866. Oliphant, David, painter, in Charleston SC, heir to grandfa David Nevay, merchant in Edinburgh, reg. 9 June 1828.

1867. Oliphant, John, in Kingston Up Can, heir to fa William Oliphant, farm servant in Wedderbrae, reg. 23 Oct.1828.

1868. Oliphant or Duffus, Magdalene, w of Adam Duffus, in Bosauquet Can, heir to fa James Watson, baker in Dundee Angus, d. 16 Feb.1843, reg. 8 Jan.1867.

1869. Oliphant of Bachilton, Janet, heir to sis Margaret Oliphant or Cumming, wid of Alexander Mackenzie in Jamaica, reg. 1801.

1870. Oliver, Thomas, smith, in America, heir to fa Thomas Oliver, nailer in Denholm Roxburghshire, reg. 28 Apr.1858.

1871. Oliver, William, dyer, in Jedburgh Roxburghshire then Edinburgh, heir to sis Mary Oliver, in NY, reg. 5 Nov.1846.

1872. Omand or Mackay, Ann, wid of William MacLeod Mackay planter, in WI, heir to fa Magnus Omand, shipmaster in Orkney then Liverpool, d. 4 Feb.1829, reg. 18 June 1879.

1873. Orme jr, Peter, shoemaker & farmer, in Kennoway Fife then Can, heir to uncle Alexander Blyth, tailor in Kennoway, d. 6 Aug.1853, reg. 2 June 1862.

1874. Ormond or Gregory, Margaret, wid of Capt Charles Gregory, in Va, heir to bro Henry Ormond, reg. 5 Nov.1790.

1875. Orr, Alexander Sneddon, in Vancouver Is, heir to fa Alexander Orr, overseer in Gartsherrie Coatbridge Lanarkshire, d. 15 Apr.1859, reg. 20 Dec.1881.

1876. Orr, Hugh, in Bridgewater America, heir to bro Robert Orr, innkeeper in Lochwinnoch Renfrewshire, reg. 17 Sep.1795.

1877. Orr, William, surgeon, in Rutland Vale Estate St Vincent, heir to fa William Orr, farmer in Busbie Renfrewshire then Irvine Ayrshire, reg. 16 Mar.1862.

1878. Osborne, James, in Up Can, heir to fa Robert Osburne, in Waterhaughs Ayrshire, d. 14 Feb.1819, reg. 3 Apr.1856.

1879. Oswald or Burns, Margaret, w of John Burns, in Can W, heir to Mary Oswald or Wilson, in Larbert Stirlingshire, reg. 19 Nov.1860.

1880. Ovans, Thomas, in Ormiston Lower Can, heir to fa David Ovans, in Ormiston, d. 26 Jan.1859, reg. 6 Nov.1862.

1881. Owen, Robert Dale, in NY, heir to fa Robert Owen, in Sevenoaks Kent , d. 17 Nov.1858, reg. 22 Dec.1874.

1882. Pagan, William, merchant, in St John NB, heir to fa William Pagan, sugar refiner in Glasgow, reg. 15 Oct.1790.

1883. Page, James, teacher, in Peterhead Aberdeenshire, heir to cousin Helenus Page, millwright in Jamaica, reg. 10 Mar.1837.

1884. Pandrich, George, farmer, in Chester Co USA, heir to mo Grizel Ramsay or Pandrich, w of W Pandrich manufacturer in Dundee Angus, d. 10 Apr.1840, reg. 8 Dec.1870.

1885. Panton, David Brooke, minister, in Jamaica, heir to mo Sophia Morrieson or Panton, wid of Archdeacon Richard Panton in Jamaica, d. 12 Aug.1863, reg. 7 Jan.1864.

1886. Panton, James, in SC, heir to uncle Alexander Panton, surgeon in Glasgow, reg. 16 Nov.1842.

1887. Park or Macauley, Agnes, wid of Robert Macauley farmer, in Can W, heir to cousin David Bowman, in Glasgow, d. 19 May 1867, reg. 15 Dec.1868.

1888. Park, David Boyd, sailmaker, in Norfolk Va, heir to fa David Park, in Peebles, reg. 31 July 1837.

1889. Park, James, planter, in Jamaica, heir to fa Walter Park, cooper in Greenock Renfrewshire, reg. 19 Sep.1807.

1890. Park, John Marcellus, in Bergen NJ, heir to grandmo Catherine Bryce, in Blairlogie, reg. 9 Mar.1835.

1891. Park or Headrick, Mary, w of Peter Headrick, in Can, heir to sis Lillias Park, in Dunoon Argyll, reg. 6 Mar.1863.

1892. Park or Headrick, Mary, w of Peter Headrick, in Can, heir to sis Margaret Park, in Dunoon Argyll, reg. 6 Mar.1863.

1893. Park, Walter, in NY, heir to gt grandfa Walter Pasley, tanner in Langholm Dumfries-shire, reg. 2 Dec.1851.

1894. Parker, James, merchant, in Va, heir to fa Patrick Parker, ship carpenter in Port Glasgow Renfrewshire, reg. 24 Aug.1754.

1895. Parker, John R, in Clam Cove Deer Is NA, heir to bro George Parker, in Clam Cove, reg. 31 Dec.1836.

1896. Parker, William, merchant, in Montreal, heir to fa Hugh Parker, merchant in Kilmarnock Ayrshire, reg. 14 Nov.1787.

1897. Parlane, Robert, in Helensburgh Dunbartonshire, heir to bro Alexander Parlane, merchant in Montreal then Liverpool, d. 12 May 1847, reg. 6 June 1851.

1898. Paterson, Archibald, farmer, in Santa Clara Cal, heir to aunt Janet Baxter or Brown, w of Peter Brown farmer in Broadoak Shropshire England, d. 9 Apr.1843, reg. 25 June 1868.

1899. Paterson, Archibald, farmer, in Santa Clara Cal, heir to aunt Christian Baxter, in Prestonpans E Lothian, d. 6 May 1860, reg. 27 May 1871.

1900. Paterson, Isobel, w of Peter Paterson merchant, in Greenock Renfrewshire, heir to uncle Andrew Spreull, merchant in Gosport Va, reg. 1 Feb.1777.

1901. Paterson or Bain, Jessie Mary, w of James Bain, in Toronto, heir to fa T Paterson, in Edinburgh, d. 21 Nov.1882, reg. 7 July 1883.

1902. Paterson, John, nailer, in St Ninian's Stirlingshire then Ill, heir to fa James Paterson, nailer in St Ninian's, reg. 11 June 1851.

1903. Paterson, John William, in Toronto, heir to fa Archibald Paterson, in Toronto, d. 15 Oct.1851, reg. 12 Jan.1865.

1904. Paterson, Joshua, MD, in Glasgow, heir to bro Charles Paterson, surgeon in Jamaica, reg. 22 May 1844.

1905. Paterson, Marion, da of William Paterson, in Jamaica, heir to grand-uncle David Milligan of Dalskairth, reg. 12 Dec.1800.
1906. Paterson, Mary, da of William Paterson, in Jamaica, heir to grand-uncle David Milligan of Dalskairth, reg. 12 Dec.1800.
1907. Paterson, William, attorney, in Jamaica, heir to mo Barbara Montgomery or Paterson, w of Robert Paterson writer in Paisley Renfrewshire, reg. 1 June 1778.
1908. Paterson, William, heir to fa Thomas Paterson, ropemaker in Leith Mid Lothian then Baltimore Md, reg. 24 Feb.1780.
1909. Paterson, William Hugh, in Little River SC, heir to fa William Paterson, ex RN in Little River, reg. 3 Dec.1832.
1910. Paterson, William Glendinning, in Albany NY, heir to mo Isabel Paterson, w of Rev James Paterson in Calcutta, reg. 5 Apr.1866.
1911. Paton, Alexander, sailor, in Greenock Renfrewshire, heir to uncle John Paton, in Jamaica, reg. 11 Sep.1838.
1912. Paton, James, porter, in Can W, heir to sis Christian Paton, grocer in Dunfermline Fife, reg. 16 May 1854.
1913. Paton, John, in Lodi Wisc, heir to cousin John Paton, in Kinross, d. 8 Jan.1876, reg. 16 Feb.1881.
1914. Paton, Thomas, banker, in Can, heir to bro Peter Paton, in Lasswade Mid Lothian, d. 8 Oct.1857, reg. 15 July 1858.
1915. Paton, William, writer, in Stirling, heir to bro John Paton, in Jamaica, reg. 11 Sep.1838.
1916. Patrick, John, in USA, heir to sis Anne Patrick, in Kirkintilloch Dunbartonshire, d. 24 Jan.1873, reg. 24 May 1875.
1917. Patrick or Henly, Margaret Easson, w of W Dandridge Henly, in Va, heir to fa William Patrick, in Beith Ayrshire then Smithfield Va, reg. 28 May 1821.
1918. Patrick or Henly, Margaret Easson, w of Dandridge Henly, in Va, heir to uncle Robert Patrick of Shotts, merchant in Bermuda, reg. 14 July 1823.
1919. Patterson or Towart, Jane, w of J Patterson teacher, in NB, heir to fa William Towart, innkeeper in Glasgow, reg. 31 Mar.1820.
1920. Paul, Alexander, in Myersdale Pa, heir to grand-uncle Thomson Paul, WS in Edinburgh, d. 12 Nov.1876, reg. 3 Dec.1878.
1921. Paul, Andrew Walter, baker, in NY, heir to aunt Jean Goodlet, in Linlithgow W Lothian then NY, reg. 6 Aug.1838.
1922. Paul, Robert, blockprinter, in Aberdeen, heir to uncle Alexander Telfer, watchmaker in Antigua, reg. 24 Jan.1806.
1923. Paxton, Adam, in Allen's Corner Montreal, heir to bro Andrew Paxton, tinsmith in Duns Berwickshire, d. 4 Aug.1861, reg. 12 Jan.1878.
1924. Paxton or Williamson, Jean, wid of William Williamson, in USA, heir to Thomas Paxton, staymaker in Raggiewhat, reg. 7 May 1852.

1925. Pearson, James, merchant, in Montreal, heir to bro William Pearson, writer in Glasgow, reg. 15 Jan.1819.

1926. Peden, Alexander, in Montreal, heir to mo Elizabeth Haddow or Peden, w of Alexander Peden wright in Newmilns Ayrshire, d. 30 July 1854, reg. 11 Oct.1881.

1927. Peebles, William, in San Francisco , heir to fa Charles Peebles, writer in Glasgow, d. 16 Jan.1844, reg. 17 Aug.1864.

1928. Penman, Andrew, in Jamaica, heir to bro David Penman, s of Andrew Penman bookseller in Glasgow, reg. 21 Jan.1846.

1929. Pennycook, Robert, in Westmoreland Jamaica, heir to uncle Robert Fullerton, in Edinburgh, reg. 16 Jan.1823.

1930. Percy, Robert, merchant, in NY, heir to mo Mary Paton or Percy, in Kilmarnock then Cornhill Ayrshire, d. 15 Apr.1860, reg. 19 Feb.1861.

1931. Perry, William Alexander, in Olathe Kan, heir to fa James Perry, MD in Jerseyville Ill, d. 18 May 1859, reg. 16 Dec.1878.

1932. Peter, Walter, merchant, in Va, heir to bro David Peter, shipmaster in Glasgow, reg. 30 Nov.1787.

1933. Peterkin, William, in America, heir to fa John Peterkin, house carpenter in Invergordon Ross & Cromarty, reg. 15 Nov.1843.

1934. Petrie, George, stove manufacturer, in NY, heir to fa James Petrie, tinsmith in Forres Morayshire, reg. 8 Apr.1837.

1935. Petrie, William, in Philadelphia, heir to grandfa Walter Lumsdane, watchmaker in Cupar Fife, reg. 28 Dec.1792.

1936. Pew, Alexander, in Jamaica, heir to fa Alexander Pew, blockmaker in Leith Mid Lothian, reg. 3 May 1819.

1937. Pewtrie, Alexander Oliphant, in Belleville Can, heir to aunt Magdalene Oliphant or Watson, wid of John Watson baker in Dundee Angus, reg. 15 Nov.1837.

1938. Philip, Alexander, builder, in Avondale NJ, heir to Isobel Graham, wid of John Graham tenant farmer in Breich W Lothian, reg. 14 July 1879.

1939. Philip, George, in Braugham Ont, heir to fa Thomas Philip, in New Byth King Edward Aberdeenshire, d. 2 Jan.1874, reg. 9 June 1880.

1940. Philip, James, in Ont, heir to sis Jane Philip, teacher in Keith Hall Aberdeenshire, d. 30 Mar.1850, reg. 16 July 1875.

1941. Philip, Richard, in Avondale NJ, heir to Isobel Graham, wid of John Graham tenant farmer in Breich W Lothian, reg. 14 July 1879.

1942. Philips, George, in Jamaica, heir to fa William Philips, mason in Hawick Roxburghshire, reg. 1 Dec.1809.

1943. Pirie, George, in Can, heir to bro Thomas Pirie, s of George Pirie merchant in Aberdeen, reg. 6 Apr.1841.

1944. Pirie, James, in Trinidad, heir to mo Ann Donaldson or Pirie, w of John Pirie merchant in Aberdeen, reg. 13 Nov.1813.

1945. Pirie, James, in Trinidad, heir to fa John Pirie, merchant in Aberdeen, reg. 13 Nov.1813.

1946. Pitbladdo, Charles Bruce, in Portsmouth NH, heir to fa Colin Pitbladdo, in Garalands Dunfermline Fife, d. 5 June 1871, reg. 10 Oct.1881.

1947. Playfair, James Spiers, merchant, in Toronto, heir to fa James Playfair, merchant in Glasgow, d. 1 Jan.1866, reg. 22 Jan.1867.

1948. Playfair, John Spiers, merchant, in Toronto, heir to fa James Playfair, merchant in Glasgow, d. 11 Jan.1866, reg. 25 Apr.1870.

1949. Pollock, John Reid, in Up Can, heir to mo Anne White or Pollock, reg. 23 Apr.1859.

1950. Pollock, John Reid, in Up Can, heir to aunt Elizabeth White, reg. 23 Apr.1859.

1951. Pollock, John Reid, in Up Can, heir to aunt Janet White or Riddoch, reg. 23 Apr.1859.

1952. Porteous or Burnet, Charlotte, w of Rev John S Burnet, in Brantford Can, heir to bro Robert Porteous, in Dumfries, reg. 2 Feb.1864.

1953. Porteous, John, merchant, in NY, heir to fa John Porteous, feuar in Muthil Perthshire, reg. 13 Aug.1793.

1954. Porteous, John, in Kirkwall Can, heir to uncle John Gillespie, in Whitletts St Quivox Ayrshire, reg. 26 Jan.1855.

1955. Porteous, William, in Kinburn Can W, heir to sis Helen Porteous or Craw, w of Alexander Heron Craw in Southport, d. 20 May 1866, reg. 14 Feb.1870.

1956. Porteous, William, in Kinburn Fitzroy Can W, heir to bro James Porteous, s of William Porteous innkeeper in Kirtlebridge Dumfries-shire, d. 1 May 1846, reg. 21 Feb.1870.

1957. Porter, Henry, in NA, heir to fa Henry Porter, printer in Edinburgh, reg. 7 July 1856.

1958. Porter, William, in Va, heir to cousin Ann Finlay, da of James Finlay of Wallyford in E Lothian, d. Nov.1809, reg. 18 Dec.1811.

1959. Porter, William, in Va, heir to cousin Janet Finlay, da of James Finlay of Wallyford in E Lothian, d. Nov.1809, reg. 18 Dec.1811.

1960. Pow, Andrew, laborer, in Innerleithen Peebles-shire, heir to cousin Robert Ferguson, in Jamaica, reg. 24 June 1856.

1961. Pow, John, weaver, in Howford, heir to cousin Robert Ferguson, in Jamaica, reg. 24 June 1856.

1962. Pringle, James, in Can, heir to aunt Margaret Monilaws or Hood, w of J Hood tenant farmer in Long Yester, reg. 1 Aug.1843.

1963. Proudfoot, Laurence, physician, in NY, heir to uncle George Proudfoot of Balbuchty, merchant in Perth, reg. 2 June 1855.

1964. Purse, John, merchant, in Quebec, heir to fa Alexander Purse, tailor in Elgin Morayshire, reg. 11 Apr.1794.

1965. Purse, John, merchant, in Quebec, heir to grandfa William Blanchill, tailor in Elgin Morayshire, reg. 11 Apr.1794.

1966. Purves, Robert Ker, seaman, in Philadelphia, heir to fa Alexander Purves, shoemaker in Dunbar E Lothian, d. 13 Dec.1861, reg. 26 Oct.1863.

1967. Purvis, John, in Columbia SC, heir to fa Burridge Purvis, in N Glassmount, reg. 16 May 1825.

1968. Rae, George, in America, heir to grandfa George Rae, blacksmith in Rosehearty Aberdeenshire, d. 1825, reg. 6 Apr.1875.

1969. Rae, George, in Dow City Ia, heir to fa Thomas Rae, weaver in Kettlebridge Fife, d. 28 Dec.1882, reg. 13 Sep.1883.

1970. Rae, James, in Raehills Can W, heir to bro John Rae, in Ecclefechan Dumfries-shire, d. 20 Feb.1843, reg. 6 Apr.1861.

1971. Rae, John, in NA then Stromness Orkney, heir to grandfa John Rae of Gorseness, in Orkney, d. 2 Oct.1834, reg. 1 Mar.1862.

1972. Rae, John, in NA then Gorseness Orkney, heir to fa William Rae of Gorseness, d. 19 Jan.1845, reg. 7 July 1862.

1973. Rae or Myrick, Louisa, w of Josiah Myrick, in Portland Ore, heir to bro John Rae of Gorseness, in Orkney, d. 6 Oct.1867, reg. 9 Sep.1870.

1974. Rae or Wygart, Margaret, w of Theodore Wygart, in Portland Ore, heir to bro John Rae of Gorseness, in Orkney, d. 6 Oct.1867, reg. 9 Sep.1870.

1975. Rae of Park, John, heir to bro William Rae of Park, merchant in Jamaica, reg. 21 July 1837.

1976. Raeburn or Morice, Catherine, w of James Morice, in Montreal, heir to grandfa Robert Marnoch, wright in Aberdeen, reg. 11 Nov.1853.

1977. Ralston, Alexander, in Bethel Vt, heir to fa Alexander Ralston, merchant in America, reg. 19 Jan.1821.

1978. Ralston, George, in Philadelphia, heir to uncle John Ralston, minister in Duns Berwickshire, reg. 12 Dec.1839.

1979. Ralston, John Campbell, VS, in Edinburgh then NY, heir to grandmo Ann McGregor or Wemyss, in Edinburgh, reg. 30 July 1855.

1980. Ramsay, John, in Mass, heir to bro James Ramsay, in Stewarton Ayrshire, reg. 8 Oct.1800.

1981. Ramsay or Allan, Mary J, w of John B Allan, in USA, heir to grandfa William Kerr, innkeeper in Ayr, reg. 25 July 1854.

1982. Ramsay, Robert, in Montreal, heir to bro David Ramsay, merchant in Leith Mid Lothian, reg. 3 May 1850.

1983. Rankin or Hyndman, Janet, w of J Hyndman, in America, heir to uncle Richard Kirkland, weaver in Airdrie Lanarkshire, d. 30 Dec.1812, reg. 10 Apr.1848.

1984. Rankin or Hyndman, Janet, w of T Hyndman, in America, heir to uncle Richard Kirkland, weaver in Airdrie Lanarkshire, d. 30 Dec.1812, reg. 10 Apr.1848.

1985. Rankin, Thomas, in Smithfield RI, heir to uncle James Rankin, mason in Auchtermuchty Fife, d. 12 Oct.1860, reg. 2 Aug.1867.
1986. Rankine, Charles, farmer, in Tiny Toronto, heir to mo Agnes Miller or Rankine, w of Thomas Rankine farmer in Toronto, d. 10 July 1858, reg. 18 Dec.1868.
1987. Rattray, Alexander, in Trinidad, heir to uncle Henry Rattray, in Jamaica, reg. 28 Oct.1807.
1988. Rattray, Andrew, in Grandview Washington Co USA, heir to bro William Rattray, builder in Falkirk Stirlingshire, d. 16 Oct.1865, reg. 23 Nov.1869.
1989. Reid, David Robert, in La, heir to fa James Reid, in La, reg. 29 Oct.1858.
1990. Reid, David William, in NY, heir to grandfa Peter Reid, MD in Edinburgh, d. 8 June 1836, reg. 13 Feb.1878.
1991. Reid, David William, in NY, heir to John Mackenzie, glazier in Edinburgh, d. 1 Dec.1849, reg. 13 Feb.1878.
1992. Reid, David William, in NY, heir to Isobel Miller or Mackenzie, wid of John Mackenzie glazier in Edinburgh, d. 27 Aug.1846, reg. 13 Feb.1878.
1993. Reid, David William, in NY, heir to grandmo Christian Arnot or Reid, w of Dr Peter Reid in Edinburgh, d. 15 Dec.1851, reg. 24 Jan.1883.
1994. Reid, Donald, in Denver Col, heir to mo Catherine Mackenzie or Reid, wid of Alexander Mackenzie in Invergordon Ross & Cromarty, d. 3 Mar.1882, reg. 8 Aug.1882.
1995. Reid or Kemp, Elizabeth, wid of William Kemp, in Fergus Ont, heir to David Reid, warper in Brechin Angus, reg. 22 Feb.1878.
1996. Reid, George Lowe, civil engineer, in Hamilton Can W, heir to fa David Reid, merchant in Dunfermline Fife, reg. 17 Dec.1860.
1997. Reid or Barker, Helen, w of Garden Barker, in Tex, heir to fa James Reid, in La, reg. 27 Oct.1858.
1998. Reid, James, in La, heir to grandfa William Reid, merchant in Lossiemouth Morayshire, d. 30 Nov.1832, reg. 24 Aug.1857.
1999. Reid, James, laborer, in Ont, heir to grandfa Thomas Nisbet, in Midcalder Mid Lothian, reg. 20 Nov.1871.
2000. Reid or Sheldon, Janet, w of Charles Sheldon, in NY, heir to aunt Jean Reid, in Port Glasgow Renfrewshire, reg. 5 Nov.1857.
2001. Reid or Sheldon, Janet, w of Charles Sheldon, in NY, heir to fa John Reid, merchant in Port Glasgow Renfrewshire then NY, reg. 5 Nov.1857.
2002. Reid jr, Daniel, in Port Huron USA, heir to uncle John Reid, sewing agent in Lochwinnoch Renfrewshire, d. 22 Apr.1867, reg. 1 Sep.1874.
2003. Reid or Scott, Margaret, in Paisley Renfrewshire, heir to bro George Reid, merchant in Wilmington NC, reg. 17 Oct.1846.

2004. Reid or Smith, Margaret, w of Willes L Smith, in USA, heir to fa James Smith, in La, reg. 29 Oct.1858.

2005. Reid, Margaret Anne, in Westminster Can, heir to fa William Reid, merchant in Llanbryde Morayshire, d. 12 May 1855, reg. 17 Dec.1875.

2006. Reid or Kerr, Mary, w of John Kerr, in NY, heir to fa John Reid, merchant in Port Glasgow Renfrewshire then NY, reg. 5 Nov.1857.

2007. Reid or Kerr, Mary, w of John Kerr, in NY, heir to aunt Jean Reid, in Port Glasgow Renfrewshire, reg. 5 Nov.1857.

2008. Renaud, Edward, in Washington NA, heir to grandfa John Craig, merchant in Glasgow, reg. 28 Nov.1865.

2009. Renfrew, John, in Greentown Pa, heir to nephew Robert Renfrew, smith in Pollockshaws Glasgow, reg. 16 Oct.1837.

2010. Renfrew, Robert, merchant, in NY, heir to fa Robert Renfrew, smith in Paisley Renfrewshire, d. 14 Nov.1831, reg. 30 Oct.1866.

2011. Rennie, William Frederick, in St John Newfoundland, heir to bro David Rennie, in London, d. 6 Feb.1865, reg. 22 Dec.1881.

2012. Renton, Alexander Haig, in America, heir to bro Robert Renton, customs officer in Leith Mid Lothian, d. 23 Oct.1874, reg. 18 May 1875.

2013. Renton, Henry, minister, in Kelso Roxburghshire then Jamaica, heir to fa William Renton, merchant in Edinburgh, reg. 10 Dec.1855.

2014. Renwick, Thomas, in Buffalo USA, heir to fa Thomas Renwick, tailor in Hawick Roxburghshire, reg. 23 Dec.1842.

2015. Renwick, William, merchant, in Davenport Ia, heir to mo Elizabeth Lockerby or Renwick, w of James Renwick in Ia, d. 4 Dec.1878, reg. 30 Nov.1882.

2016. Reoch, Robert, colormaker, in Riverpoint RI, heir to Bethia Tennant or Reoch, wid of Robert Reoch calico printer in Grahamston Renfrewshire, reg. 17 Sep.1875.

2017. Riach, Alexander Fridge, in NY, heir to fa Peter Riach, merchant in Forres Morayshire, d. 30 Aug.1864, reg. 14 Apr.1877.

2018. Riach, John James, farmer, in Emmetsburg Ia, heir to fa James Riach, minister in Clither, d. 16 Sep.1862, reg. 30 June 1882.

2019. Richardson or Hogg, Ann, w of George Hogg wright, in America, heir to fa John Richardson, smith in Edinburgh, reg. 21 Apr.1802.

2020. Richardson, William, in America, heir to uncle Matthew Richardson , in Guileburn Dumfries-shire, d. 19 Jan.1846, reg. 10 Sep.1846.

2021. Richardson, William, draper, in Liverpool, heir to uncle William Richardson, MD in WI, reg. 10 Aug.1857.

2022. Riddell, John, in Can W, heir to bro Robert Riddell, tea dealer in Glasgow, d. 19 Oct.1858, reg. 6 July 1859.

2023. Riddell, John, builder, in York Can, heir to Alexander Brownlee
       Hamilton, mason in Strathaven Lanarkshire, d. 5 Aug.1866, reg.
       16 Aug.1876.
2024. Riddell, Robert, mason, in Richmond Va, heir to fa Thomas Riddell,
       mason in Selkirk, d. 8 July 1853, reg. 3 July 1869.
2025. Riddell, William, tailor, in Can, heir to fa Walter Riddell, tailor in
       Hawick Roxburghshire, d. 11 Feb.1849, reg. 26 Sep.1856.
2026. Riddie, Andrew, merchant, in Jamaica, heir to sis Mary Riddie or
       Semple, wid of Gavin Semple in Castleview Avondale
       Lanarkshire, d. 18 Feb.1881, reg. 18 July 1881.
2027. Riddle, William, tailor, in Can W, heir to fa Robert Riddle, merchant
       in Galashiels Selkirkshire, reg. 30 July 1857.
2028. Riddler, John Jamieson, in Ill, heir to fa John Riddler, gardener in
       Aberdeen, d. 25 Nov.1843, reg. 4 Dec.1850.
2029. Ridley, David, in NB, heir to grand-uncle James Ridley sr, merchant in
       Leith Mid Lothian, d. 1804, reg. 14 Feb.1862.
2030. Rintoul, David, yeoman, in Beverly Can, heir to fa David Rintoul, in
       Beverly Can, d. 8 June 1872, reg. 21 Aug.1874.
2031. Rintoul or Kennedy, Helen, in NY, heir to bro Thomas Rintoul, saddler
       in Perth, reg. 24 Dec.1833.
2032. Rintoul, James Renwick, in Beverly Can, heir to fa David Rintoul, in
       Beverly Can, d. 8 June 1872, reg. 21 Aug.1874.
2033. Rintoul, James Renwick, in Beverly Can, heir to sis Janet Rintoul or
       Dykeman, w of Peter Dykeman in Galt Ont, d. 29 Dec.1872, reg.
       21 Aug.1874.
2034. Rintoul or Grummet, Margaret, w of Thomas Grummet, in Galt Ont,
       heir to fa David Rintoul, in Beverly Can, d. 8 June 1872, reg. 21
       Aug.1874.
2035. Rintoul, Robert, in Can E, heir to fa William Rintoul, minister in Up
       Can, reg. 2 Feb.1859.
2036. Rintoul, William, in Galt Can, heir to fa David Rintoul, in Beverly Can,
       d. 8 June 1872, reg. 21 Aug.1874.
2037. Ritchie, Adam, farmer, in Can, heir to fa John Ritchie, in Johnstone
       Renfrewshire, reg. 6 Mar.1838.
2038. Ritchie, Archibald Tucker, agent, in London, heir to fa Archibald Ritchie,
       merchant in Trinidad, reg. 11 May 1859.
2039. Ritchie, Archibald, in Reigate NA, heir to bro John Ritchie, shoemaker
       in Port Glasgow Renfrewshire then Boroondara Victoria, d. 22
       Mar.1860, reg. 11 Mar.1861.
2040. Ritchie, John, in Lynden Ont, heir to fa Alexander Ritchie, in Can, d. 17
       May 1862, reg. 17 Oct.1871.
2041. Ritchie, John, traveller, in Montreal, heir to mo Jessie Robertson or
       Ritchie, w of William Ritchie manufacturer in Ayr, d. 22
       Dec.1856, reg. 13 Oct.1873.

2042. Ritchie or Ronald, Margaret, w of James Ronald cabinetmaker, in America, heir to bro William Ritchie, sailor in Irvine Ayrshire, reg. 20 Feb.1807.

2043. Ritchie, William, in Baltimore, heir to bro James Ritchie, weaver in Perth, reg. 14 Aug.1799.

2044. Ritchie, William Alexander, in Lancaster USA, heir to granduncle John Ritchie, merchant in Govan Glasgow, reg. 19 Oct.1842.

2045. Ritchie, William Alexander, in Lancaster USA, heir to cousin Alexander Ritchie, in Govan Glasgow, reg. 19 Oct.1842.

2046. Ritchie, William Alexander, in Lancaster USA, heir to cousin John Ritchie, in Govan Glasgow, reg. 9 Nov.1842.

2047. Rob, Francis, surgeon, in Alexandria Jamaica, heir to remote cousin James McFarlane, farmer in Boghead, reg. 22 Sep.1840.

2048. Robb, Edmund Boyd, in NB, heir to uncle William Robb, clerk in Glasgow, d. 13 Apr.1845, reg. 26 Apr.1862.

2049. Robb, James, in King's College NB, heir to bro William Robb, clerk in Glasgow, reg. 24 Apr.1861.

2050. Robb, James, in Can W, heir to aunt Mary Robb or Adam, wid of George Adam in Aberdeen, d. 7 Oct.1872, reg. 17 Apr.1873.

2051. Roberts, Allen, in Airdrie Lanarkshire, heir to bro James Roberts, carter in Craig then America, reg. 27 Mar.1840.

2052. Robertson, Alexander, farmer, in Can W, heir to fa Donald Robertson, tenant farmer in Dalreich Inverness-shire, d. 22 May 1859, reg. 18 Oct.1861.

2053. Robertson, Alexander, bank manager, in London, heir to fa James Robertson, in Jamaica then Elgin Morayshire, d. 31 July 1816, reg. 12 Nov.1863.

2054. Robertson, Anthony, saddler, in Patterson NJ, heir to fa George Robertson, in Biggar Lanarkshire, d. 5 Sep.1847, reg. 20 Oct.1866.

2055. Robertson, Charles, in Point Livy Que, heir to sis Mary Robertson, in Ruthrieston Aberdeenshire, d. 21 May 1861, reg. 6 Aug.1861.

2056. Robertson, Daniel, in San Francisco, heir to fa John Robertson, weaver in Paisley Renfrewshire, d. 21 Oct.1873, reg. 3 June 1876.

2057. Robertson or Sully, Elizabeth, wid of M Sully, in Richmond USA, heir to James Gilchrist, architect in Edinburgh, reg. 10 Sep.1827.

2058. Robertson or Sully, Elizabeth, wid of M Sully, in Richmond USA, heir to sis Margaret Robertson or Gilchrist, wid of J Gilchrist architect in Edinburgh, reg. 10 Sep.1827.

2059. Robertson, Frederick William, in Waterloo Ia, heir to grand-aunt Elizabeth Archibald, in Portobello Mid Lothian, d. 4 June 1873, reg. 19 Sep.1877.

2060. Robertson, George, in Detroit Mich, heir to sis Jane Robertson, in Edinburgh, d. 3 Dec.1878, reg. 27 Jan.1880.

2061. Robertson, James, in Glenloin Arrocher Dunbartonshire, heir to uncle George Ogilvie, in Jamaica then Dundee Angus, reg. 2 Feb.1842.

2062. Robertson, James Duncan, teacher, in Jamaica, heir to bro William Robertson, in Jamaica, reg. 22 June 1859.

2063. Robertson, James Duncan, teacher, in Jamaica, heir to bro John Robertson, saddler in Jamaica, reg. 22 June 1859.

2064. Robertson, James, clerk, in Antigua, heir to grand-aunt Isabella Robertson, in Kinross, reg. 19 Dec.1867.

2065. Robertson, James, clerk, in Antigua, heir to grand-aunt Susan Robertson, in Kinross, reg. 19 Dec.1867.

2066. Robertson, Janet, in Wisc, heir to mo Elizabeth Wilson or Robertson, in Middleton, reg. 8 Apr.1852.

2067. Robertson or Boswell, Jessie Nettles, w of James Philip Boswell, in Camden SC, heir to fa Adam Robertson, in Camden SC, d. 11 Oct.1854, reg. 13 June 1873.

2068. Robertson, John, baker, in Philadelphia, heir to fa James Robertson, tenant farmer in Hill of Fortrose Ross & Cromarty, reg. 3 Sep.1832.

2069. Robertson, John, in Belton Bell Co Tex, heir to fa Johnston Robertson, watchman in Govan Silk Factory Glasgow, d. 23 Mar.1864, reg. 13 June 1867.

2070. Robertson, John, in Can, heir to mo Isabella Watson or Robertson, d. 25 June 1857, reg. 28 Aug.1874.

2071. Robertson, John, in Can, heir to David Robertson, chamberlain in Edinburgh, d. 24 Oct.1871, reg. 31 July 1874.

2072. Robertson, John, joiner, in San Francisco, heir to fa John Robertson, gardener in Govan Glasgow, d. 9 Sep.1845, reg. 3 Aug.1878.

2073. Robertson or Watt, Mary, w of James Watt baker, in NY, heir to cousin Catherine Blyth, in Abernethy, d. 7 Feb.1868, reg. 29 Apr.1868.

2074. Robertson, Methven, in Millbury Worcester USA, heir to aunt Margaret Methven or Whyte, wid of Robert Whyte in Leslie Fife, reg. 6 Nov.1856.

2075. Robertson of Struan, Alexander Gilbert, in Jamaica, heir to nephew George Robertson of Struan, in Perthshire, d. 3 Apr.1864, reg. 7 Feb.1868.

2076. Robertson or White, Pamela Hiler, w of C L White, in America, heir to Jane Robertson or Livingstone, wid of J Livingstone merchant in South Bridge Edinburgh, reg. 9 Feb.1860.

2077. Robertson, Peter, merchant, in Belleville Can, heir to fa David Robertson, minister in Kilmaurs Ayrshire, d. 10 June 1846, reg. 13 July 1848.

2078. Robertson or White, Rachael, wid of William White merchant, in Aberdeen, heir to bro Adam Topp, in Jamaica, d. 26 Aug.1868, reg. 11 Nov.1868.

2079. Robertson, Robert David, in Staten Is NY, heir to uncle David
Robertson, tax inspector in Kelso Roxburghshire, reg. 26 June
1860.
2080. Robertson, Sarah Ann, in Camden SC, heir to fa Adam Robertson, in
Camden SC, d. 11 May 1854, reg. 13 June 1873.
2081. Robertson, Thomas, in Greenwich NA, heir to mo Mary Alexander or
Robertson, wid of John S Robertson in Greenwich NA, d. 8
Feb.1857, reg. 4 June 1863.
2082. Robertson, William, planter, in NJ, heir to bro Patrick Robertson, Major
Scots Greys, reg. 27 Jan.1739.
2083. Robertson, William, in Petersburg Va, heir to grandfa James Mudie,
merchant in Arbroath Angus, reg. 29 Jan.1806.
2084. Robertson, William, in Petersburg NA, heir to fa William Robertson,
writer in Forfar Angus, reg. 17 May 1816.
2085. Robertson, William, merchant, in Va, heir to uncle David Robertson,
merchant in Arbroath Angus, reg. 28 Jan.1818.
2086. Robertson, William, yeoman, in Lanark Up Can, heir to bro John
Robertson, cook in HMS Duncan, reg. 26 July 1832.
2087. Robinson, John Hey, in Ellerslie Baltimore, heir to grand-aunt Janet
Duncan, in Newbigging Musselburgh Mid Lothian, d. 10 June
1865, reg. 6 Mar.1871.
2088. Robson, Charles, merchant, in NS, heir to fa James Robson, minister in
NS, d. 8 Dec.1838, reg. 22 June 1859.
2089. Robson, James, saddler, in St John NB, heir to grandfa Alexander Smith,
gardener in Potachy, reg. 17 Jan.1827.
2090. Robson, James, saddler, in St John NB, heir to grand-aunt Ann Clerihew,
da of John Clerihew forester in Potachy, reg. 21 Feb.1827.
2091. Rodger or Johnston, Agnes Berry, w of John Johnston farmer, in
Chatham Can, heir to grandfa Andrew Rodger, farmer in St
Monance Fife, reg. 16 Sep.1851.
2092. Rodger or Johnston, Agnes Berry, w of John Johnston farmer, in
Chatham Can, heir to gt grandfa David Rodger, merchant in St
Monance Fife, reg. 16 Sep.1851.
2093. Rodger or Johnston, Agnes Berry, w of John Johnston farmer, in
Chatham Can, heir to grandfa Andrew Rodger, weaver & merchant
in St Monance Fife, d. 19 Feb.1819, reg. 1 Nov.1853.
2094. Rodger, Euphame, heir to cousin Janet Rodger or Cuthill, wid of Adam
Cuthill sailor in Jamaica, reg. 1803.
2095. Rodger, Grizel, heir to cousin Janet Rodger, wid of Adam Cuthill sailor
in Jamaica, reg. 1803.
2096. Rodger, Isabella, heir to cousin Janet Rodger or Cuthill, wid of Adam
Cuthill sailor in Jamaica, reg. 1803.
2097. Rodger, James, in Cincinnati, heir to grandfa James Rodger, tailor in
Tranent Mid Lothian, d. 6 Jan.1845, reg. 12 Mar.1862.

2098. Rodger, John, merchant, in NB, heir to aunt Margaret Scott, in Greenock Renfrewshire, reg. 26 July 1839.
2099. Rodgers, Edward Bain, minister, in Toronto, heir to fa James Rodgers, in Kincardine-on-Forth Fife, d. 4 Mar.1871, reg. 3 Feb.1883.
2100. Rose, James, in Newmarket Cambridge England, heir to mo Catherine Miller or Rose, in Jamaica, d. 25 Dec.1861, reg. 9 Oct.1876.
2101. Rosier or Ross, Edward James, sailor, in Va, heir to grandfa Edward Rosier or Ross, in Sucquoy S Ronaldsay Orkney, reg. 9 Apr.1801.
2102. Ross or Garge, Alexander, dyker, in Kirkwall Orkney, heir to fa William Ross or Garge, in New Scotland Barbados, reg. 19 Nov.1683.
2103. Ross, Charles, merchant, in Antigua, heir to fa Walter Ross, WS, reg. 7 Dec.1789.
2104. Ross, Donald Proctor, NP, in Toronto, heir to uncle Donald Ross, merchant in Montreal, d. 1 Dec.1851, reg. 2 July 1868.
2105. Ross or Dewar, Fanny, in Oshawa Can, heir to fa James Ross, in Blainlie Roxburghshire, d. 25 Feb.1832, reg. 18 Aug.1874.
2106. Ross, George, planter, in Jamaica, heir to bro John Ross, advocate in Aberdeen, reg. 19 Aug.1797.
2107. Ross or Watson, Helen, w of James Watson ship carpenter, in America, heir to fa David Ross, wright in Anstruther Fife, reg. 23 Dec.1839.
2108. Ross, James, in Salt Lake Ut, heir to fa James Ross, weaver in Dunning Perthshire, d. 13 Nov.1868, reg. 20 Apr.1869.
2109. Ross, James Robertson, in Oshawa Can, heir to grandfa James Ross, in Blainslie Roxburghshire, d. 25 Feb.1832, reg. 22 July 1874.
2110. Ross, James, farmer, in Ross Ranch BC, heir to mo Agnes Livingston or Ross, w of Douglas Ross spirit dealer in Pollockshaws Glasgow, d. 19 July 1868, reg. 16 Feb.1880.
2111. Ross, John, merchant, in Charleston SC, heir to fa Henry Ross, writer in Lerwick Shetland, reg. 25 Feb.1808.
2112. Ross, John, in NB, heir to fa David Ross, cooper in Pultneytown Wick Caithness, d. 23 May 1822, reg. 22 Aug.1874.
2113. Ross, Philip Simpson, merchant, in Montreal, heir to fa Philip Ross, in Port Dundas Glasgow, reg. 18 Aug.1859.
2114. Ross, Roderick, in Can, heir to fa Donald Ross, dyker in Hill of Fortrose Ross & Cromarty, reg. 4 Sep.1855.
2115. Ross, William, in Montreal then Baltimore, heir to grand-uncle Hector Gallie, farmer in Easter Rarichies, reg. 7 Oct.1859.
2116. Ross or Cooper, William, in Ardgay Ross & Cromarty, heir to uncle James Ross or Cooper, in St Mary's Jamaica, d. 14 Feb.1844, reg. 12 Aug.1863.

2117. Ross, William, in Wilton Waseca Co Minn, heir to fa Donald Ross, cooper in Invergordon Ross & Cromarty, d. 12 Sep.1856, reg. 18 Dec.1869.

2118. Rossie, William Sutherland, in Ill, heir to fa John Rossie, fish curer in Orkney, d. 2 June 1856, reg. 14 Sep.1857.

2119. Rowand, Andrew, farmer, in Pollo Ill, heir to grandfa John Park, farmer in Gockston, d. 18 Aug.1828, reg. 22 July 1868.

2120. Rowat, John, in Can, heir to fa David Rowat, farmer in Campsie Stirlingshire, reg. 14 Mar.1845.

2121. Rowe, Robert, cabinetmaker, in NY, heir to mo Margaret Youngson or Rowe, w of Robert Rowe porter in Edinburgh, reg. 27 July 1818.

2122. Rowsay, John, goldsmith & jeweller, in Va, heir to uncle John Rowsay, s of John Rowsay of Dishes in Stronsay Orkney, reg. 1 June 1773.

2123. Roxburgh, Euphemia, in Up Can, heir to aunt Marjory Melville or Dun, reg. 19 May 1854.

2124. Roxburgh, William, merchant, in Quebec, heir to fa William Roxburgh, weaver in Kilmarnock Ayrshire, reg. 16 Dec.1783.

2125. Roy, Alexander, in Winona Miss, heir to mo Jean Duff or Roy, w of John Roy mason in Dundee Angus, d. 24 Dec.1867, reg. 3 July 1874.

2126. Russell or Rutan, Catherine, w of David Rutan, in NJ, heir to William Russell jr of Whiteside, reg. 31 Mar.1813.

2127. Russell or Rutan, Catherine, w of David Rutan, in NJ, heir to grandfa William Russell of Whiteside, reg. 31 Mar.1813.

2128. Russell, Hector, merchant, in Montreal, heir to fa John Russell, merchant in Montreal, reg. 11 Apr.1854.

2129. Russell, Janet, in Binnymyre East Barony of Kilsyth Stirlingshire, heir to cousin William Russell, surgeon in Jamaica, reg. 17 Oct.1766.

2130. Russell, John, in NJ, heir to fa William Russell, portioner in West Craig, reg. 17 Nov.1786.

2131. Russell, John, in San Francisco, heir to mo Janet Campbell or Russell, wid of David Russell weaver in Gallatown Kirkcaldy Fife, reg. 19 Apr.1853.

2132. Russell, John, in Kingston NY, heir to bro William Russell, in Grahams Rd Falkirk Stirlingshire, reg. 22 Oct.1860.

2133. Russell, John, in Grafton Can W, heir to sis Catherine Russell, in Tain Ross & Cromarty, d. 23 Dec.1861, reg. 6 Oct.1863.

2134. Russell, Robert, in Porter's Hill Can W, heir to fa James Russell, weaver in Longcroft Burn Denny Stirlingshire, d. 25 May 1814, reg. 3 Jan.1870.

2135. Russell or Drake, Ruhanna, w of Peter Drake, in NJ, heir to grandfa William Russell of Whiteside, reg. 31 Mar.1813.

2136. Russell or Drake, Ruth, w of Peter Drake, in Sussex NJ, heir to William Russell jr of Whiteside, reg. 6 July 1814.

2137. Russell or Sutton, Sarah, w of J Sutton, in Byram NA, heir to grandfa William Russell of Whiteside, reg. 31 Mar.1813.

2138. Russell or Sutton, Sarah, w of J Sutton, in Byram NA, heir to William Russell jr of Whiteside, reg. 6 July 1814.

2139. Russell, Thomas, in Can W, heir to mo Janet Paton or Russell, w of Thomas Russell in Can W, reg. 1 Sep.1859.

2140. Rutherford, James, miller, in Greely America, heir to grandfa Peter Black, mason in Crieff Perthshire, d. May 1849, reg. 6 July 1878.

2141. Rutherford, Janet Kirkwood, in Hamilton Can W, heir to fa James Rutherford, in Bo'ness W Lothian, d. 20 Feb.1859, reg. 4 June 1870.

2142. Rutherford or Coutts, Marion, w of John Coutts, in Hamilton Can W, heir to fa James Rutherford, in Bo'ness W Lothian, d. 20 Feb.1859, reg. 4 June 1870.

2143. Rutherford, William, merchant, in London, heir to bro James Rutherford, saddler in Fisherrow Edinburgh then NY, d. 1 Aug.1835, reg. 22 Jan.1855.

2144. Ruxton, William, in Lower Woolwich Can, heir to aunt Agnes Ruxton, in Arbroath Angus, d. 4 Apr.1868, reg. 7 Apr.1869.

2145. Saddler or Harries, Mary, w of Richard Harries, in Woollaston Gloucester England, heir to bro William Saddler, merchant in St Kitts, reg. 21 Feb.1781.

2146. Sampson, Samuel, currier, in Petersburg Va, heir to grand-uncle William Sampson, merchant in London, reg. 1 Dec.1828.

2147. Samson, Thomas, in Richmond Va, heir to sis Margaret Samson, in Edinburgh, d. 19 Dec.1860, reg. 2 July 1872.

2148. Sanders, William Blair, merchant, in Toronto, heir to cousin William Sanders, in Perth, d. 17 Sep.1860, reg. 7 Feb.1876.

2149. Sanderson, John, manufacturer, in Can W, heir to uncle John Sanderson, shoemaker in Galashiels Selkirkshire, d. 30 Apr.1847, reg. 10 Sep.1863.

2150. Sangster, John, in Trinidad, heir to fa James Sangster, in Mains of Pitrichie Old Meldrum Aberdeenshire, reg. 19 Nov.1808.

2151. Sangster, William, clerk, in Montreal, heir to grandfa John Christie, feuar in Macduff Banffshire, reg. 16 Feb.1810.

2152. Sanson, James, merchant, in Edinburgh then Can W, heir to bro Alexander Sanson, Inland Revenue in Portobello Edinburgh, d. 5 Sep.1863, reg. 11 Feb.1864.

2153. Saunders, William, gardener, in Baltimore, heir to fa David Saunders, gardener in Balgarvie, d. 8 July 1849, reg. 18 May 1852.

2154. Scobie, William, in Boston USA, heir to grandmo Catherine Tainsh or Scobie, in Auchterarder Perthshire, reg. 5 Mar.1830.

2155. Scott or McCallum, Ann H, in Quebec, heir to Janet Morrison or Orr, wid of Thomas Orr shipmaster in Greenock Renfrewshire, reg. 2 Apr.1830.

2156. Scott, Charles Robert, planter, in Alexandria America, heir to aunt Elizabeth Scott, in Edinburgh, reg. 29 Mar.1797.

2157. Scott, David, tailor, in NY, heir to fa David Scott, shoemaker in Arbroath Angus, reg. 30 May 1831.

2158. Scott, Elizabeth, heir to fa William Scott, in Edinburgh then Savannah USA, reg. 6 June 1831.

2159. Scott, James N, planter, in Jamaica, heir to fa John Scott, planter in Jamaica, reg. 23 Nov.1820.

2160. Scott, John, in Caledonia NA, heir to fa Robert Scott, miller in Roughheugh, reg. 10 Mar.1826.

2161. Scott, John, in Fredericksburg America, heir to sis Margaret Scott, in Greenock Renfrewshire, reg. 2 Oct.1840.

2162. Scott, John, in Can W, heir to bro James Scott, divinity student in Annan Dumfries-shire, reg. 15 Dec.1857.

2163. Scott, Kezia, heir to fa William Scott, in Edinburgh then Savannah USA, reg. 6 June 1831.

2164. Scott, Rebecca, wid of Adam Scott, in Jamaica, heir to grandfa Alexander Campbell, merchant in Glasgow, reg. 24 Nov.1817.

2165. Scott, Robert, watchmaker, in Va, heir to fa George Scott, baker in N Leith Mid Lothian, reg. 21 May 1779.

2166. Scott, Robert, cabinetmaker, in Boston, heir to fa William Scott, slater in Hawick Roxburghshire, d. 3 Feb.1866, reg. 18 June 1866.

2167. Scott, Robert, saddler, in Scotland Oakland Cal, heir to sis Isabella Scott, in Jedburgh Roxburghshire, d. 24 July 1867, reg. 10 Jan.1868.

2168. Scott, Thomas, in Jamaica, heir to fa John Scott, in Flowerbank Sanquhar Dumfries-shire, reg. 22 Apr.1839.

2169. Scott, Walter, in Ayr Can, heir to mo Janet Tillie or Scott, wid of William Scott in Newhallmains Middleburn, reg. 20 Apr.1855.

2170. Scott, Walter, in Ayr Can, heir to fa William Scott, in Newhallmains Middleburn, reg. 20 Apr.1855.

2171. Scott, William John, clerk, in Newfoundland, heir to fa James Scott, coastguard in Cornwall England, reg. 29 Apr.1843.

2172. Scott, William, in NY, heir to fa Walter Scott, weaver in Hawick Roxburghshire then Dovemount, reg. 17 Feb.1845.

2173. Scott, William, yeoman, in Wilmot Can, heir to bro David Scott, in United Cottages Holborn Pl Aberdeen, reg. 18 July 1864.

2174. Scott, William, yeoman, in Wilmot Can, heir to bro James Scott, farmer in Achath Aberdeenshire, d. 18 Jan.1815, reg. 10 Oct.1864.

2175. Scott, William, carpenter, in Oneonta NY, heir to mo Mary Armstrong or Scott, w of Robert Scott in Hamden, d. 1 June 1865, reg. 8 Apr.1878.

2176. Seaton, John Smith, in Yarmouth NS, heir to grandmo Janet Cowan or Smith, wid of Andrew Smith in Longmyre, d. 1825, reg. 4 Apr.1866.

2177. Seatter, James, farmer, in Holland Berkeley Ont, heir to fa James Seatter, shoemaker in Kirkwall Orkney, d. 1855, reg. 23 June 1873.

2178. Sellick, Francis William, in Paw Paw Mich, heir to fa James Sellick, excise supervisor in Burntisland Fife, d. 8 Apr.1876, reg. 7 Mar.1877.

2179. Semple or Choate, Christina, w of Henry Choate machinist, in S Danvers NA, heir to mo Mary Robertson or Semple, w of James Semple currier in Ipswich NA, d. 5 Aug.1857, reg. 13 July 1864.

2180. Semple or Caldwell, Janet Ralph, wid of J Caldwell leathermerchant, in Salem, heir to mo Mary Roberton or Semple, w of J Semple currier in Ipswich NA, d. 5 Aug.1857, reg. 13 July 1864.

2181. Semple, John Roberton, in Charlestown NA, heir to mo Mary Roberton or Semple, w of James Semple leather merchant in Ipswich NA, d. 5 Aug.1857, reg. 13 June 1864.

2182. Seton, John, s of William Seton WS, heir to bro William Seton, surgeon in Jamaica, reg. 17 Apr.1781.

2183. Seton, John Gordon, farmer, in Quebec, heir to aunt Sarah Seton or Robertson, w of William Robertson dyer in Largs Ayrshire, d. 12 Dec.1838, reg. 18 June 1872.

2184. Shand, William, in Jefferson Co Oh, heir to fa John Shand, tenant farmer in Wolfstar E Lothian, d. 14 Nov.1859, reg. 28 Jan.1869.

2185. Shand, William, in Jefferson Co Oh, heir to gt grandfa John Mathieson, tenant farmer in Kippielaw St Boswells Roxburghshire, d. pre 10 Jan.1787, reg. 13 June 1870.

2186. Shand, William, in Crichton Mains Edinburgh then Columbus Oh, heir to fa John Shand, tenant farmer in Wolfstar E Lothian, reg. 25 Aug.1875.

2187. Shankland or McKinlay, Janet, in America, heir to fa Mungo McKinlay, heritor in Rothesay Bute, reg. 28 Mar.1832.

2188. Shannon, Alexander, in Carbondale America, heir to grandfa James Thomson, in Dalbeattie Kirkcudbrightshire, d. 1816, reg. 17 Oct.1866.

2189. Sharpe, John, planter, in Jamaica, heir to mo Emilia Stennet or Sharpe, w of John Sharpe of Grantham in Jamaica, reg. 5 Oct.1860.

2190. Shaw, David, shipping agent, in Montreal, heir to mo Agnes Jamieson or Shaw, in Helensburgh Dunbartonshire, d. 19 May 1862, reg. 19 Mar.1872.

2191. Shaw, George, in NY, heir to fa George Shaw, hotelkeeper in Nairn, d. 2 Feb.1879, reg. 21 May 1879.

2192. Shaw or Shawfield, Jane, w of Alexander Shaw or Shawfield physician, in Va, heir to grandfa John Shawfield, merchant in Edinburgh, reg. 10 Apr.1799.

2193. Shaw, Jessie, in NB, heir to George Shaw, minister in Hamilton Lanarkshire, reg. 14 July 1858.

2194. Shaw, Margaret, in NB, heir to George Shaw, minister in Hamilton Lanarkshire, reg. 14 July 1858.

2195. Shaw, Mary, in NB, heir to George Shaw, minister in Hamilton Lanarkshire, reg. 14 July 1858.

2196. Shaw, Rebecca, in NB, heir to George Shaw, minister in Hamilton Lanarkshire, reg. 14 July 1858.

2197. Sheddan, John, in Abingdon NA, heir to fa John Sheddan, baker in Perth, reg. 30 Jan.1788.

2198. Shedden, Matthew, baker, in Glasgow, heir to uncle Robert Shedden, merchant in Montreal, reg. 20 Feb.1854.

2199. Shedden, Robert, merchant, in Va, heir to fa William Shedden, merchant in Beith Ayrshire, reg. 17 Nov.1767.

2200. Shedden, William, merchant, in Va, heir to fa John Shedden, merchant in Beith Ayrshire, reg. 20 Dec.1771.

2201. Sheriffs, John, in Whiteburn NS, heir to bro James Sheriffs, courthouse keeper in Aberdeen, reg. 10 June 1841.

2202. Sherwood, William, in Graniteville Nev, heir to sis Ann Sherwood or Simpson, in Torwood Dunipace Stirlingshire, d. 27 Aug.1874, reg. 7 Jan.1878.

2203. Shields, Henry, merchant, in Charleston USA, heir to fa Henry Shields, farmer in Coaltown of Balmull Fife, reg. 6 Oct.1819.

2204. Shiels, John, in Can, heir to fa George Shiels, tenant farmer in Gilliestongues, reg. 2 May 1854.

2205. Shirra, Nicol, in Rodgerville Huron Co Can W, heir to sis Janet Shirra or Harvey, in Shirtgarton Kippen Stirlingshire, reg. 3 Oct.1870.

2206. Shirreff, Alexander, in London, heir to bro John Shirreff, merchant in Up Can, reg. 17 Oct.1849.

2207. Shirreff, John, merchant, in NB, heir to uncle Patrick Shirreff, Commander RN, d. 6 Dec.1863, reg. 26 May 1864.

2208. Shirreff, Robert, in Fitzroy Can W, heir to fa Charles Shirreff, merchant in Leith Mid Lothian then Fitzroy, reg. 17 Oct.1849.

2209. Shirreff, Robert, in Fitzroy Can W, heir to grand-uncle Robert Menzies, in Devon England, reg. 1 Nov.1849.

2210. Short or Gow, Agnes, wid of Robert Gow, in Edinburgh, heir to uncle Robert Gow, planter in Jamaica, reg. 5 Apr.1854.

2211. Simpson, Ada, in Pittston America, heir to uncle Alexander Simpson, spirit merchant in Falkirk Stirlingshire, d. 3 July 1874, reg. 30 June 1876.

2212. Simpson, Alexander, in USA, heir to uncle Peter Simpson, acid manufacturer in Camelon Stirlingshire, d. 16 Feb.1856, reg. 10 Nov.1856.
2213. Simpson, David, in Galt Ont, heir to aunt Maria Simpson, w of John Simpson in Chirnside Kelso Roxburghshire, d. 1 Feb.1873, reg. 21 Oct.1873.
2214. Simpson, Elizabeth, in Pittston America, heir to uncle Alexander Simpson, spirit merchant in Falkirk Stirlingshire, d. 3 July 1874, reg. 30 June 1876.
2215. Simpson, James, in Charleston SC, heir to grandfa James Tibbers, reg. 1 Aug.1770.
2216. Simpson or Dietrick, Janet, w of Albert W Dietrick, in Pittston America, heir to uncle Alexander Simpson, spirit merchant in Falkirk Stirlingshire, d. 3 July 1874, reg. 30 June 1876.
2217. Simpson, Joseph, in Grenada, heir to aunt Christian Bennet or Durward, wid of William Durward merchant in Aberdeen, reg. 18 Jan.1800.
2218. Simpson or Wallace, Margaret, w of Christopher Wallace, in Wilkes Barre Pa, heir to uncle Alexander Simpson, spirit merchant in Falkirk Stirlingshire, d. 3 July 1874, reg. 30 June 1876.
2219. Simpson or Adams, Mary Ann, w of John Adams manufacturer, in SC, heir to grandfa James Simpson, shipmaster in Greenock Renfrewshire, reg. 16 Jan.1857.
2220. Simpson, Peter, tanner, in NY, heir to fa Peter Simpson, tanner in Dalkeith Mid Lothian, reg. 1 Aug.1842.
2221. Simpson, Peter, tanner, in NY, heir to uncle Benjamin Simpson, reg. 1 Aug.1842.
2222. Simpson, William Kinnear, in Silver City Ut, heir to fa David Simpson jr, in Dundee Angus, d. 15 Mar.1856, reg. 20 Aug.1873.
2223. Simpson, William, storekeeper, in Chicago, heir to grandfa James Geddes, minister in Cambuslang Lanarkshire, reg. 23 Aug.1880.
2224. Simson, Walter, in Can W, heir to mo Helen Reddie or Simson, w of William Simson customs officer in Limekilns Fife, reg. 28 Sep.1847.
2225. Sinclair, Finlay, farmer, in Can, heir to bro Daniel Sinclair, in Edinburgh, reg. 22 Sep.1857.
2226. Sinclair, Hannah, in Lasswade Mid Lothian, heir to bro William Sinclair, in St Vincent, d. 2 Oct.1853, reg. 13 Nov.1854.
2227. Sinclair, James, in Boston America, heir to mo Isobell Lamont or Sinclair, w of Donald Sinclair merchant in Inveraray Argyll, reg. 26 Apr.1790.
2228. Sinclair or Grierson, Janet, wid of Rev Dr J Grierson, in Cockpen Mid Lothian, heir to bro William Sinclair, in St Vincent, d. 2 Oct.1853, reg. 13 Nov.1854.

2229. Sinclair, John, baker, in NY, heir to sis Mary Sinclair, da of Graham
    Sinclair in New Kilpatrick Dunbartonshire, reg. 29 Sep.1827.
2230. Sinclair, John, baker, in NY, heir to sis Agnes Sinclair, da of Graham
    Sinclair in New Kilpatrick Dunbartonshire, reg. 29 Sep.1827.
2231. Sinclair, John, baker, in NY, heir to sis Janet Sinclair, da of Graham
    Sinclair in New Kilpatrick Dunbartonshire, reg. 29 Sep.1827.
2232. Sinclair, John, in Culloden Inverness-shire then NS, heir to Donald
    MacPherson, farmer in Balchree of Petty then Blarnaphat
    Inverness-shire, reg. 5 July 1851.
2233. Sinclair of Stempster, Benjamin, heir to bro Archibald Sinclair, in
    Jamaica, reg. 9 Dec.1778.
2234. Sinclair, Peter, in Ramsay Can, heir to fa Finlay Sinclair, farmer in
    Ramsay Can, d. 12 Nov.1857, reg. 1 Sep.1858.
2235. Sinclair, Robert, sailor then merchant, in Albany NA, heir to grand-uncle
    Thomas Rankine jr, sailor in Greenock Renfrewshire, reg. 15
    Jan.1762.
2236. Sinclair, Thomas, in Eastaquoy Orkney, heir to bro William Sinclair,
    Hudson Bay Co, reg. 20 Sep.1826.
2237. Sinclair, William, in St Vincent, heir to William Sinclair, s of Andrew
    Cassels Howden WS, reg. 12 Feb.1844.
2238. Sinclair, William, in St Vincent, heir to Alexander Sinclair, s of Andrew
    Cassels Howden WS, reg. 12 Feb.1844.
2239. Sivright, John, in MacLelland's Brook Pictou NS, heir to fa James
    Sivright, shoemaker in Fife Keith, reg. 6 Aug.1853.
2240. Skeaf or Gordon, Mary, w of Andrew Gordon saddler, in Ballater
    Aberdeenshire then Can, heir to grandfa Joseph Skeaf, quill
    mnufacturer in Edinburgh, d. 4 Mar.1833, reg. 10 June 1861.
2241. Skene, Charles, in Parry Sound Ont, heir to sis Mary Skene, in
    Aberdeen, d. 22 May 1882, reg. 8 Feb.1883.
2242. Skinning, John, carpenter, in America, heir to grandfa Andrew McMaster,
    in Whitecrook, reg. 12 June 1838.
2243. Sleigh or Howse, Margaret, w of Alfred Richard Howse, in Victoria
    Vancouver Is, heir to sis Eleanor Sleigh or Sheriff, wid of Walter
    Brown Sheriff in Rutherglen Lanarkshire, d. 3 Jan.1873, reg. 24
    Jan.1883.
2244. Sloan, William James, postmaster, in Holland Landing Can W, heir to fa
    James Sloan, excise officer in Stranraer Wigtownshire, d. 12 June
    1807, reg. 6 Apr.1866.
2245. Sloane, James William, clerk, in Holland Landing Can W, heir to fa
    William Sloane, postmaster in Holland Landing, d. 19 Sep.1867,
    reg. 7 Dec.1869.
2246. Sloane or Carson, Jane, farmer, in Respin, heir to bro Alexander Sloane,
    in New Orleans then Whithorn Wigtownshire, reg. 22 Oct.1861.

2247. Sloane or Carson, Jane, farmer, in Respin, heir to bro Anthony Sloane, in New Orleans, d. 3 Jan.1844, reg. 14 Oct.1861.
2248. Sloane or Carson, Jane, farmer, in Respin, heir to bro Peter Sloane, in New Orleans, d. 18 May 1849, reg. 14 Oct.1861.
2249. Sloane or Brown, Mary, in Garrarie Kirkcudbrightshire, heir to bro Peter Sloane, in New Orleans, d. 18 May 1844, reg. 22 Oct.1861.
2250. Sloane or Brown, Mary, in Garrarie Kirkcudbrightshire, heir to bro Anthony Sloane, in New Orleans, d. 3 Jan.1844, reg. 22 Oct.1861.
2251. Sloane or Brown, Mary, in Garrarie Kirkcudbrightshire, heir to uncle Alexander Sloane, in New Orleans then Whithorn Wigtownshire, d. 13 Dec.1835, reg. 22 Oct.1861.
2252. Smart, David, founder, in NY, heir to uncle David Smart, slater in Strathmiglo Fife, reg. 7 Nov.1775.
2253. Smart, David, in Mich, heir to John Smart, manufacturer in Bridgetown of Innertiel Kirkcaldy Fife, reg. 8 Apr.1852.
2254. Smellie, John, merchant, in Kingston Jamaica, heir to fa John Smellie, merchant in Glasgow, reg. 2 May 1729.
2255. Smith, Agnes, in Mass, heir to grandfa Archibald Barr, farmer in Linn of Cathcart Glasgow, reg. 4 Jan.1812.
2256. Smith, Agnes, heir to bro John Smith, doctor in St Vincent, reg. 13 Feb.1816.
2257. Smith or De Blaquire, Agnes, in Can, heir to mo Agnes Briggs or Smith, w of Alexander Smith in Perth, reg. 16 Oct.1855.
2258. Smith, Andrew, in Can, heir to mo Agnes Briggs or Smith, w of Alexander Smith in Perth, reg. 16 Oct.1855.
2259. Smith or Gammack, Ann, wid of James Gammack, in London Ont, heir to bro Alexander Smith, watchmaker in Turriff Aberdeenshire, d. 26 Nov.1878, reg. 3 July 1879.
2260. Smith, Donald, in Cambridge USA, heir to fa James Smith, farm servant in Inverness, reg. 21 Mar.1842.
2261. Smith, Edward, in NS, heir to sis Isabel Smith or Reid, wid of William Reid manufacturer in Fochabers Morayshire, reg. 23 Aug.1845.
2262. Smith or Hutcheon, Elizabeth, w of R Hutcheon farmer, in Corncaterach, heir to bro George Smith, in Ga, reg. 6 Nov.1850.
2263. Smith, George, engineer, in Oh, heir to bro Robert Smith, chemist in Glasgow, reg. 29 Jan.1852.
2264. Smith, James, minister, in Nashville Ky, heir to uncle James Smith, s of Peter Smith merchant in Doune Stirlingshire, reg. 28 Aug.1835.
2265. Smith, James, saddler, in Can, heir to fa Alexander Smith, feuar in MacDuff Banffshire, reg. 22 Dec.1852.
2266. Smith, James Graham, in Glasgow then America, heir to fa James Smith of Craigend, reg. 14 Nov.1853.

2267. Smith, James, saddler, in Can, heir to grandfa Andrew Smith, overseer in Orchardton Kirkcudbrightshire, reg. 6 Apr.1858.

2268. Smith, James, in Philadelphia, heir to sis Jean Smith, in Kilmarnock Ayrshire, d. Apr.1841, reg. 7 Apr.1859.

2269. Smith, James, in Sackville NB, heir to bro Alexander Smith, staff surgeon in MacDuff Banffshire, d. 21 July 1848, reg. 15 June 1863.

2270. Smith or Dawson, Jean, w of A Dawson, in Colithie, heir to bro George Smith, in Ga, reg. 6 Nov.1850.

2271. Smith or McTavish, Jean, w of Henry McTavish shoemaker, in Brantford Can, heir to fa George Smith, woolcomber in Spittal, reg. 24 June 1864.

2272. Smith, John, in Va, heir to grandfa John Smith, in Drongan Ayrshire, reg. 16 Jan.1779.

2273. Smith, John Lyon, in Middleton America, heir to uncle John Lyon, in Society Hopetoun House W Lothian, reg. 3 May 1860.

2274. Smith, John Fleming, in Brandywine NA, heir to cousin Gavin Smith, in Concraig Aberdeenshire, d. 4 Jan.1843, reg. 26 Mar.1863.

2275. Smith, John Duncan, in Rochester NA, heir to sis Jessie Smith, in Edinburgh, d. 25 June 1863, reg. 7 July 1864.

2276. Smith, John, in Tarbolton Fitzroy Harbor Can W, heir to bro Andrew Smith, Lt RN, d. 18 Mar.1864, reg. 18 Aug.1864.

2277. Smith, John, hardware merchant, in New Orleans, heir to fa George Smith, wright in Hilltown Dundee Angus, d. 1850, reg. 20 Feb.1868.

2278. Smith, John Malcom, surgeon, in Edinburgh, heir to fa John Smith, minister in Queen's College Kingston Can W, d. 8 Aug.1856, reg. 5 Nov.1872.

2279. Smith, John, carpenter, in Ashtabula Oh, heir to fa John Smith, mariner in Dundee Angus, d. Nov.1853, reg. 2 Apr.1874.

2280. Smith, John, carpenter, in Ashtabula Oh, heir to uncle George Smith, carpenter in Dundee Angus, d. 5 Nov.1852, reg. 2 Apr.1874.

2281. Smith, Mary, wid of P Smith, in Albany NY , heir to fa Alexander Smith, tailor in Aberdeen, d. 15 June 1870, reg. 29 Sep.1870.

2282. Smith, Peter, in Halifax NS, heir to fa Peter Smith, miller in Lundin Mill Fife, d. 3 Sep.1871, reg. 22 Sep.1875.

2283. Smith, Robert Cumming, in NY, heir to fa Peter Smith, coppersmith in NY, reg. 27 July 1858.

2284. Smith, Robert, in W Barnet NA, heir to fa Hugh Smith, feuar & boardsmith, d. July 1850, reg. 29 Oct.1861.

2285. Smith, Thomas Baikie, in Kirkwall Orkney then Haiti, heir to bro William Smith, s of William Smith of Furmistown in Orkney, d. Mar.1799, reg. 14 Nov.1853.

2286. Smith, William, in St Vincent, heir to James Steinson, schoolmaster in King Edward Aberdeenshire, reg. 26 Aug.1856.

2287. Smith, William Ebenezer, engineer, in Aurora Ill, heir to bro Henry Smith, photographic artist in Edinburgh, d. 8 Feb.1868, reg. 17 Nov.1868.

2288. Soutter, Peter William, clerk, in Calcutta, heir to uncle William Soutter, in Cal, d. 21 Nov.1863, reg. 2 Apr.1873.

2289. Soutter, William, in Cal, heir to aunt Catherine Soutter, in Kinblethmont Angus, reg. 7 Oct.1856.

2290. Speden, William, in Washington USA, heir to fa Robert Speden, s of Robert Speden feuar in Bowden in Washington USA, reg. 11 July 1819.

2291. Spence, Andrew Bishop, heir to fa Andrew Spence, dentist in Philadelphia, reg. 28 Mar.1820.

2292. Spence, John, ship carpenter, in Stromness Orkney then Vancouver Is, heir to uncle John Spence, merchant in Stromness , d. 30 Dec.1833, reg. 24 Sep.1862.

2293. Spence, Thomas, in Fea Birsay Orkney, heir to fa Nicol Spence, Hudson Bay Co, reg. 22 Mar.1859.

2294. Spiers, James, engineer, in San Francisco, heir to fa James Spiers, in Levernbank Neilston Renfrewshire, d. 29 Sep.1865, reg. 18 May 1882.

2295. Spiers, John, in Waterloo Can, heir to grandfa James Willison, baker in Denny Stirlingshire, d. Oct.1815, reg. 19 Sep.1851.

2296. Sproat, Robert, in NJ, heir to bro William Sproat, in Kirkpatrick Durham Kirkcudbrightshire, reg. 18 Aug.1856.

2297. Sprott, James, minister, in Musquedaboit NS, heir to fa James Sprott, in Caldon Park, reg. 14 Aug.1826.

2298. Stalker, Donald, in America, heir to mo Marion Davidson or Stalker, in Peebles, reg. 16 July 1844.

2299. Steel, Hugh, shipmaster, in Bo'ness W Lothian then Philadelphia, heir to bro Archibald Steel, farmer in Stanley Perthshire then Saltcoats Ayrshire, reg. 23 June 1759.

2300. Steel or Freeman, Lillias, w of James A Freeman, in Genessee America, heir to aunt Helen Steel, in Longshot, d. 16 Mar.1859, reg. 29 July 1868.

2301. Steele, Andrew, organ-builder, in NY, heir to sis Jane Steele, grocer in Elphinstone Tranent E Lothian, d. 25 May 1870, reg. 7 Dec.1871.

2302. Stennet, Emily, heir to mo Emily Fordyce or Stennet, w of John Stennet physician in Jamaica, reg. 5 July 1819.

2303. Stennet, Francis, heir to mo Emily Fordyce or Stennet, w of John Stennet physician in Jamaica, reg. 5 July 1819.

2304. Stephen or Thomson, Betsy Gibb, w of William Thomson merchant, in Toronto, heir to bro Robert Stephen, in Dundee Angus, d. 5 Apr.1883, reg. 18 Oct.1883.

2305. Steuart, William John, in Binnia Plains NSW, heir to mo Anne Kennedy or Steuart, in WI then Edinburgh, d. 28 May 1844, reg. 21 Feb.1872.

2306. Steven or Russell, Jean, in Garbethill Cumbernauld Dunbartonshire, heir to bro John Steven, millwright in Trinidad, reg. 20 Mar.1845.

2307. Steven, John, in New Providence, heir to fa James Steven, merchant tailor in Glasgow, reg. 18 Nov.1803.

2308. Steven, William, in St John NB, heir to bro James Steven, in Glasgow, d. 25 May 1853, reg. 10 Dec.1853.

2309. Stevens, James, s of John Stevens, in Fisherford of Auchterless Aberdeenshire, heir to cousin John Brown, s of Alexander Brown in St Kitts, reg. 23 May 1767.

2310. Stevenson or Henderson, Barbara, w of John Henderson cabinetmaker, in Can, heir to mo Catherine Kirkwood or Stevenson, reg. 1 July 1858.

2311. Stevenson, Joan, w of H Stevenson, in Jamaica, heir to grandfa William Bell, cooper in Leith Mid Lothian, reg. 25 June 1782.

2312. Stevenson, John, shoemaker, in Edinburgh then NY, heir to fa James Stevenson, in Canongate Edinburgh, reg. 24 Dec.1838.

2313. Stevenson, John, in Up Can then Park, heir to fa James Stevenson, weaver in Hilltown Dundee Angus, reg. 28 Nov.1848.

2314. Stevenson, Robert, joiner, in Sparta Randulf Co Ill, heir to uncle Matthew Stevenson, feuar in Neilston Renfrewshire, d. 16 Dec.1867, reg. 22 May 1868.

2315. Stewart, Albert, heir to fa James Stewart, merchant in Mexico then Wellhall Hamilton Lanarkshire, reg. 23 Sep.1851.

2316. Stewart, Archibald, in St Andrews Fife, heir to fa James Stewart, merchant in Mexico then Wellhall Hamilton Lanarkshire, reg. 23 Sep.1851.

2317. Stewart, Charles Haggart, in Melbourne, heir to fa James Stewart, merchant in Mexico then Wellhall Hamilton Lanarkshire, reg. 23 Sep.1851.

2318. Stewart, Charles, in Cincinnati, heir to bro Alexander Stewart jr, clerk in NY, d. 31 Aug.1854, reg. 23 Nov.1865.

2319. Stewart, Daniel, in Dominica, heir to gt grandfa Alexander Erskine, factor to Marquis of Tweedsdale, reg. 18 Jan.1787.

2320. Stewart, Dunbar Douglas, in Halifax NS, heir to fa James Stewart, judge in Halifax NS, reg. 2 July 1832.

2321. Stewart, George, farmer & weaver, in Dundee Angus then Can, heir to fa James Stewart, weaver in Hilltown Dundee Angus, reg. 28 Nov.1848.

2322. Stewart, George, in Up Can, heir to fa William Stewart, farmer in Henshelwood, reg. 23 Mar.1858.

2323. Stewart, Helen, in St Andrews Fife, heir to fa James Stewart, merchant in Mexico then Wellhall Hamilton Lanarkshire, reg. 23 Sep.1851.

2324. Stewart, Isett, in St Andrews Fife, heir to fa James Stewart, merchant in Mexico then Wellhall Hamilton Lanarkshire, reg. 23 Sep.1851.

2325. Stewart, James, in Jamaica, heir to bro William Stewart, writer in Perth, reg. 23 Dec.1814.

2326. Stewart, James Hinton, heir to fa James Stewart, merchant in Mexico then Wellhall Hamilton Lanarkshire, reg. 23 Sep.1851.

2327. Stewart, James Alexander, in NY, heir to mo Helen Glass or Stewart, wid of Dr John Stewart in Blair Atholl Perthshire, reg. 28 Feb.1853.

2328. Stewart, James, in Huntly Aberdeenshire, heir to bro John Stewart, in WI, reg. 20 Nov.1854.

2329. Stewart or Haldane, Jane, wid of David Haldane, in Grenada, heir to bro George Stewart, seaman in Edinburgh, reg. 10 Aug.1854.

2330. Stewart or McIntosh, Jane, wid of Alexander McIntosh merchant, in Berbice, heir to uncle Norman Stewart, merchant in Va, reg. 5 May 1858.

2331. Stewart, John, in Albany NY, heir to fa Alexander Stewart, tenant farmer in Pitkerral Bridge of Dull Perthshire, reg. 19 Mar.1798.

2332. Stewart, John, in Jamaica then Fort William Inverness-shire, heir to fa Dugald Stewart, in Fort William, reg. 10 June 1858.

2333. Stewart, John, carpenter, in Blantyre Lanarkshire, heir to bro William Stewart, clerk in NY, d. Nov.1848, reg. 13 Dec.1866.

2334. Stewart or Montgomery, Marcella, in Can W, heir to bro Hugh Stewart, in Jordanbank Edinburgh, d. 29 May 1867, reg. 7 May 1874.

2335. Stewart, Mary, in NY, heir to gt grandfa John Brough of Boghall, reg. 5 June 1811.

2336. Stewart, Mary, da of P Stewart merchant, in NY, heir to grandmo Mary Brough of Boghall, reg. 20 Nov.1816.

2337. Stewart, Nancy, in St Andrews Fife, heir to fa James Stewart, merchant in Mexico then Wellhall Hamilton Lanarkshire, reg. 23 Sep.1851.

2338. Stewart, Octavius, heir to fa James Stewart, merchant in Mexico then Wellhall Hamilton Lanarkshire, reg. 23 Sep.1851.

2339. Stewart, Patrick, in Mexico, heir to fa James Stewart, merchant in Mexico then Wellhall Hamilton Lanarkshire, reg. 23 Sep.1851.

2340. Stewart, Peter, contractor, in Can, heir to fa Peter Stewart, innkeeper in Strichen Aberdeenshire, reg. 30 Jan.1839.

2341. Stewart, William, heir to fa James Stewart, merchant in Mexico then Wellhall Hamilton Lanarkshire, reg. 23 Sep.1851.

2342. Stewart, William, in Exeter Mich, heir to uncle William Stewart, carrier in Dalmellington Ayrshire, d. 26 Aug.1875, reg. 24 Dec.1877.

2343. Stirling or McGregor, Jane, in Guelph Can, heir to bro Thomas
Stirling, s of Rev Dr Alexander Stirling in Tillicoutry
Stirlingshire, reg. 7 July 1847.

2344. Stirling, Michael Finlayson, merchant, in Belize Honduras, heir to mo
Helen Rose or Stirling, wid of John Stirling surgeon in Glasgow,
reg. 13 May 1853.

2345. Stirling, William, merchant, in Jamaica, heir to fa James Stirling of
Stair, merchant in London, reg. 20 May 1823.

2346. Stirrat, David, in Baltimore, heir to cousin Elizabeth Gavin, in Beith
Ayrshire, reg. 11 Jan.1834.

2347. Stirrat, David, in Motthaven NA, heir to fa David Stirrat, sewed muslin
manufacturer in Kilwinning Ayrshire, d. 27 Oct.1859, reg. 15
Dec.1865.

2348. Stiven or Black, Helen, in Falkirk Stirlingshire, heir to bro John Stiven,
millwright in Trinidad, reg. 21 Mar.1845.

2349. Stobbie or Ferguson, Elizabeth, w of John Stobbie, in Elliotshead, heir
to bro John Ferguson, baker in Jamaica, reg. 4 Dec.1798.

2350. Stocks, James, in Elora Wellington Can, heir to Ann Hutton, in Perth,
reg. 20 Jan.1851.

2351. Stocks, James, in Elora Wellington Can, heir to gt grandfa John Hutton,
baker in Perth, reg. 8 June 1853.

2352. Stocks, Jeannie, in Hamilton Can, heir to fa James Stocks, in Perth, d.
27 Feb.1857, reg. 4 Sep.1866.

2353. Stocks, Jeannie, in Hamilton Can, heir to uncle Jedidiah Stocks, in
Perth, d. 23 Feb.1849, reg. 4 Sep.1866.

2354. Stocks, Jessie, in Hamilton Can, heir to fa James Stocks, in Perth, d. 27
Feb.1857, reg. 4 Sep.1866.

2355. Stocks, Jessie, in Hamilton Can, heir to uncle Jedidiah Stocks, in Perth,
d. 23 Feb.1849, reg. 4 Sep.1866.

2356. Stoddart, John, in Waupon Fond-du-Lac Wisc, heir to mo Ann Reid or
Stoddart, w of John Stoddart in Fond-du-Lac, d. 5 Feb.1852, reg. 9
Feb.1865.

2357. Storrar, Michael, maltster, in Auchtermuchty Fife, heir to bro Lawrence
Storrar, in Lucca Jamaica then Auchtermuchty, reg. 22 Mar.1848.

2358. Stott, William, in Philadelphia, heir to sis Jane Stott, da of James Stott
leather-merchant in Edinburgh, d. 31 May 1856, reg. 19 May
1869.

2359. Strachan, John, in Tenbrookfarm NY, heir to grandfa John Strachan of
Campfield, reg. 7 Aug.1822.

2360. Strachan, Margaret S, in NY, heir to grandfa John Strachan, laborer in
Edentown, d. 26 June 1858, reg. 12 Feb.1879.

2361. Strachan, Mary Helen, in NY, heir to grandfa John Strachan, laborer in
Edentown, d. 26 June 1858, reg. 12 Feb.1879.

2362. Strachan or Mitchell, Susan, w of John Mitchell merchant, in Va, heir to bro John Strachan, in Aberdeen, reg. 20 May 1797.

2363. Strange, John Maxwell, s of James M Strange, in Toronto, heir to grand-aunt Barbara Strange or Marshall, w of William Marshall surgeon in Cambuslang Lanarkshire, reg. 28 Oct.1859.

2364. Strange, John Maxwell, in Toronto, heir to fa James Strange, in Toronto, d. 27 Mar.1854, reg. 2 Oct.1862.

2365. Strange, John Maxwell, in Toronto, heir to aunt Eliza Strange or Watkins, w of John Watkins in Kingston Can W, reg. 2 July 1867.

2366. Strange, Maxwell William, in Up Can, heir to aunt isabella Strange or Hyndman, w of Archibald Campbell Hyndman in Lesmahagow Lanarkshire, reg. 27 Sep.1859.

2367. Strathearn, James, in Lassa Ill, heir to grandmo Agnes Rayburn or Brown, w of David Brown in Irvine Ayrshire, d. 13 Nov.1871, reg. 4 June 1877.

2368. Stratton, John, in Cambridge NY, heir to fa Peter Stratton, carrier in Lilliesleaf Roxburghshire, reg. 13 June 1820.

2369. Struthers, Andrew, in Can W, heir to fa Alexander Struthers, cotton waste dealer in Glasgow, reg. 12 Nov.1852.

2370. Struthers, Gavin, corporal 42nd regiment, in Bermuda, heir to fa Alexander Struthers, weaver in Strathaven Lanarkshire, d. 1 Jan.1851, reg. 6 June 1851.

2371. Summers, John, surgeon 3rd WI Regiment, heir to mo Elizabeth Mitchell or Summers, in London, reg. 4 Dec.1850.

2372. Summers, Robert Thomson, merchant, in Toronto, heir to fa Robert Summers, in Hamilton Lanarkshire, d. 21 May 1880, reg. 2 Nov.1880.

2373. Summers, William Thomas, in Va, heir to gt gt grandfa James Shaw, horseletter in Port Glasgow Renfrewshire, reg. 18 July 1836.

2374. Sutherland, George, in NY, heir to fa William Sutherland, in Halkirk Caithness, d. 10 Nov.1841, reg. 4 July 1865.

2375. Sutherland, James, plasterer, in Boston USA, heir to aunt Margaret Watt, feuar in Fochabers Morayshire, d. 14 July 1867, reg. 3 Oct.1870.

2376. Sutton, Mary, da of John Sutton, in St Croix, heir to gt grandfa William Fife, in Gilcomston, reg. 29 Jan.1756.

2377. Swan, John, merchant, in Baltimore, heir to fa John Swan, in Scarig, reg. 21 Apr.1792.

2378. Swan, John, in NY, heir to grandfa John Swan of Craigfod, in Strathmiglo Fife, reg. 12 Jan.1853.

2379. Swanson, John Goodfellow, rigger, in San Francisco, heir to mo Janet Goodfellow or Swanson, w of Donald Swanson in Langside Peebles, reg. 16 Nov.1867.

2380. Swanston or Ovens, Agnes, in Montreal, heir to fa John Swanston, mason in Bowden Newton St Boswells Roxburghshire, reg. 27 May 1843.

2381. Swanston or Bain, Margaret, in Montreal, heir to fa John Swanston, mason in Bowden Newtown St Boswells Roxburghshire, reg. 27 May 1843.

2382. Swinton, George Steel, in Sandwich Is, heir to mo Jean Steel or Swinton, w of H Swinton merchant in Grangemouth Stirlingshire, reg. 21 Dec.1847.

2383. Syme, David, principal, in Brooklyn Public School, heir to fa William Syme, merchant in Auchterarder Perthshire, reg. 4 July 1853.

2384. Syme, David, in Brooklyn NY, heir to bro Peter Syme, in Australia, d. 27 Mar.1860, reg. 6 Dec.1861.

2385. Symmers, Alexander, in Montreal, heir to fa George Symmers, attorney in Dublin then Galway Ireland, d. Dec.1839, reg. 8 July 1863.

2386. Symmers, James, in Hamilton Ont, heir to uncle James Symmers, teacher in Dollar Clackmannanshire, d. 31 Oct.1880, reg. 22 June 1882.

2387. Symson, Alexander, Baron of the Exchequer, in Grenada, heir to cousin Alexander Symson of Concraig, reg. 1 Nov.1769.

2388. Tait, Ann Shiells, in Quebec, heir to fa Peter Tait, farmer in Edinburgh, reg. 2 Mar.1859.

2389. Tait or Garrioch, Catherine, w of John Garrioch carter, in Kirkwall Orkney, heir to fa William Tait, Hudson Bay Co in Stromness Orkney, d. 5 Oct.1826, reg. 27 June 1861.

2390. Tait, David, in Quebec, heir to bro James Tait, in Lauder Berwickshire, d. 24 Jan.1867, reg. 16 Dec.1872.

2391. Tait, James, WS, in NY, heir to mo Isabella Sanders or Tait, w of J R Tait baker in Edinburgh, d. 14 Aug.1862, reg. 30 July 1868.

2392. Tait or Barron, Jean, w of John Barron plasterer, in Stromness Orkney, heir to fa William Tait, Hudson Bay Co in Stromness, d. 5 Oct.1826, reg. 27 June 1861.

2393. Tait or Gibson, Margaret, in Rockford Ill, heir to fa John Tait, in Cartyloop Minnigaff Kirkcudbrightshire, reg. 3 Feb.1838.

2394. Tait, Thomas, farmer, in Crichie Aberdeenshire, heir to uncle John Tait, cooper in Jamaica then Aberdeen, reg. 27 Nov.1858.

2395. Tarbat, Alexander, in Cal, heir to mo Marjery Rose or Tarbat, in Forfar Angus, reg. 30 Sep.1857.

2396. Tate, William A, in Red River Settlement, heir to Jean Tate or Spence, w of John Spence in Red River Settlement, reg. 4 May 1860.

2397. Taylor, George, merchant, in Kingston Jamaica, heir to bro John Taylor, s of John Taylor of Kirktonhill, reg. 18 July 1827.

2398. Taylor, James Scott, heir to fa John Taylor, merchant in Glasgow then NY, reg. 21 Dec.1838.

2399. Taylor, James, mason, in NY, heir to aunt Janet Taylor, in Auchterarder Perthshire, reg. 27 Dec.1850.
2400. Taylor, James, mason, in NY, heir to aunt Susan Taylor, in Auchterarder Perthshire, reg. 27 Dec.1850.
2401. Taylor, James, engineer, in Amboy USA, heir to sis Mary Taylor, in Newton, d. 6 Jan.1858, reg. 12 June 1873.
2402. Taylor, John, tailor, in Kelso Roxburghshire then Troy NY, heir to fa William Taylor, tailor in Kelso, reg. 10 Nov.1832.
2403. Taylor, John William, in Rochester NY, heir to fa John Taylor, carpet manufacturer in Rochester NY, d. 20 Aug.1853, reg. 4 Aug.1863.
2404. Taylor, Peter Arnot, cooper, in Sparta NA, heir to fa John Taylor, laborer in Tillicoutry Clackmannanshire, reg. 27 Nov.1865.
2405. Taylor, Peter Arnot, cooper, in Sparta NA, heir to mo Christian Arnot, reg. 27 Nov.1865.
2406. Tedcastle, John, in Center Hill Hudson City NA, heir to mo Janet Hope or Tedcastle, w of Thomas Walker in Maxwelltown Dumfries-shire, reg. 27 June 1864.
2407. Telfer, William, wright, in Hawick Roxburghshire then Can, heir to mo Isabel Nichol or Telfer, reg. 21 Oct.1844.
2408. Tennant, John, in Walkerton Can W, heir to uncle James Tennant, surgeon in Brighton England, d. 16 June 1851, reg. 19 Oct.1866.
2409. Thom, Archibald, surgeon, in Perth Can, heir to mo Ann Bodie or Thom, w of Alexander Thom farmer in Old Aberdeen, reg. 31 Aug.1821.
2410. Thom, Charles, in Plainfield NJ, heir to grandfa Charles Thom, in Charleston Paisley Renfrewshire, d. 10 June 1845, reg. 28 July 1879.
2411. Thom, Eliza, in Ascog Bute, heir to William Thom, in Dundas Can W, d. 4 May 1860, reg. 13 May 1861.
2412. Thom, Robert, in Ascog Bute, heir to William Thom, in Dundas Can W, d. 4 May 1860, reg. 13 May 1861.
2413. Thom, William, schoolmaster, in Quebec, heir to fa James Thom, youth instructor in Quebec, d. 25 Feb.1849, reg. 27 Sep.1867.
2414. Thom, William, schoolmaster, in Quebec, heir to aunt Jane Thom or Smillie, w of James Smillie jeweller in Quebec, d. 4 Feb.1840, reg. 27 Sep.1867.
2415. Thomas, John, in America, heir to sis Janet Thomas or Torrie, w of James Torrie in Shawfield Bank Rutherglen Lanarkshire, reg. 9 May 1849.
2416. Thompson, Dougald, farmer, in Birchville NA, heir to grandfa Donald Thompson, farmer in Greenock Renfrewshire, d. 22 Jan.1839, reg. 28 Jan.1864.
2417. Thomson, Daniel, tailor, in Merion Pa, heir to James Davidson, weaver in Glasgow, reg. 17 June 1803.

2418. Thomson, David, s of Andrew Thomson, in Baad, heir to uncle David Henderson, in Bertie NC, reg. 16 Aug.1737.

2419. Thomson, George, merchant, in NY, heir to fa James Thomson, writer in Cupar Fife, reg. 14 Dec.1859.

2420. Thomson, George, in St Louis NA, heir to sis Jane Thomson, in High Buckholmside Galashiels Selkirkshire, d. 19 Apr.1863, reg. 18 Jan.1869.

2421. Thomson, Grizel, in Baad, heir to uncle David Henderson, in Bertie NC, reg. 16 Aug.1737.

2422. Thomson, Isobel, da of Andrew Thomson, in Baad, heir to uncle David Henderson, in Bertie NC, reg. 16 Aug.1737.

2423. Thomson, James, in Can, heir to remote cousin Mary Milliken, in Lyndoch St Glasgow, d. 16 Mar.1872, reg. 7 Oct.1874.

2424. Thomson, James, in Can, heir to remote cousin Christina Milliken, in Glasgow, d. 24 May 1873, reg. 7 Oct.1874.

2425. Thomson, James, in Chicago, heir to bro John Thomson, merchant in Aberdeen, d. 1858, reg. 14 Oct.1882.

2426. Thomson, John, s of Andrew Thomson, in Baad, heir to uncle David Henderson, in Bertie NC, reg. 16 Aug.1737.

2427. Thomson, John, in Montreal, heir to mo Margaret Robertson or Thomson, wid of John Thomson merchant in Leith Mid Lothian, reg. 6 Jan.1834.

2428. Thomson or Inglis, Margaret, in Linton Roxburghshire, heir to bro James Thomson, in Jamaica, reg. 1 Mar.1833.

2429. Thomson, Mary, da of Andrew Thomson, in Baad, heir to uncle David Henderson, in Bertie NC, reg. 16 Aug.1737.

2430. Thomson, Mary Ann, in Edinburgh, heir to fa George Thomson, millwright in New Mills Jamaica, d. 1838, reg. 10 Dec.1874.

2431. Thomson, Matthew, shoemaker, in America, heir to fa David Thomson, shoemaker in Edinburgh, reg. 27 Nov.1843.

2432. Thomson, Robert, clerk, in NY, heir to fa John Thomson, printer in Edinburgh, reg. 7 Mar.1851.

2433. Thomson, Samuel, in Burns Alleghany Co NY, heir to bro Hugh Thomson, blacksmith in Strathaven Lanarkshire, d. 9 Mar.1871, reg. 20 Sep.1873.

2434. Thomson, Thomas, s of Andrew Thomson, in Baad, heir to uncle David Henderson, in Bertie NC, reg. 16 Aug.1737.

2435. Thomson, Thomas, in Montreal, heir to grandfa Thomas Thomson, in Farnham Montreal, reg. 11 Jan.1843.

2436. Thomson, William, merchant, in Newfoundland, heir to remote cousin William Gemmell, Lt Col in Greenock Renfrewshire, reg. 9 Jan.1829.

2437. Thomson, William Alexander, in Buffalo America, heir to grandfa
William Thomson, in Thornbank Duchrae Kirkcudbrightshire, reg.
10 Dec.1838.
2438. Thomson, William, in Clinton Ia, heir to fa James Thomson, tailor in
Arbroath Angus, d. 28 Feb.1871, reg. 24 June 1872.
2439. Thomson, William, farmer, in Sandy Ut, heir to fa William Thomson, in
Rumford Stirlingshire, d. 9 May 1879, reg. 26 Oct.1881.
2440. Thorburn, Adam William, in Clarendon Jamaica, heir to grand-uncle R
Thorbrand or Thorburn, carrier in Hawick Roxburghshire, reg. 18
Oct.1824.
2441. Thornton, Peter, engineer, in Hamilton Can W, heir to bro William
Thornton, engineer in America, d. 10 June 1856, reg. 8 July 1863.
2442. Tod, Alexander, merchant, in Philadelphia, heir to sis Helen Tod or
Stewart, wid of John Stewart merchant in Edinburgh, reg. 3
Mar.1790.
2443. Tod or Toddie, Andrew, in London, heir to Lindsay Tod or Toddie, cotton
planter in America, reg. 25 Feb.1833.
2444. Tod or Toddie or McGregor, Betty, in London, heir to Lindsay Tod or
Toddie, cotton planter in America, reg. 25 Mar.1833.
2445. Tod or Toddie or Murdoch, Elspeth, in Dyce Aberdeenshire, heir to
Lindsay Tod or Toddie, cotton planter in America, reg. 25
Mar.1833.
2446. Tod, George, in Holm Orkney then Caroline Co Va, heir to grandfa
George Tod, minister in Holm Orkney, reg. 23 Jan.1765.
2447. Tod, James, physician & surgeon, in Jamaica, heir to grandfa James Tod,
tenant farmer in Wemyss Fife, reg. 24 July 1789.
2448. Tod or Toddie or Kidd, Janet, in Edinburgh, heir to Lindsay Tod or
Toddie, cotton planter in America, reg. 25 Mar.1833.
2449. Tod or Toddie or Arnott, Katherine, w of W Arnott, in Auchtermuchty
Fife, heir to bro Lindsay Tod or Toddie, cotton planter in Fla, reg.
5 Aug.1826.
2450. Tod or Toddie or Arnot, Margaret, in Inglis Hall, heir to Lindsay Tod or
Toddie, cotton planter in America, reg. 25 Mar.1833.
2451. Tomison, William, heir to uncle William Tomison, in Hudson Bay then
S Ronaldsay Orkney, reg. 19 Nov.1838.
2452. Torbett, David, in Markham York Ont, heir to fa John Torbett, laborer in
Crofthead Whitburn W Lothian, d. 1 Dec.1881, reg. 15 Nov.1882.
2453. Torrance, Agnes, in Edinburgh, heir to uncle Andrew Jackson, in USA,
reg. 13 Dec.1854.
2454. Tower, Alexander, in St Croix then Torquay England, heir to fa George
Tower, merchant in Aberdeen, d. 17 Dec.1811, reg. 6 Aug.1861.
2455. Tran, Hugh, merchant, in St Kitts, heir to mo Elizabeth Warden or Tran,
w of Arthur Tran merchant in Glasgow, reg. 12 Feb.1768.

2456. Trent, John, s of Laurence Trent merchant, in Barbados, heir to uncle William Trent, in Newbattle Midlothian, d. July 1689, reg. 28 July 1703.

2457. Trotter, Robert, blacksmith, in NY then Kelso Roxburghshire, heir to fa John Trotter, meal dealer in Kelso Roxburghshire, reg. 29 Mar.1849.

2458. Troup, William, minister, in Hamilton Can W, heir to fa William Troup, in Dalbhadie Aberdeenshire, d. 1 Mar.1858, reg. 2 July 1872.

2459. Tudhope, Robert, skinner, in Philadelphia, heir to grandfa Robert Tudhope, flesher in Selkirk, reg. 27 July 1836.

2460. Tudhope, Robert, skinner, in Philadelphia, heir to gt grandfa Alexander Tudhope, flesher in Selkirk, reg. 1 Feb.1837.

2461. Tulloch, David, in Trenton Falls NY, heir to bro William Tulloch, shopman in Glasgow, d. 21 June 1872, reg. 25 Oct.1876.

2462. Turnbull, Robert, minister, in Hartford NA, heir to fa George Turnbull, in Dennyloanhead Stirlingshire, d. 21 July 1866, reg. 19 Feb.1867.

2463. Turnbull, Thomas Thomson, merchant, in Montreal, heir to mo Christina Thomson or Turnbull, wid of Alexander Turnbull in Leith Mid Lothian, d. 19 Jan.1880, reg. 15 Mar.1880.

2464. Turnbull, William John, in Montreal, heir to mo Christina Thomson or Turnbull, wid of Alexander Turnbull in Leith Mid Lothian, d. 19 Jan.1880, reg. 15 Mar.1880.

2465. Turner, Henry Castle, printer, in Can, heir to cousin James Castle, goldsmith & jeweller in Edinburgh, d. 26 May 1867, reg. 5 Oct.1869.

2466. Turner, James, in Tenn, heir to grandfa James Turner of Gateside, reg. 25 May 1852.

2467. Turner, John Visey, merchant, in Seymour Can, heir to fa Alexander Turner, Major HEICS, d. 6 Mar.1832, reg. 16 June 1848.

2468. Urquhart, John, wagonmaker, in Stoufville Ont, heir to Donald Munro, merchant in Invergordon Ross & Cromarty, reg. 22 July 1880.

2469. Vallance or Ashley, Agnes, in Dansville America, heir to fa David Vallance, weaver in Cumnock Ayrshire, reg. 24 Aug.1842.

2470. Veitch or Grinton, Catherine, w of William Grinton draper, in Edinburgh then NA, heir to bro James Veitch, in Can, d. 9 Sep.1832, reg. 22 Apr.1862.

2471. Veitch or Grinton, Catherine, w of William Grinton draper, in Edinburgh then NA, heir to bro John Veitch, merchant in Edinburgh, reg. 7 Apr.1862.

2472. Vincent, John, in Hudson Bay, heir to fa Thomas Vincent, in Innertown Stromness Orkney then Hartlypool England, reg. 22 Jan.1839.

2473. Waddell, James, merchant, in Jamaica, heir to fa William Waddell, mason in Dumfries, reg. 7 Jan.1809.
2474. Waddell, James, in Kingston Jamaica, heir to sis Katherine Waddell, in Edinburgh, reg. 18 Dec.1818.
2475. Waddell, James, merchant, in Can, heir to fa James Waddell of Leadloch, in Auchtermuir Lanarkshire, reg. 14 Aug.1854.
2476. Waddell, James, merchant, in Kingston Can W then Glasgow, heir to fa James Waddell of Deadloch, d. 5 Oct.1852, reg. 4 Nov.1867.
2477. Walker, Alexander Gordon, in Mercer Co Va, heir to fa James Walker, in Edinburgh, reg. 6 July 1853.
2478. Walker, Alexander Gordon, in Logan Co America, heir to grandfa William Gibb jr, in Edinburgh, d. 3 May 1829, reg. 29 Nov.1877.
2479. Walker, George, in Birkenhead England, heir to bro James Walker, in Glasgow then Antigua, d. 27 Oct.1835, reg. 29 Nov.1867.
2480. Walker, James, weaver, in Johnstone Renfrewshire then Can, heir to fa James Walker, cotton spinner in Johnstone then America, reg. 16 Nov.1859.
2481. Walker, John, in PEI, heir to fa John Walker, flaxdresser in Aberdeen, reg. 11 Mar.1853.
2482. Walker, John Geddes, Major RA, heir to sis Agnes Walker, da of James Walker merchant & customs collector in Leith Mid Lothian then Bahamas, reg. 13 Sep.1853.
2483. Walker, John Black, in Rochford Ill, heir to uncle Matthew Walker, writer in Glasgow, d. 10 Mar.1876, reg. 19 Dec.1877.
2484. Walker jr, James, heir to fa James Walker, house carpenter in New Aberdour Aberdeenshire, reg. 6 June 1870.
2485. Walker jr, James, in Uxbridge Ont, heir to mo Jessie Kerr or Walker, w of James Walker in New Aberdour Aberdeenshire, reg. 6 June 1870.
2486. Walker, Madeleine Hay, in Edinburgh, heir to sis Agnes Walker, da of James Walker merchant & customs collector in Leith Mid Lothian then Bahamas, reg. 13 Sep.1853.
2487. Walker, Matthew, carter, in Burnside then Montreal, heir to fa William Walker, in Cowcaddens Glasgow then Quebec, reg. 18 Jan.1826.
2488. Walker, Peter, merchant, in Stirling then NY, heir to uncle Robert Walker, merchant in Aberdeen, reg. 3 Jan.1835.
2489. Walker, Peter, in Tenn, heir to bro Charles Walker, in Arbroath Angus, d. 3 Jan.1869, reg. 3 Oct.1883.
2490. Walker, Robert, in Jamaica, heir to cousin Gilbert Barrie, skinner in Newton Stewart Wigtownshire, reg. 24 Mar.1790.
2491. Walker, William M, minister, in Huntingdon Lower Can, heir to fa Thomas Walker, surgeon in Irvine Ayrshire, reg. 7 Jan.1836.
2492. Walker, William Montgomery, minister, in Can, heir to grandmo Mary Montgomery or Fleming, in Irvine Ayrshire, reg. 12 May 1843.

2493. Walkinshaw, Robert, in Rancho del Oro Mexico, heir to bro William Walkinshaw, Capt HEICS, reg. 30 Aug.1827.

2494. Walkinshaw, Robert, in Mexico, heir to cousin Euphemia Moffat, in Grangehill then Kinghorn Fife, reg. 16 Nov.1846.

2495. Wallace or Rigsby, Agnes, in Nottingham England, heir to bro William Wallace, in Jamaica, reg. 16 Feb.1788.

2496. Wallace, James, in Barnet USA, heir to fa John Wallace, farmer in East Threepwood Roxburghshire, reg. 22 June 1842.

2497. Wallace, Thomas, merchant, in Charleston USA then Kilmaurs Ayrshire, heir to aunt Marion Wallace, in Kilmaurs, reg. 29 Aug.1842.

2498. Walls, Lawrence, in Lather Can, heir to fa Lawrence Walls, mason in Can, reg. 4 Oct.1854.

2499. Wand or Beck, Janet, wid of John N Beck planter, in Antigua, heir to grandfa William Wand, portioner of Pitgober, reg. 26 Mar.1794.

2500. Wanless, David, in USA, heir to grandfa David Baxter, manufacturer in Dundee Angus, reg. 4 Mar.1859.

2501. Wardin, William H, in Philadelphia, heir to uncle James Wardin, in Port Stewart Londonderry, reg. 2 Apr.1857.

2502. Wards, James, in Ont, heir to fa John Wards, farmer in Goodwalter Rendall Orkney, d. 6 Jan.1869, reg. 26 Dec.1882.

2503. Waterston, Robert, merchant, in Boston, heir to grandmo Mary Tait or Cassie, w of Robert Cassie weaver in North Berwick E Lothian, reg. 13 Dec.1847.

2504. Watson or Chapman, Agnes, w of James Chapman, in Westfield NA, heir to fa Henry Watson, mason in Limekilns Fife, d. Dec.1825, reg. 23 Sep.1867.

2505. Watson, Alexander, in Mooretown Ont, heir to mo Ann Watson, w of David Watson in Dundee Angus, d. 13 Jan.1840, reg. 5 May 1879.

2506. Watson, David, in Dundas Ont, heir to mo Ann Watson, w of David Watson in Dundee Angus, d. 13 Jan.1840, reg. 5 May 1879.

2507. Watson, Henry, mariner, in Cal, heir to aunt Margaret Watson, in Hawkhill Dundee Angus, d. Apr.1837, reg. 15 Dec.1864.

2508. Watson, Henry, mariner, in Downie Villa Cal, heir to fa Henry Watson, shipmaster in Dundee Angus then Leith Mid Lothian, d. 24 Apr.1839, reg. 12 Jan.1865.

2509. Watson, James Pyot, shipmaster, in NY, heir to aunt Margaret Ogilvie of Friock, in Angus, reg. 22 July 1812.

2510. Watson, James, in Toronto, heir to mo Ann Watson, w of David Watson in Dundee Angus, d. 13 Jan.1840, reg. 5 May 1879.

2511. Watson or McGlashan, Margaret, in Conima Ont, heir to mo Ann Watson, w of David Watson in Dundee Angus, d. 13 Jan.1840, reg. 5 May 1879.

2512. Watson, Robert, in Victoria Vancouver Is, heir to fa Robert Watson, merchant in Aberdeen, d. 21 Feb.1849, reg. 1 Dec.1869.
2513. Watson, William, in Jamaica, heir to fa Alexander Watson, merchant in Aberdeen, reg. 1 July 1769.
2514. Watson, William, in NY, heir to fa Joseph Watson, clothier in Chirnside Berwickshire then NY, reg. 13 Oct.1845.
2515. Watson, William, Capt, in America, heir to mo Isabel Dalgleish or Watson, wid of T Watson of Shields in Peebles-shire, d. 21 Apr.1848, reg. 21 Oct.1848.
2516. Watson, William, wood merchant, in Can E, heir to sis Janet Watson or Thomson, wid of James Thomson in Douglas Lanarkshire, reg. 2 Oct.1857.
2517. Watson, William, butcher, in Lafayette NY, heir to fa Alexander Watson, clerk in Clyde Ironworks Glasgow, d. 20 Dec.1865, reg. 17 July 1872.
2518. Watson, William, baker, in London Ont, heir to fa John Watson, in Polwarth Berwickshire, d. 19 May 1873, reg. 10 May 1880.
2519. Watt, Alexander, in New Deer Aberdeenshire then Can, heir to mo Isabella Norrie or Watt, in Auchreddie Aberdeenshire, reg. 20 Aug.1836.
2520. Watt, Archibald, merchant, in NY, heir to fa Thomas Watt, in Denmiln, reg. 11 Aug.1841.
2521. Watt or Townsley, Forbes, in Yorkville Can W, heir to uncle Charles Watt, solicitor in Banff, d. 20 Sep.1845, reg. 20 July 1865.
2522. Watt, George Darling, reporter, in Salt Lake City Ut, heir to grandfa Andrew Watt, in Waulkmill of Skyreburn Kirkcudbrightshire, d. 3 Sep.1849, reg. 24 June 1867.
2523. Watt, James, merchant, in Va, heir to fa James Watt, merchant in Panbride Angus, reg. 22 Nov.1775.
2524. Watt or Orsali, Margaret, w of Thomas Orsali, in Montreal, heir to grandfa Thomas Watt, tailor in Cambusnethan Lanarkshire, reg. 22 Apr.1854.
2525. Watt, Thomas, in Haarlem NY, heir to aunt Jane Watt, in Skene Tce Aberdeen, d. 18 Oct.1869, reg. 21 Dec.1870.
2526. Watt, William, in Chicago, heir to uncle John Watt, in Kirbuster Orkney, d. 21 Jan.1872, reg. 29 Nov.1873.
2527. Waugh, James, in Chilicothe Oh, heir to bro John Waugh, feuar in Kelso Roxburghshire, reg. 25 May 1833.
2528. Webster or Duncan, Ann, w of James Duncan farmer, in Tillyhouse Aberdeenshire, heir to uncle Alexander Naughton, in Tobago, reg. 21 Dec.1865.
2529. Webster or Winchester, Catherine, w of C Winchester, in Aberdeen, heir to bro James Webster, in Content Est Jamaica, reg. 12 Apr.1827.

2530. Webster, James Frederick, minister, in Greenville SC, heir to fa James Webster, in Cheltenham England, d. 6 Dec.1858, reg. 5 Mar.1877.

2531. Webster, Robert Yeoman, in NB, heir to grandfa Robert Yeoman, machine maker in Kintore Aberdeenshire, d. 5 Nov.1877, reg. 17 Apr.1880.

2532. Webster, William, baker, in NY, heir to mo Margaret Maxwell or Webster, wid of James Webster in Arbroath Angus, d. 3 Apr.1865, reg. 24 Aug.1865.

2533. Wedderspoon, David, in Otsego USA, heir to aunt Elizabeth Wedderspoon, in Auchterarder Perthshire, d. 9 Nov.1849, reg. 8 Nov.1850.

2534. Weekes, Thomas Pym, s of William B Weekes, in Nevis, heir to gt grandfa Walter Stewart, minister in Ellon Aberdeenshire, reg. 6 Aug.1766.

2535. Weir, Alexander, painter, in Edinburgh, heir to bro Robert Weir, painter in Edinburgh then Jamaica, reg. 22 Oct.1761.

2536. Weir, Elizabeth Moffat, da of A Weir surgeon, in Jamaica, heir to cousin William Hunter, in Swintonhill, reg. 29 Mar.1810.

2537. Weir, John Blackwood, in Torwoodhall Can, heir to mo Helen Blackwood or Weir, w of John Weir in Grahamston Falkirk Stirlingshire, reg. 14 Nov.1853.

2538. Weir, John Blackwood, in Torwoodhall Can, heir to bro James Weir, merchant in Dundas Wentworth Can, reg. 12 Dec.1853.

2539. Weir or Hindman, Margaret, w of James Hindman plasterer, in NY, heir to fa Robert Weir, Capt HEICS in Edinburgh, d. 20 Nov.1851, reg. 17 Jan.1872.

2540. Welsh, James, in St Kitts, heir to fa James Welsh, postal worker in Edinburgh, d. 10 May 1850, reg. 13 Apr.1865.

2541. Welsh, James, in St Kitts, heir to mo Jane Begbie or Welsh, wid of James Welsh, d. 27 Apr.1852, reg. 13 Apr.1865.

2542. Welsh, James, blacksmith, in Pittston Pa, heir to bro John Welsh, in Dalmellington Ayrshire, d. 13 Jan.1873, reg. 22 Sep.1880.

2543. Whan, Thomas, merchant, in Can, heir to fa James McWhan, weaver in Stranraer Wigtownshire, reg. 29 Nov.1850.

2544. White, Alexander Charles, in Woodbine Kan, heir to fa James White, tenant farmer in Ayton Law Berwickshire, d. 14 Jan.1858, reg. 11 Feb.1873.

2545. White, Alexander, in Lake Forest Ill, heir to fa Alexander White of Rosedale, in Lake Forest Ill, d. 18 Mar.1872, reg. 23 June 1873.

2546. White, Elizabeth, in Goshen Dereham Can W, heir to Mary Lang or Rennie, w of William Rennie in Kilsyth Stirlingshire, d. 27 May 1832, reg. 30 July 1867.

2547. White, Janet, in Goshen Can W, heir to grand-aunt Mary Lang or
Rennie, w of William Rennie in Kilsyth Stirlingshire, d. 27 May
1832, reg. 1 May 1868.

2548. White, John, s of Robert White surgeon, in Va, heir to uncle John White
of Whitepark, Depute Clerk of Session, d. 24 Nov.1760, reg. 6
Jan.1762.

2549. White, Margaret, in Brooklyn USA, heir to grandfa John White,
portioner in Duns Berwickshire, reg. 8 May 1856.

2550. White, Melissa, in Goshen Dereham Can W, heir to Mary Lang or
Rennie, w of William Rennie in Kilsyth Stirlingshire, d. 27 May
1832, reg. 30 July 1867.

2551. White, Robert, in Goshen Dereham Can W, heir to Mary Lang or
Rennie, w of William Rennie in Kilsyth Stirlingshire, d. 27 May
1832, reg. 30 July 1867.

2552. White, Robert, in Goshen Can W, heir to grand-aunt Mary Lang or
Rennie, w of William Rennie in Kilsyth Stirlingshire, d. 27 May
1832, reg. 1 May 1868.

2553. White, Thomas, baker, in Brooklyn USA, heir to grandfa John White,
portioner in Duns Berwickshire, reg. 8 May 1856.

2554. Whiteford, William, in Montreal, heir to grandmo Jane Whiteford, in
Lesmahagow Lanarkshire, reg. 18 Oct.1852.

2555. Whitton, George, merchant, in Marshalltown Ia, heir to fa John Whitton,
surgeon in Ia, reg. 19 July 1870.

2556. Whitton jr, James, inspector, in NY, heir to grandmo Margaret Day or
Dempster, vintner in Dundee Angus, d. 10 July 1878, reg. 28
Oct.1881.

2557. Whyte, James Robertson, in Brooklyn NY, heir to aunt Agnes Whyte, in
Forfar Angus, d. Mar.1839, reg. 16 Apr.1873.

2558. Whyte, James Robertson, in Brooklyn NY, heir to uncle Alexander
Whyte, in Forfar Angus, d. 10 Oct.1827, reg. 16 Apr.1873.

2559. Whyte, John, in Montreal, heir to bro William Whyte, MD in Banff, d.
17 Nov.1864, reg. 24 May 1865.

2560. Whyte jr, Robert, carpenter, in Ottawa, heir to mo Janet Robb or Whyte,
w of Robert Whyte carpenter in Ottawa, reg. 8 July 1869.

2561. Whyte jr, William, in NY, heir to fa William Whyte, cabinetmaker in
Glasgow, d. 17 Dec.1872, reg. 6 Dec.1875.

2562. Whyte, Patrick, in Sidney Can, heir to bro Alexander Whyte,
manufacturer in Dundee Angus, d. 7 Jan.1844, reg. 5 Apr.1866.

2563. Whyte, Robert, in America, heir to mo Christian Dick or Whyte, w of
David Whyte manufacturer in Kinross, d. Apr.1829, reg. 27
Sep.1876.

2564. Whytlaw, John, in Miss, heir to uncle John Whytlaw, merchant in
Glasgow then Bay Is NZ, reg. 9 May 1853.

2565. Wight, Andrew, farmer, in Madison Co Mo, heir to aunt Beatrice Wight, in Edinburgh, reg. 2 Feb.1831.

2566. Wightman, John Stanhope, in Rusk NA, heir to mo Sarah Cairns or Wightman, wid of William Wightman in Hamburgh NA, reg. 6 June 1860.

2567. Wighton, George Dickson, clerk, in Col, heir to fa William Wighton, watchmaker in Edinburgh, d. 7 Nov.1866, reg. 2 Nov.1881.

2568. Wilkie, Helen, in St Kitts, heir to grandmo Helen Napier or Forrester, w of J Forrester in Stirling Castle, reg. 22 Jan.1816.

2569. Wilkie, William, in Rantoles Ridge SC, heir to fa Peter Wilkie, grocer in Glasgow, reg. 12 Oct.1832.

2570. Wilkie, William Peter, in SC, heir to grandfa Peter Wilkie, grocer in Glasgow, reg. 9 Sep.1844.

2571. Williamson, Alexander, farmer, in NY, heir to uncle James Williamson, mason in Forres Morayshire, reg. 30 Sep.1857.

2572. Williamson, Andrew, in Banksville Pa, heir to aunt Janet Williamson, in College Fordell Fife, d. 10 May 1867, reg. 16 Sep.1882.

2573. Williamson or McKedie, Catherine, in Quebec, heir to mo Catherine Williamson, wid of John Williamson in Auchnagarry, d. 18 June 1870, reg. 3 Sep.1873.

2574. Williamson or Markless, Elizabeth, w of Findlay Markless, in Glasgow, heir to cousin John Williamson, planter in Va, reg. 17 Sep.1785.

2575. Williamson or Libberton, Euphemia, w of Robert Libberton, in Abbeyhill, heir to cousin John Williamson, planter in Va, reg. 17 Sep.1785.

2576. Williamson, George, clerk, in Edinburgh, heir to grand-uncle Alexander Naughton, in Tobago, d. 1829, reg. 21 Dec.1865.

2577. Williamson, James, mason, in Can, heir to grandfa James Williamson, in St Fergus Aberdeenshire, reg. 15 Mar.1838.

2578. Williamson or Hutchison, Maria L, w of Robert Hutchison, in NY, heir to aunt Janet Williamson, in Baldridge Dunfermline Fife, d. Oct.1850, reg. 24 Feb.1876.

2579. Williamson, Robert, mason, in NY, heir to fa James Williamson, mason in Gattonside Roxburghshire, reg. 28 Sep.1848.

2580. Williamson, Walter, surgeon, in Stafford Co Va, heir to fa Walter Williamson of Chapeltoun, reg. 14 Aug.1761.

2581. Wilson, Alexander, in NY, heir to fa William Wilson, mason in Edinburgh, reg. 9 Apr.1821.

2582. Wilson, Daniel, DL, in Toronto University, heir to uncle Peter Wilson, in Edinburgh, d. 26 Jan.1864, reg. 8 Nov.1864.

2583. Wilson, David, blacksmith, in Boston, heir to mo Margaret Miller or Wilson, w of John Wilson cabinetmaker in Dundee Angus, reg. 23 Jan.1871.

2584. Wilson or Scott, Gage, w of William Scott, in NB, heir to uncle John Alexander, mason in Castle Douglas Kirkcudbrighthshire, reg. 3 Apr.1846.

2585. Wilson, George, s of David Wilson merchant, in Coupar-Angus Perthshire, heir to uncle James Crockett, MD in SC, d. 16 Apr.1765, reg. 11 Oct.1765.

2586. Wilson, Henry, in NS, heir to mo Isabella Strachan or Wilson, in Inverkeithing Fife, reg. 10 Apr.1839.

2587. Wilson or Milner, Jacobina, w of Pate Mills Milner planter, in NC, heir to fa John Wilson, storekeeper in Va, reg. Feb.1771.

2588. Wilson, James, farmer, in Wisc, heir to fa Robert Wilson, in Neuckfoot, reg. 13 Jan.1852.

2589. Wilson, James, in NY, heir to fa William Wilson, weaver in Johnstone Renfrewshire, reg. 28 Apr.1857.

2590. Wilson or Norfleck, Janet, w of Thomas Norfleck overseer, in Va, heir to fa John Wilson, storekeeper in Va, reg. Feb.1771.

2591. Wilson, John, millwright, in NY, heir to fa J Wilson, farm servant in Carlinwark then Buchan Aberdeenshire, reg. 18 Aug.1834.

2592. Wilson, John, in Berwick then Oskawa Can, heir to grand-aunt Margaret Wilson or Gibson, w of Adam Gibson watchmaker in Duns Berwickshire, reg. 3 Apr.1851.

2593. Wilson, John, in Philadelphia, heir to fa Robert Wilson, laborer in Beith Ayrshire, d. 1 Jan.1844, reg. 4 Dec.1862.

2594. Wilson, John, tenter, in Boston, heir to mo Margaret Miller or Wilson, w of John Wilson cabinetmaker in Dundee Angus, reg. 23 Jan.1871.

2595. Wilson, Matthew, in Mendota America, heir to mo Catherine Paterson or Wilson, in Glasgow, d. 10 Mar.1871, reg. 28 Jan.1878.

2596. Wilson, Robert, in Cincinnati Oh, heir to fa William Wilson, in Toledo Oh, d. 7 Jan.1859, reg. 6 Feb.1871.

2597. Wilson, Robert, in Cincinnati Oh, heir to aunt Betty Wilson, dressmaker in Temple Dalkeith Mid Lothian, d. 17 Apr.1854, reg. 6 Feb.1871.

2598. Wilson, Robert, in New Annan NS, heir to mo Mary Arbuckle or Wilson, w of David Wilson in New Annan NS, d. 11 Sep.1869, reg. 29 Jan.1878.

2599. Wilson, Robert Denholm, in Philadelphia, heir to bro William Wilson, carriage painter in Northampton England, d. 15 July 1874, reg. 28 Mar.1882.

2600. Wilson, Thomas Alexander, in Can W, heir to fa Lawrence Wilson, in Dunfermline Fife then Can W, reg. 10 May 1871.

2601. Wilson, Thomas Alexander, in Can W, heir to mo Janet Alexander, in Dunfermline Fife then Can W, reg. 10 May 1871.

2602. Wilson, William, in Halifax NS, heir to mo Marjory Gerrie or Wilson, w of George Wilson mariner in Aberdeen, reg. 3 Oct.1873.

2603. Wilson, William, in Halifax NS, heir to fa George Wilson, mariner in Aberdeen, reg. 3 Oct.1873.

2604. Winning or Jackson, Ellen, w of William Jackson farmer, in Handcock Ill, heir to fa Thomas Winning, portioner in Balmore Stirlingshire, d. 6 Oct.1852, reg. 3 Oct.1861.

2605. Winning, William Balfour, s of R Winning 82nd Regt, heir to uncle Samuel Dalgleish, in Basseterre Guadaloupe, reg. 18 Aug.1815.

2606. Wise, Charles, bookbinder, in NY, heir to fa Charles Wise, in Newcastle, reg. 5 Apr.1854.

2607. Wishart, Colin, in Arbroath Angus, heir to bro John Wishart, builder in Jamaica, reg. 13 Nov.1844.

2608. Wishart or Ray, Elizabeth, w of James Ray, in NY, heir to fa George Wishart, shipmaster in Bo'ness W Lothian, reg. 21 Nov.1777.

2609. Wishart, George, in Kan, heir to bro John Wishart, s of George Wishart in Howaback Sandwick Orkney, d. Aug.1873, reg. 3 Nov.1872.

2610. Wishart, John, carpenter, in Portsmouth Can W, heir to uncle Edward Wishart, in Oback Orkney, reg. 23 June 1864.

2611. Woddrop, William, merchant, in Tappahannock Va, heir to fa John Woddrop, writer in Edinburgh, reg. 22 Jan.1772.

2612. Wood, Andrew, doctor, in Ipswich England, heir to uncle Andrew Baird, bookseller in Edinburgh then Jamaica, reg. 7 Sep.1827.

2613. Wood, Frederic George, in Rotherham England, heir to mo Johanna Adam or Wood, in Antigua, reg. 19 Jan.1860.

2614. Wood, George, ship carpenter, in St John NB, heir to grandfa Andrew Wood, weaver in Drumeldrie Muir Fife, d. 1 Aug 1824, reg. 1 Aug.1849.

2615. Wood, George, insurance agent, in Philadelphia, heir to fa Alexander Wood of Woodcot, in Mid Lothian, d. 18 July 1864, reg. 21 Dec.1865.

2616. Wood, George, agent Royal Insurance Co, in Philadelphia, heir to grand-uncle Sir Alexander Wood, in Edinburgh, d. 18 Mar.1847, reg. 24 May 1867.

2617. Wood, James, in America, heir to grandmo Elspeth Anderson or Wood, w of James Wood in Dundee Angus, reg. 3 July 1849.

2618. Wood, James, in Newhaven Ct, heir to uncle Joseph Wood, engineer in Havanna Cuba, d. 1 July 1867, reg. 27 Sep.1870.

2619. Wood or Moxey, Janet Mary, w of John Gray Moxey baker, in Philadelphia, heir to fa John Wood, in Edinburgh, reg. 20 Apr.1853.

2620. Wood, Robert Walker, engraver, in Edinburgh, heir to bro Thomas Wood, in Magnolia New Orleans, d. 18 Oct.1857, reg. 13 Apr.1865.

2621. Wood, William, provision merchant, in Edinburgh, heir to mo Margaret Clark or Wood, w of Simon Wood in America, d. 1 Sep.1849, reg. 18 June 1879.

2622. Woodhouse, Sarah Jane, in St Croix, heir to grandfa William Mitchell, merchant in St Croix, d. 1834, reg. 4 June 1883.

2623. Woodhouse, Sarah Jane, in St Croix, heir to grand-aunt Ann Mitchell or Bowman, w of John Bowman in St Vigeans Arbroath Angus, d. 1 Sep.1798, reg. 8 June 1883.

2624. Wotherspoon, Charlotte Bruce, in Bavaria, heir to bro James Wotherspoon, in NY, reg. 8 June 1857.

2625. Wotherspoon or Calder, Margaret, w of John Calder, in Australia, heir to bro James Wotherspoon, in NY, reg. 8 June 1857.

2626. Wren, William, engineer, in USA, heir to mo Agnes Kerr or Wren, w of William Wren collier in Ayr, reg. 11 Mar.1858.

2627. Wright, Alexander Malcolm, in NY, heir to fa Alexander Wright, in Pilrig St Edinburgh, d. 23 Sep.1866, reg. 27 Oct.1873.

2628. Wright, Archibald John, in Newark NJ, heir to mo Jean Wilson or Wright, wid of Charles Wright wheelwright in Elgin Morayshire, d. 14 Mar.1860, reg. 31 July 1861.

2629. Wright or D'Arusmont, Francesca, in Cincinnati, heir to cousin Margaret Wright, in Dundee Angus, reg. 29 Apr.1845.

2630. Wright or D'Arusmont, Francesca, in Cincinnati, heir to cousin Katherine Wright, in Dundee Angus, reg. 29 Apr.1845.

2631. Wright or Lockie, Jessie, w of William Lockie, in Carloville USA, heir to mo Louisa Crawford or Wright, wid of Malcom Wright butler in Edinburgh, d. 15 May 1881, reg. 27 July 1881.

2632. Wybar, James, painter, in NY, heir to fa George Wybar, sawyer in Edinburgh, reg. 9 Dec.1857.

2633. Wylie, David, grocer, in Glasgow, heir to Andrew Smith, in Jamaica, reg. 1 July 1829.

2634. Wylie, John, farmer, in Glover Orleans Co NA, heir to uncle Thomas Morrison, chandler in Whitburn W Lothian, d. 17 Dec.1853, reg. 24 June 1864.

2635. Wyllie, Robert, in NY, heir to fa Andrew Wyllie, shoemaker in Kinross, reg. 18 Dec.1845.

2636. Wyllie, Robert Crichton, in Hazelbank Sandwich Is, heir to aunt Agnes Crichton, shopkeeper in Holm Ayrshire, d. July 1843, reg. 30 Jan.1861.

2637. Wyllie, William Fleming, farmer, in Utica Ill, heir to bro James Wyllie, in Fullwood Stewarton Ayrshire, d. 29 Jan.1870, reg. 16 Aug.1879.

2638. Yarrel, Elizabeth, w of Capt G Yarrel, in NC, heir to grand-uncle W Begbie of Giffordvale, reg. 6 Nov.1827.

2639. Young, Andrew Houstoun, merchant, in Quebec, heir to gt grandfa James Howison, portioner of Hindford, reg. 14 Oct.1836.

2640. Young, Andrew, in Up Can, heir to uncle John Richmond, in Houletburn Louden Castle Ayrshire, reg. 9 Feb.1848.

2641. Young or Bissett, Ann, w of James Bissett machinist, in NJ, heir to mo Ann Gunn or Young, wid of Alexander Young in Dundee Angus, reg. 7 Dec.1871.

2642. Young or David, Deuchars, w of Thomas Davis, in NJ, heir to mo Ann Gunn or Young, wid of Alexander Young mechanic in Dundee Angus, reg. 7 Dec.1871.

2643. Young, George, stockbroker, in USA, heir to grandfa James Scott, wright in Kelso Roxburghshire, reg. 29 May 1854.

2644. Young, George, in Fitzroy Can W, heir to uncle Alexander Jack, merchant in Perth, d. 24 July 1810, reg. 12 Jan.1863.

2645. Young, George, in Fitzroy Can W, heir to fa John Young, glover in Perth, d. 6 Oct.1810, reg. 12 Jan.1863.

2646. Young, Helen Clarke, in America, heir to fa James Young, in Lilliesleaf Roxburghshire then Edinburgh, reg. 24 Nov.1848.

2647. Young, Hugh, stonecutter, in NY, heir to aunt Janet Young, in Kilmarnock Ayrshire, d. 28 Aug.1859, reg. 7 Mar.1861.

2648. Young, Hugh, stonecutter, in NY, heir to fa James Young, mason in Kilmarnock Ayrshire, d. 26 Apr.1860, reg. 7 Mar.1861.

2649. Young, James, in Port Huron USA, heir to fa James Young, portioner in Torwoodhead Stirlingshire, d. Apr.1818, reg. 7 Aug.1850.

2650. Young, James, seaman, in Cal, heir to mo Janet Brown or Young, w of Archibald Young watchmaker in Dundee Angus, d. May 1838, reg. 10 May 1871.

2651. Young or Reid or Clarke, Jane Anne, w of Charles Clarke, in Toronto, heir to David Reid, warper in Brechin Angus, reg. 22 Feb.1878.

2652. Young, John, physician, in Montserrat, heir to gt aunt Rebecca Gibbon or Fraser, wid of John Fraser merchant in Aberdeen, reg. 18 Feb.1792.

2653. Young, John, plasterer, in NY, heir to fa George Young, plasterer in Perth then Can, reg. 15 Apr.1828.

2654. Young, John, cooper, in Griffen Town Montreal, heir to uncle John Young, farmer in Blackston then Bishoptown Renfrewshire, d. 28 Jan.1843, reg. 11 June 1861.

2655. Young or Dawson, Mary, w of William Dawson distiller, in Cotmuir, heir to fa David Young, planter in Grenada, reg. 2 Apr.1783.

2656. Young or Millar, Mary, w of Joseph Millar, in St John NB, heir to mo Isabella Cowden or Miller, wid of William Millar carter in Glencaple Dumfries-shire, reg. 17 July 1869.

2657. Young, William, in Northampton Va, heir to fa James Young, merchant in Glasgow, reg. 22 May 1749.

Adair, John 1
Adam, James 4
Adam, Johanna 2613
Adam, John 2, 3
Adam, Robert 5
Adamson, Margaret 130
Adamson, William 8
Addison, James 9
Agnew, James 10
Agnew, Thomas 1489
Aiken, Janet 698
Aikman, Alexander 11
Ainslie, Janet 12
Aird, Alexander 14
Aitchison, Adam 21
Aitchison, Andrew 19, 20
Aitchison, William 1370
Aitken, James 25
Aitken, Jean 23
Aitken, Mary 24
Aitken, William 22
Alexander of Drumnachrim, Quintin 1529, 1613
Alexander of Menstrie, Sir William 725
Alexander, George 29
Alexander, James 28
Alexander, Janet 513, 1595, 2601
Alexander, John 2584
Alexander, Marie Jean 26, 32, 40
Alexander, Mary 1556, 2081
Alexander, Robert 37
Alexander, Robertina 27, 34
Alexander, William 33, 35, 36, 1637
Allan, Archibald 42
Allan, George 44, 54
Allan, James 43, 45
Allan, Margaret 60

Allan, Robert 49, 50
Allason, William 56
Allen, Christien 57
Allison, James 58
Allison, John 59
Alves of Shipland, Thomas 61
Anderson, Alexander 66
Anderson, Alexandrina 68
Anderson, Andrew 70, 1726
Anderson, Barbara 83
Anderson, David 86, 74, 87
Anderson, Elizabeth 1724
Anderson, Elspeth 2617
Anderson, George 73, 90
Anderson, Helen 1734
Anderson, Henry 96
Anderson, James 72, 80, 81, 82, 89, 1725
Anderson, Janet 1443, 1446, 1444, 1450, 1451, 1452
Anderson, Jean 93
Anderson, John 64, 77, 62, 84, 85
Anderson, Margaret 94
Anderson, Mary 95
Anderson, Rachel 92
Anderson, Robert 67, 88
Anderson, Thomas 69
Anderson, William 78, 91, 71, 97, 458
Annan, John 100
Arbuckle, Mary 2598
Archer, Andrew 102
Archibald, Elizabeth 1759, 2059
Archibald, John 103, 104
Armour, Hugh 105
Armour, William 106
Armstrong, Elizabeth 107
Armstrong, Mary 2175

143

Arnot, Christian 1993, 2405
Arnot, Janet 450
Arnot, John 108
Arnott, George 109
Arnott, John 110
Arrol, Margaret 112
Arrol, Thomas 111
Arthur, Archibald 114
Arthur, Cecilia Young 115
Arthur, Henry Monteath 116
Arthur, James Young 117
Athol, John 122
Auchenvole, Alexander 123
Auchterlonie, Thomas 124
Auld, Ann 155
Auld, James 125
Auld, Mary 426
Austin of Kilspindie, Joseph 126
Austin, Margaret Isabella 127
Baillie of Meikle Dunragget,
    Alexander 1225, 1697
Baillie, Margaret 129
Baillie, Martha 707
Bain, Archibald 133
Bain, George 138
Bain, John 131
Bain, Thomas 132
Baine, Anderson 137
Baine, Colin 135
Baine, Susan 136
Baird, Andrew 139, 2612
Baird, Archibald 144
Baird, John 143
Bald, Adam 145
Balderstone, Ann 1187
Ballantine, Helen 1131
Ballantyne of Kelly, Archibald 1382
Ballantyne, James 147
Ballingall of Denoon, John 1237
Ballingall, James 148, 1236
Ballingall, Laurence 150
Ballingall, William 149
Balmanno, Helen 151
Balmer, Richard 152
Bankhead, Jane 662
Banks, James 1058
Baptist, John 510
Barclay of Cairnes, George 161

Barclay of Ury, Robert 55
Barclay, Andrew 164
Barclay, Charles 156, 158
Barclay, Henry 166
Barclay, James 157, 162, 163
Barclay, John 159
Barclay, Thomas 160
Barclay, William 165
Barland, John 167
Barr, Archibald 170, 169, 2255
Barr, Janet 415
Barrie, Gilbert 2490
Barrowman, John 808
Bartholemew, Ann 261
Bartholemew, George 260
Bartlett, James 173
Baxter, Christian 1899
Baxter, David 175, 2500
Baxter, Janet 1898
Baxter, John 1169
Beaton, Alexander 180
Beattie, Francis 179
Beattie, James 178
Begbie of Giffordvale, W 2638
Begbie of Giffordvale, William 181,
    182
Begbie, Jane 2541
Begrie, Alexander 183
Begrie, David 185
Begrie, William 184
Beith, John 186, 187
Bell , Jean 192
Bell, Benjamin 1834
Bell, Catherine 188
Bell, David 191
Bell, Margaret 277, 923
Bell, Mary 142
Bell, Thomas 194
Bell, William 195, 197, 190, 189,
    193, 1035, 1813, 2311
Bennet, Christian 2217
Bennett, James Henry 201
Bennie, Elisabeth Willison 390
Berford, Ann Mary 202
Berrie of Thomaston, James 203
Bertram, William 204
Berwick, David 205
Berwick, Newall 206, 207

Bethune, Eleanora 1824
Beveridge, Francis 209
Beveridge, Matthew 1711
Birrell, Mary 212
Birrell, William 213
Bisset, Jane 214
Black, Ann 218
Black, Archibald 216
Black, David 222
Black, Helen 1032
Black, Isabella 1126
Black, James 223
Black, Janet 38
Black, Jessie 220
Black, Marian Scotland 219
Black, Mary 217
Black, Peter 2140
Black, Quintin 39
Black, William 211
Blackburn, Hugh 224
Blacklock, Helen 227
Blacklock, James 228
Blackwood, Helen 2537
Blaikie, Francis 231
Blain, James 234
Blain, Joseph 235
Blain, Margaret 233
Blair of Merchiston, Archibald 237
Blair, Agnes 176, 241
Blair, Ann 969
Blair, Dugald 238
Blair, Elizabeth 240
Blair, James 236, 239
Blair, Thomas 1119
Blanchill, William 1965
Bland, Alexander 243
Blount, Samuel 244, 246
Bluntach, John 247
Blyth, Alexander 1873
Blyth, Catherine 2073
Blyth, Jane 249
Blyth, John 609
Blyth, Thomas 248
Boag, Jean 250
Bodie, Ann 2409
Bogie, Isabella 7
Bone, Edward 134
Bone, Janet 1406

Bonnar, Thomas 253
Bontein, William 254
Borthwick, David 257
Boswell, David 258, 259
Boswell, Margaret 807, 809
Bowman, David 265, 1887
Bowman, John 262, 264
Bowman, Margaret 263
Bowman, William 268
Boyce, Joseph 272
Boyd, Alexander 273
Boyd, Janet 1042, 1092, 1093, 1095, 1097
Boyd, William 274
Boyle, John 276
Brander, Jean 278
Brands, Robert 287, 288, 289, 290
Brasnell, William 291
Breakinridge, Thomas 292
Brebner, Alexander 294
Bremner, George 295, 619
Briggs, Agnes 2257, 2258
Brims, Donald 296
Brodie, Andrew 299
Brotherstone, William 301
Brough of Boghall, John 2335
Brough of Boghall, Mary 2336
Brown, Alexander 313, 323, 328
Brown, David 308
Brown, Dr John 324
Brown, Gustavus 309
Brown, Helen 316
Brown, Henry 329
Brown, James 322
Brown, Janet 2650
Brown, John 327, 2309
Brown, Margaret 1325, 1560
Brown, Thomas 320
Brown, William 317, 330
Brown, William James 311
Brownlee Hamilton, Alexander 2023
Bruce, Alexander 333
Bruce, Andrew 334
Bruce, Mary 332
Bruce, William 335
Bryan, William 336
Bryce, Catherine 1890
Bryce, Mary 1628

150

Graham, Hugh 943
Graham, Isobel 1938, 1941
Grahame, Duncan 686
Grainger, William 953, 954
Grant of Kilgraston, John 965
Grant, Alexander 968
Grant, Elizabeth 966
Grant, Emily 967
Grant, Hugh 971
Grant, Katherine 297
Grant, Margaret 1794
Grant, Robert 955
Grant, Robert Charles 957
Gray of Shirvadike, William 975
Gray, Andrew 338, 980
Gray, Charles 972
Gray, David 977
Gray, Hugh 982
Gray, Jean 973
Gray, Margaret 974
Gray, William 976, 979
Gray-Morison of Craigend, John 1766
Greenfield, Agnes 1752, 1753
Greenlaw, John 983, 984
Gregory, Elizabeth Mary 848
Greig, Benjamin 210
Greig, George 985, 986
Greig, Simon 987
Grierson, Margaret 1401
Grieve, James 989
Grindlay, Jean 337, 794
Gunn, Ann 665, 1727, 2641, 2642
Haddow, Elizabeth 1926
Haggart, David 993
Haining, Jane 1594
Halket jr, William 995
Hall, Mary 997
Hall, William 996, 998
Halley, William 999
Halliday, Alexander 1006
Halliday, David 1001, 1004, 1005
Halliday, Hugh 1003
Halliday, John 433
Hally, Charles 1007
Halyburton, Ann 1008
Hamilton of Broomfield, John 732, 733, 735

Hamilton of Dowan, Lt James 1014, 1016, 1018
Hamilton, Ann B 731, 736, 737
Hamilton, James 1009, 1017
Hamilton, John 1011, 1015
Hamilton, Rebecca 1012
Hamilton, Robert 1010
Hamilton, William 496
Hannah, Peter 1019
Hardie, James 1020
Harlaw, Alexander 1021
Harley, Archibald 1022
Hart, James 392, 393
Hartley, Mary 1028
Harvey, Charles 1030
Harvey, John 1029
Harvie, James 1031
Hawkins, Janet 1034
Hawks, Henry 1036
Hay, Andrew 1041
Hay, Elizabeth 1038
Hay, William 1040
Heatherington, Catherine 508
Heddle of Quildon, William 1044
Heddle, Hugh Leask 1043
Heddle, William 1045
Hempsed, John 1046
Henderson of Cleughbrae, John 1050
Henderson of Laverockhall, James 632
Henderson of Rosebank, James 1053
Henderson, Ann 1378
Henderson, Balfour 505
Henderson, Daniel 1047
Henderson, David 2418, 2421, 2422, 2426, 2429, 2434
Henderson, Grizel 1051
Henderson, James 1055
Henderson, Jessie 1059
Henderson, John 1057
Hendry jr, Alexander 1063
Hendry, Duncan 1062
Hendry, Elizabeth 1061
Hendry, Isabella 497
Henry, Elizabeth Cross 1065
Henry, George 661, 1064
Henry, John 1066
Hepburn, John 805

153

Laurie, James 1306, 1590
Laurie, Margaret 1341
Law, Bethia 1510
Lawrie of Isles, Robert 1309
Lawrie, David 1307
Lawrie, Matthew 1308
Lawson of Cuparhead, George 1314
Lawson of Knockhornock, George 1313
Lawson, George 1310
Lawson, John 1311
Layton, Margaret Anne 1316
Learmount, Mary 1246
Leask, John 1318
Leckie, John 1320
Ledgerwood, Mary 1191
Lees, John 1322
Leggat, Andrew 1323
Leighton, Francis 1324
Leitch, Andrew 1326
Leith of Blair, John 1327
Lennox of Dalscairth, James 1329
Lennox, James 1330
Lenox of Dalscairth, James 1332
Lenox, David 1331
Lerrie, James 1333
Leslie of Powis, Hugh 1336
Leslie of Powis, John 1335
Leslie, Arabella 1337
Leslie, Isobel 1773
Liddell, Charles 1002
Liddell, Robert 1339
Liddle, Janet 1340
Lillie, Jess 1343, 1344
Lillie, John 1342
Lindsay, Alexander 1347
Lindsay, David 429
Lindsay, Elizabeth 992
Lindsay, Margaret 466
Lithgow, Helen 1338
Lithgow, Mary 1351
Little, Bryce 1352
Littlejohn, John 1353
Livingston, Agnes 2110
Livingstone, Archibald 1355, 1357
Livingstone, James 1356, 1358
Lockerbie, Jean 1359
Lockerbie, William 1360

Lockerby, Elizabeth 2015
Lockerby, Isabella 1853
Lockhart of Tarbrax, Norman 1362
Lockhart, Samuel 1364
Logan, John 1365
Logan, William 1367, 1368
Loudon, Agnes 1372
Lovell, James 1374
Lovie, Elizabeth 1856
Lovie, George 1181
Low, James 1376
Low, John 1377
Low, William 1375
Lowson, H 367
Lowson, Helen 1129, 1758
Lumgair, James 1379
Lumsdane, Walter 1935
Lumsden of Pitcaple, Alexander 575
Lumsden, David 1380, 1381
Lumsden, Isabella 271
Lumsden, Isabelle 1137
Lumsden, Jean 831
Lyall of Gallery, David 1383
Lyle, Robert 154, 1384, 1385, 1386
Lyon, James 1388
Lyon, Janet 1391
Lyon, John 339, 2273
Lyon, Margaret 1448
McAdie, David 1392
Macalister, John 1395
Macalister, Robert 1394
McAllister, Patrick 1396
MacAlpine, John 1397, 1398
McArthur, Duncan 230
McArthur, Mary 1399
McArthur, Robert 1400
McAskell, Allan 1402
McAulay, Henry 1403
McBeath, James 1404
McCallum, Jean Henderson 897
McCandlish, Blair 1408
McCandlish, Elizabeth 420, 1407
McClune, James 1665
McClure, James 1412
McClure, William 1413
McClusky, Alexander 1414
McCoull, Christiana 1416
MacCraire, Robina 1054

McCredie, Hugh 1418
McCrorie, Grizel 1419
McCulloch jr, John 1423
McCulloch, Andrew 1421
McCulloch, Archibald 1422
McCulloch, David 946
McCulloch, James 1420
McDiarmid, John 1424
MacDonald of Morar Inverness-shire,
 Major Simon 1432
MacDonald, Allan 1431
McDonald, Daniel 1428
McDonald, Hannah 1508, 1517
McDonald, Hugh 1427
McDonald, James 1828
MacDonald, John 1429
McDonald, John 1433
MacDonald, John 1426
McDonald, Mary 645, 994
McDonald, Ronald 1425
McDonald, William 929
McDougall, Alexander 1438
McDougall, Robert 1435
McDougall, William 1434, 1437
McDowall, Robert 1439
McEwan, John 1442
McEwan, William 1441
McFarlane, Duncan 1449
McFarlane, James 2047
McFarlane, John 1123
McFarlane, Peter 1445
McGeachy, Duncan 1453
McGill, Jean 1455
McGillivray of Dalcrombie, Farquhar
 1456
McGillivray of Dunmaglass, John
 1457
McGlashan, A 1461
McGlashan, Grizel Grace 942
McGlashan, James 1459, 1462
McGlashan, William 1460
MacGoun, Duncan 1464, 1466
MacGoun, John 1465
MacGoun, Robert 1467, 1463, 1468
McGowan, Andrew 1470
McGowan, Elizabeth 1471
McGowan, John 1469
McGregor of Balhaldie, Donald 689

McGregor of Balholdie, Donald 1454
McGregor, Ann 1979
MacGregor, David 1473
MacGregor, James 1476
McGregor, John 849, 1477
MacGregor, Margaret 1474
McGregor, Mary 1472
McGregor, Peter 1475
McGregor, William 1478
McGrigor, Frances 1802
MacGrigor, Robert 1479
McHoull, William 1480
McIldoe, James 730, 815
McIndoe, James 1481
McIntosh, James 1485
McIntosh, Nicholas 1458
McIver, Colin 1488
MacIver, Farquhar 398
McJannet, Samuel Watkinson 1490
Mack, Hamilton 1491
Mack, William 1492, 1493
McKarchar, John 1494
McKay, Charles 1500
Mackay, Elizabeth 798
McKay, Hugh 1502
Mackay, John 168, 1499
Mackay, Peter 1497
Mackay, Thomas 1495
Mackay, William 1496, 1498
McKean, James 1503
McKechnie, Peter 1505
McKen, Thomas 1506
Mackenzie of Forret, James 1513
McKenzie, Alexander 1516
MacKenzie, Alexander 1294
Mackenzie, Ann 1511
Mackenzie, Catherine 1994
Mackenzie, Daniel 1507
Mackenzie, George 15, 17
Mackenzie, Jemima 1519
Mackenzie, John 1089, 1518, 1991
McKenzie, John 1755
Mackenzie, Kenneth 1512
Mackenzie, Margaret 16
Mackenzie, Roderick 1509
McKerrell, Archibald 1772
McKewn, Barbara 245
Mackie of Barmore, Patrick 1088

Mackie, Charles 1525, 1534
Mackie, David 1157
Mackie, Marion 1158
Mackie, Robert 1533
Mackinlay, Matthew 1535
McKinlay, Mungo 2187
Mackirdy, John 1537
MacKnaight, Thomas 1538
McLachlan of Cameron, Hugh 1541
McLachlan, Allan 1539, 1540
McLachlan, James 1542
McLaren, Alexander 1545
McLaren, Donald 608, 1544, 1546, 1547, 1548
McLaren, William 1549
McLarne, Robert 1265
McLaughlan, George 1550
McLea, Robert 1551
MacLean, Ann 493
MacLean, Christina 1536
MacLean, James 1554
McLeary, Samuel 1557
McLehose, John 1558
McLeish, David 1559
McLennan, Thomas 1561
McLeod, George 1562, 1563, 1564
MacLure, Margaret 1565
McMaster, Andrew 2242
McMillan, George 1567
McMillan, Gilbert 1568
McMillan, Marion 221, 1566
McMurdo, Mary 340
MacNab, John 1570
McNab, John 742
McNaught, Daniel 863
McNaughton, Daniel 1571
McNaughton, John 1572
McNicol, Robert 1577
McNiven, Alexander 1580
McOmish, John 1581
McOwan, Peter 1583
MacPherson, Donald 2232
McPherson, Donald 699
McPherson, Duncan 1585
McPherson, George 1584
McRitchie, David 1588
McRonald, Thomas 1589
Mactavish, Dugald 1591

McVicar, Elizabeth 1592
McVity, James 1593
McWhan, James 2543
MacWilliam, James 1597
McWilliam, John 229, 1596
Maguire, John 1598
Mailer, Andrew 1601
Main, James 1602, 1603
Mair, James 1604
Maitland, Lillias 1605
Malcolm, Janet Gordon 760
Malloch, Andrew 1608
Maltman, John 1609
Manson, Daniel 1037, 1048, 1049
Mark, Alexander 1612
Marnie, Sarah 1672
Marnoch, Robert 1976
Marquis, John 1614
Marshall, David 1616
Marshall, Francis 1621
Marshall, George 1617
Marshall, James 570, 970, 1615
Marshall, John 1622, 1623
Marshall, Joseph 1618
Marshall, William 1620
Martin, Alexander 1636
Martin, George 1627
Martin, James 1625, 1635
Martin, Marion 1317
Martin, Peter 1638
Martin, Robert 1633
Martin, William A 1626, 1631
Mason, Robert 1639
Masson, Elizabeth 1641
Mathieson, John 2185
Mathison, Helen 1189
Mathison, James 1190
Mathison, Janet 1188
Matthews, Alexander 1654
Matthewson, John 1655
Maull, James 1656
Maurice, Alexander 1657
Mavor, Jane 1520
Maxwell, Alexander 1658
Maxwell, Charles 1659, 1663
Maxwell, James 1660
Maxwell, John Strange 1664
Maxwell, Margaret 2532

156

Maxwell, William 1661
Meikle, James 1666
Mein, Alexander 99
Mein, Andrew 1161
Mein, Robert 1155
Meldrum, Andrew 1668, 1667, 1669
Melrose, Robert 1670
Melville, Andrew 1671
Melville, Marjory 2123
Menzies, James 1673
Menzies, Robert 2209
Mercer, James 1674
Merrilees, Fletcher 1675
Metcalfe, Penelope 1677
Methven, Margaret 1678, 2074
Millar, Alexander 1680, 1686, 1681,
    1682, 1679, 1687, 1690, 1691,
    1693
Millar, Archibald 1685
Millar, David 1694
Millar, James 585, 1683
Millar, John 1689, 1684, 1692
Millar, Joseph 1688
Millar, Lillias 1569
Miller, Agnes 1700, 1025, 1986
Miller, Alexander Crumm 1714
Miller, Ann 1703
Miller, Catherine 2100
Miller, Daniel 1709
Miller, George 1701, 1710, 1712
Miller, Helen 1624
Miller, Isobel 1992
Miller, James 1695, 1698, 1707
Miller, Joseph 1706
Miller, Margaret 2583, 2594
Miller, Philip 1702
Miller, Thomas 1705
Milligan of Dalskairth, David 1905,
    1906
Milliken, Christina 2424
Milliken, Mary 2423
Milln, John 1715
Miln, John 1716
Milne, Charles 1719
Milne, Francis 1718
Milne, Helen 722, 724
Milne, John 1717
Milne, Robert 1721

Milne, William 1720, 1722
Minnoch jr, Alexander 1823
Mitchell of Blairgetts, James 1735
Mitchell sr, James 1732
Mitchell, Ann 2623
Mitchell, David 1728
Mitchell, Elizabeth 2371
Mitchell, George 1733
Mitchell, Jessie 1729
Mitchell, Robert 1723
Mitchell, Thomas 1176
Mitchell, William 2622
Mitchell, Young 1737, 1738
Moar, Peter Clouston 1739
Moffat, Euphemia 1736, 2494
Moffat, George 1742
Moffat, John 1743
Monach, James 1746
Monach, Janet 1748
Monach, Margaret 1747
Monilaws, Margaret 1962
Monro, Catherine 1749
Monteath, Margaret 1751
Montgomery of Nettlehurst &
    Mosshead, John 1754
Montgomery, Barbara 1907
Montgomery, Mary 2492
Moodie, James 1756, 1757
Morin of Morintown, John 1760
Morin of Morintown, William 1761
Morison, John 1762, 1763, 1764
Morison, Margaret 30
Morison, Nathaniel 1587
Morison, Robert 1765
Morrieson, Sophia 1885
Morrin, Samuel 526
Morris, Alexander 1767, 1770, 1771
Morris, James 1768
Morris, Thomas 1769
Morrison of Craighead, William 1777
Morrison, Janet 312, 307, 315, 325,
    2155
Morrison, Margaret 753
Morrison, Mary 1745
Morrison, Susanna 752
Morrison, Thomas 1774, 2634
Morton, Frances 1842
Morton, John 314

158

Pagan, William 1882
Page, Helenus 1883
Paisley, Walter 1143
Panton, Alexander 1886
Park, David 1888
Park, John 2119
Park, Lillias 1891
Park, Margaret 1892
Park, Walter 1889
Parker, George 1895
Parker, Hugh 1896
Parker, Patrick 1894
Parlane, Alexander 1897
Pasley, Walter 1893
Paterson, Alison 1082
Paterson, Archibald 1903
Paterson, Catherine 2595
Paterson, Charles 1904
Paterson, Isabel 1910
Paterson, James 1902
Paterson, John 140
Paterson, Peter 1775
Paterson, T 1901
Paterson, Thomas 1908
Paterson, William 1909
Patison, Robert 1393
Paton, Catherine 1543
Paton, Christian 1912
Paton, Janet 2139
Paton, John 981, 1911, 1913, 1915
Paton, Mary 1930
Paton, Peter 1914
Patrick of Shotts, Robert 1918
Patrick, Anne 1916
Patrick, William 1917
Patterson, Charles 1321
Patterson, Thomas 1166
Paul, Thomson 1920
Paxton, Andrew 1923
Paxton, Jean 944, 945
Paxton, Thomas 1924
Pearson, William 1925
Peebles, Charles 1927
Penman, David 1928
Penman, Rebecca 866
Pennell, Jane 717
Perrie, Anna 1056
Perry, James 1931

Peter, David 1932
Peterkin, John 1933
Petrie, James 1934
Pew, Alexander 1936
Philip, Elizabeth 65
Philip, Jane 1940
Philip, Thomas 1939
Philips, William 1942
Phillips, David 374
Philp of Greenlaw, James 522
Pillans, William 962, 961, 963, 964
Pirie, John 1945
Pirie, Thomas 1943
Pitbladdo, Colin 1946
Playfair, Barbara 208
Playfair, James 1947, 1948
Porteous, Helen 1955
Porteous, James 1956
Porteous, John 1953
Porteous, Robert 1952
Porter, Henry 1957
Proudfoot of Balbuchty, George 1963
Purse, Alexander 1964
Purves, Alexander 1966
Purvis, Burridge 1967
Rae of Gorseness, John 1971, 1973, 1974
Rae of Gorseness, William 1972
Rae of Park, William 1975
Rae, George 1968
Rae, John 1970
Rae, Thomas 1969
Rainnie, John 448
Ralston, Alexander 1977
Ralston, John 1978
Ramsay, David 1982
Ramsay, Grizel 1884
Ramsay, James 1980
Rankin, Daniel 1371
Rankin, James 1985
Rankine jr, Thomas 2235
Rattray, Henry 1987
Rattray, William 1988
Rayburn, Agnes 2367
Read, William 1023
Reddie, Helen 2224
Reid, Ann 2356
Reid, David 1996, 1995, 2651

159

Reid, Elizabeth 894
Reid, George 2003
Reid, James 1989, 1997
Reid, Jean 1060, 2000, 2007
Reid, John 2002, 2001, 2006
Reid, Mainie 1369
Reid, Margaret 1553
Reid, Peter 1990
Reid, William 1998, 2005
Renfrew, Robert 2009, 2010
Rennie, David 2011
Renton, Robert 2012
Renton, William 2013
Renwick, Robert 196
Renwick, Thomas 2014
Riach, James 2018
Riach, Peter 2017
Richardson , Matthew 2020
Richardson, John 2019
Richardson, William 2021
Richmond, John 2640
Riddell, Robert 2022
Riddell, Thomas 2024
Riddell, Walter 2025
Riddie, Mary 2026
Riddle, Robert 2027
Riddler, John 2028
Ridley sr, James 2029
Rintoul, David 2030, 2032, 2034, 2036
Rintoul, Janet 2033
Rintoul, Thomas 1226, 2031
Rintoul, William 2035
Ritchie, Alexander 2040, 2045
Ritchie, Andrew 488
Ritchie, Archibald 2038
Ritchie, James 2043
Ritchie, John 2039, 2037, 2044, 2046
Ritchie, William 2042
Robb, Janet 2560
Robb, Mary 2050
Robb, William 2048, 2049
Roberton, Mary 2180, 2181
Roberts, James 2051
Robertson of Fascally, George 702
Robertson of Struan, George 2075
Robertson, Adam 2067, 2080

Robertson, Ann 883
Robertson, Cardelia 375
Robertson, Catherine 141, 727
Robertson, Christian 569, 1782
Robertson, David 2079, 2071, 2077, 2085
Robertson, Donald 2052
Robertson, Elizabeth 319
Robertson, George 2054
Robertson, Isabella 2064
Robertson, James 2053, 1831, 2068
Robertson, Jane 2060, 2076
Robertson, Jean 1024
Robertson, Jessie 2041
Robertson, John 2063, 2056, 2072, 2086
Robertson, Johnston 2069
Robertson, Margaret 2058, 2427
Robertson, Marion 318
Robertson, Mary 2055, 2179
Robertson, Patrick 2082
Robertson, Susan 2065
Robertson, William 2062, 2084
Robson, James 2088
Robson, John 729
Rodger, Andrew 2091, 2093
Rodger, David 2092
Rodger, James 2097
Rodger, Janet 2094, 2095, 2096
Rodgers, James 2099
Ronald, Agnes 709
Rose, Helen 2344
Rose, Marjery 2395
Rosier, Edward 2101
Ross, Alexander 1440
Ross, David 2107, 2112
Ross, Donald 2104, 2114, 2117
Ross, Henry 2111
Ross, James 2109, 2105, 2108, 2116
Ross, John 2106
Ross, Philip 2113
Ross, Walter 2103
Ross, William 2102
Rossie, John 2118
Rowat, David 2120
Rowsay, John 2122
Roxburgh, William 2124
Rumgay, John 888

161

Sloane, Peter 1522, 1531, 1526, 2248, 2249
Sloane, William 2245
Smart, David 2252
Smart, John 2253
Smellie, John 2254
Smith of Craigend, James 2266
Smith, Alexander 2259, 2089, 2265, 2269, 2281
Smith, Andrew 2267, 2276, 2633
Smith, Gavin 2274
Smith, George 1652, 2262, 76, 2270, 2271, 2277, 2280
Smith, Henry 2287
Smith, Hugh 2284
Smith, Isabel 2261
Smith, James 2260, 2004, 2264
Smith, Jean 2268
Smith, Jessie 2275
Smith, John 671, 607, 2256, 2272, 2278, 2279
Smith, Margaret 343
Smith, Mary 873
Smith, Peter 2282, 2283
Smith, Robert 2263
Smith, William 2285
Sneddon, Janet 947
Souter, Elizabeth 930
Soutter, Catherine 2289
Soutter, William 2288
Speden, Robert 2290
Spence, Andrew 2291
Spence, John 2292
Spence, Nicol 2293
Spiers, James 2294
Spreull, Andrew 1900
Sproat of Portmary, David 1328
Sproat, Helen 933
Sproat, William 2296
Sprott, James 2297
Stalker, James 1346
Stalker, Margaret 1345
Stark, Sarah 1315
Steel, Archibald 2299
Steel, Christiana 1163
Steel, Helen 2300
Steel, Jean 2382
Steele, James 1220

Steele, Jane 2301
Steinson, James 2286
Stennet, Emilia 2189
Stephen, Robert 2304
Steven, James 2307, 2308
Steven, John 101, 2306
Stevens, Janet 1128
Stevenson, Ann 650, 651, 652
Stevenson, Elizabeth 1501
Stevenson, James 2312, 2313
Stevenson, Matthew 2314
Stewart jr, Alexander 2318
Stewart, Alexander 499, 2331
Stewart, Anne 113
Stewart, Dugald 2332
Stewart, Duncan 501
Stewart, Esther 539
Stewart, George 2329
Stewart, Hugh 2334
Stewart, James 2315, 2316, 2321, 2320, 275, 1574, 1575, 2317, 2323, 2324, 2326, 2337, 2338, 2339, 2341
Stewart, John 2328
Stewart, Mary 818, 1185, 1515
Stewart, Norman 2330
Stewart, Peter 2340
Stewart, Robert 427
Stewart, Walter 2534
Stewart, William 2322, 41, 2325, 2333, 2342
Stirling of Stair, James 2345
Stirling, Thomas 2343
Stirrat, David 2347
Stirrat, Margaret 952
Stiven, John 2348
Stocks, James 2352, 2354
Stocks, Jedidiah 2353, 2355
Storrar, Lawrence 2357
Stott, Jane 2358
Strachan of Campfield, John 2359
Strachan, Isabella 2586
Strachan, John 879, 877, 2360, 2361, 2362
Strange, Barbara 2363
Strange, Eliza 2365
Strange, isabella 2366
Strange, James 2364

Stratton, Peter 2368
Struthers, Alexander 2369, 2370
Stuart, Marjory 1305
Summers, Robert 2372
Sutherland, William 2374
Swan of Craigfod, John 2378
Swan, John 2377
Swan, Marion 1275
Swanston, John 2380, 1611, 2381
Syme, Peter 2384
Syme, William 2383
Symmers, George 2385
Symmers, James 2386
Symson of Concraig, Alexander 2387
Tainsh, Catherine 2154
Tait, James 2390
Tait, John 2393, 2394
Tait, Mary 2503
Tait, Peter 2388
Tait, William 2389, 2392
Tate, Jean 2396
Taylor, Anstruther 1521
Taylor, James 690
Taylor, Janet 2399
Taylor, John 2397, 2398, 2403, 2404
Taylor, Mary 2401
Taylor, Susan 2400
Taylor, William 2402
Telfer, Alexander 1922
Tennant, Bethia 2016
Tennant, James 2408
Thom, Charles 2410
Thom, James 2413
Thom, Jane 2414
Thom, William 2411, 2412
Thomas, Janet 2415
Thompson, Donald 2416
Thompson, Jane 119
Thomson, Agnes 560
Thomson, Catherine 1619
Thomson, Christina 2463, 2464
Thomson, David 2431
Thomson, George 2430
Thomson, Hugh 2433
Thomson, James 310, 2419, 2188,
    2428, 2438
Thomson, Jane 2420
Thomson, John 2425, 2432

Thomson, Margaret 874
Thomson, Mary 269, 270
Thomson, Thomas 2435
Thomson, William 267, 1125, 1124,
    1127, 2437, 2439
Thorbrand, R 2440
Thornton, William 2441
Tibbers, James 2215
Tillie, Janet 2169
Tod, George 2446
Tod, Helen 2442
Tod, James 2447
Tod, Lindsay 2449, 2444, 2443,
    2445, 2448, 2450
Todd, David 903
Todd, Ellen 793
Toddie, Lindsay 1255
Tomison, William 2451
Topp, Adam 2078
Torbett, John 2452
Torrie, Jean 417
Towart, William 1919
Tower, Elizabeth 364
Tower, George 2454
Tower, John 1052
Trent, William 2456
Trotter, John 2457
Troup, William 2458
Tudhope, Alexander 2460
Tudhope, Robert 2459
Tulloch, Jean 637
Tulloch, William 2461
Turnbull of Longraw, William 728
Turnbull, Agnes 613
Turnbull, Anne 543
Turnbull, George 2462
Turner of Gateside, James 2466
Turner, Alexander 2467
Turner, Coll 353, 500, 1027
Urie, Elizabeth 215
Vair, Thomas 146
Vallance, David 2469
Vallance, Jean 587
Veitch, James 2470
Veitch, John 2471
Vincent, Thomas 2472
Virtue, Daniel 298
Waddell of Deadloch, James 2476

163

164

165

CPSIA information can be obtained at www.ICGtesting.com
Printed in the USA
BVOW04s0019070415

394980BV00011B/81/P